Finding Truth in Fiction

Finding Truth in Fiction

What Fan Culture Gets Right—And Why It's Good to Get Lost in a Story

KAREN E. DILL-SHACKLEFORD

AND

CYNTHIA VINNEY

UNIVERSITY PRESS

Oxford University Press is a department of the University of Oxford. It furthers
the University's objective of excellence in research, scholarship, and education
by publishing worldwide. Oxford is a registered trade mark of Oxford University
Press in the UK and certain other countries.

Published in the United States of America by Oxford University Press
198 Madison Avenue, New York, NY 10016, United States of America.

© Oxford University Press 2020

All rights reserved. No part of this publication may be reproduced, stored in
a retrieval system, or transmitted, in any form or by any means, without the
prior permission in writing of Oxford University Press, or as expressly permitted
by law, by license, or under terms agreed with the appropriate reproduction
rights organization. Inquiries concerning reproduction outside the scope of the
above should be sent to the Rights Department, Oxford University Press, at the
address above.

You must not circulate this work in any other form
and you must impose this same condition on any acquirer.

Library of Congress Cataloging-in-Publication Data
Names: Dill-Shackleford, Karen E., 1969– author. | Vinney, Cynthia, 1978– author.
Title: Finding truth in fiction : what fan culture gets right - and why
it's good to get lost in a story / Karen E. Dill-Shackleford, Cynthia Vinney, editors.
Other titles: Truth in fiction
Description: New York : Oxford University Press, 2020. | Includes
bibliographical references and index. | Summary: Provided by publisher.
Identifiers: LCCN 2019036484 (print) | LCCN 2019036485 (ebook) |
ISBN 9780190643607 (hardback) | ISBN 9780190643614 | ISBN 9780190643621
(epub) | ISBN 9780190643638
Subjects: LCSH: Fiction—Psychological aspects. | Motion pictures—Psychological aspects. |
Television programs—Psychological aspects. |
Fans (Persons)—Psychology. | Identity (Psychology) |
Self-actualization (Psychology) | Mass media—Social aspects. | Truth—Psychological aspects.
Classification: LCC PN3352.P7 D55 2020 (print) |
LCC PN3352.P7 (ebook) | DDC 808.3—dc23
LC record available at https://lccn.loc.gov/2019036484
LC ebook record available at https://lccn.loc.gov/2019036485

9 8 7 6 5 4 3 2 1

Printed by Sheridan Books, Inc., United States of America

To Agatha Christie and Jane Austen
K.E.S.

To my parents for encouraging my love of fiction,
and my husband for being as big a fan as I am
C.V.

CONTENTS

1. Truth in Fiction 1
2. It Matters: Finding Meaning in Stories 35
3. On Actors and Their Roles: The Social Psychology of Narrative Person Perception 62
4. Mental Models of Fiction: The Mechanics of Getting Lost in a Story 91
5. The Timelessness of Stories 120
6. Story and Identity: How Stories Influence Who We Are 151
7. Story and Life Stage: Turning to Stories Throughout Our Lives 182
8. On Prejudice and Values 216
Epilogue: Coping, Well-Being, and the Future of Fiction 243

NAME INDEX 263
SUBJECT INDEX 275

1
Truth in Fiction

> The magic and the danger of fiction is that it allows us to see through other eyes. It takes us to places we have never been, allows us to care about, worry about, laugh with, and cry for people who do not, outside of the story, exist. There are people who think that things that happen in fiction do not really happen. Those people are wrong.
> —Neil Gaiman (2011) Afterword to
> Evelyn Evelyn: A Tragic Tale In Two Tomes, ¶1

When the lights go down in a movie theater as the film starts, when we turn on the TV to watch our favorite show, when we binge-watch the latest streaming series, or open the pages to the latest novel, something magical happens. We travel to new places. We meet new people and have new relationships. Through the power of fiction, we can become someone else and experience things we might never experience in our real lives. Often, we come back changed. Maybe we are just more relaxed and content because we spent some much-needed time away from our troubles. Sometimes we develop deeper insight into who we are and how to navigate our real-life challenges, whatever they may be.

Even though we usually don't think about it that much, fictional stories are powerful forces in our lives. And today we have more access to stories of all kinds than ever before. Whatever our mood or desire, we can find

Finding Truth in Fiction. Karen E. Shackleford and Cynthia Vinney, Oxford University Press (2020).
© Oxford University Press.
DOI: 10.1093/oso/9780190643607.001.0001

something that suits our tastes and interests. We believe this makes understanding the impact of stories on our lives more important than ever before. From our earliest days, stories are one of the few things we all have in common. Regardless of our personal preferences, most of us has experienced the power of a story, and whether we share it or not, each of us has a story of our own to tell.

And no matter how many times we read or see them, iconic story moments excite our emotions, spark our memories, and make our hearts race. Do you ever find yourself wishing that Rick hadn't let Ilsa get on that plane in *Casablanca*? How good did it feel when Harry discovered he was a wizard in *Harry Potter and the Sorcerer's Stone*? Have you ever compared your struggles to the quest for the ring in the *Lord of the Rings*? If these and other iconic moments get you every time, then you are like most of us fans and enthusiasts of great stories, be they on the page or screen.

As fans of popular stories, we've been to these same places: We know the joy of standing on the Titanic with our arms in the wind, the shock of hearing that Darth Vader is our father. Maybe we understood what Diana may have felt when, after being told what she can't do for too long, she said, "It's what *I'm* going to do" before taking matters into her own hands in *Wonder Woman*. Although we did not experience these things firsthand, we've been inside those story worlds in our imagination. And imagination is one of the most powerful and exciting things about being human. Technically, we were never a Jedi learning about our long-lost parents or an Amazon using our fighting skills to defend the down-trodden, but we have been there in our imagination. However you make sense of it, we argue in this book that the experience of knowing another's journey is very useful to us in our own lives. In other words, taking in a story has real value.

THEIR STORY IS OUR STORY

In her *Book Retreat* mystery series, author Ellery Adams describes the fictional town of Storyton, where guests stay in Storyton Hall, a book lovers' haven where technology is banned and story books abound.

> Jane locked the door to the Mystery Suite and glanced at the brass key nestled in her palm. Like all of Storyton Hall's guest room keys, its tag was engraved with the image of an open book and the Steward family motto. Written in Latin, the motto, *De Nobis Fabula Narratur*, roughly translated to *Their Story is Our Story*. (Adams, 2014, p. 86)

The Storyton motto is our motto for the book you hold in your hands: Their story is our story. What it means for us as psychologists is that when we watch a great story unfold, we bind ourselves to the characters, we feel what they feel, and their experiences become our experiences. We are bound by imagination and common humanity. There's no such thing as "It's only a story."

Story is everything. Being on the television screen, being a movie, or being popular doesn't diminish the value of the story. What matters is that the story takes ahold of our imagination, that we bind to it and belong to it in some way. We are stories; stories are who we are.

Thus, the book you hold in your hands is about the meaning of fiction in our lives, both what happens in our hearts and minds when we watch or read a story and what we share with others who have experienced the same stories that we have. From committed fans of franchises like *Star Trek* or *The Hunger Games*, or enthusiasts of single stories like *The Big Lebowski* or *The Rocky Horror Picture Show*, to the eagerly awaited next book in George R. R. Martin's *A Song of Ice and Fire* series, we explore how we can use beloved characters and stories for growth, exploration, and, of course, pleasure. In short, we explore what we gain from immersing ourselves in the films, TV shows, and books we love or at least find compelling. Everything we are talking about relates to the psychology of audiences—whether you consider yourself a "fan" of a story or you just loved or appreciated a particular story, this is about you.

We are two media psychologists who have spent years investigating the psychology of story, including audience members' psychological reactions to stories, how "into" stories people get, and the difference it can make in our real lives. Among other things, our research has revealed how being a fan of popular culture is related to overall well-being and how writing fanfiction can help writers explore the human condition. Throughout the book, we explore the different ways stories affect our lives, and what our connections to a story world and its characters mean to us. As psychologists, we draw evidence from social science research and related disciplines, as well as other scholars. But it doesn't matter what your background is. This book is for anyone who has loved a story and felt it enriched their life in both small and large ways. This is something we've experienced many times—we hope you have too.

Just to be clear, sometimes we call ourselves a fan of a story and sometimes, although we like a film, show, or book, we don't give ourselves that label. For instance, even if we think a film like *La La Land*, *Life Is Beautiful*, or *The Pursuit of Happyness* changed who we are or how we see the world, we wouldn't necessarily say we're a "fan" of it. We might instead say something like, "Oh, you should really watch that!" or "What a tough but important film." But we don't look for a fan website or attempt to find a conference where we can meet the film's stars. Part of it might be that we're more inclined to call ourselves a fan of a series (of shows, films, books, etc.) than if there is only a single film or book involved. We can love a single film like *Big Fish*, *The Artist*, or *Hidden Figures* but we may not use the word "fan" to describe our relationship to the story.

Whether we'd call ourselves fans or not, if a story makes us feel complex emotions and strikes us as having some wisdom to impart, scenes and moments from that story may flash before our eyes when we are in a situation that reminds us of it. What are those moments for you? Who do you think of when you need to summon up courage, fight against the bad guys, or learn when to let go? In *Harry Potter and the Sorcerer's Stone*, Neville Longbottom, a student at the Hogwarts School of Witchcraft and Wizardry, gets an award from Headmaster Dumbledore for standing up to his friends, which Dumbledore notes sometimes takes the most courage. In *The Shawshank Redemption*, a film about a wrongfully imprisoned man suffering and then breaking free, both Tim Robbins's and Morgan Freeman's characters eventually find they are able to liberate their souls. Some version of these feelings is universal, so there may be times in your life when you felt like the kid who stood up to his friends or a prisoner who is set free (see Figure 1.1).

Truth in Fiction

Figure 1.1 Feeling liberated: Throughout our lives, we may think of iconic screen moments and connect them with our own experiences. Here we see Tim Robbins in *The Shawshank Redemption* just after escaping from prison.

Our research highlights the intimacy of our relationship to stories, regardless of whether we're studying fans or audiences more generally. Our passion is to show how choosing and using stories helps us develop and evolve in our real lives. Historically, when psychologists have studied popular culture audiences, they have often focused on concepts like celebrity worship, which centers on the potential for our interest in popular culture to become pathological (e.g., Giles & Maltby, 2006; Maltby, Day, McCutcheon, Houran, & Ashe, 2006; McCutcheon, Lange, & Houran, 2002). It's true that some fans' fascination with popular celebrities, stories, or characters can become psychologically unhealthy and even destructive—for examples we need look no further than the former Beatles fan who murdered John Lennon or the man who attempted to assassinate then-President Ronald Reagan to impress Jodie Foster. Yet, we believe that for most people, being a popular culture fan and watching and reading stories is a positive and healthy part of life. Rather than sneering at fans for the ways a story touches them or getting concerned about their inability to distinguish fantasy from reality, we instead celebrate the variety of good that a wonderful story can inspire.

For example, Claire Handscombe, *The West Wing* superfan and editor of *Walk with Us: How* The West Wing *Has Changed Our Lives* (Handscombe, 2014b) gives examples of how the show crossed from the screen into the everyday lives of its fans:

> Couples have walked down the aisle to the show's theme music. An iPhone app, pets and even children have been named after the characters. Some fans say that the show has helped them crawl out of depression or that it's deepened friendships among those who've watched it together. Others say it has renewed their political idealism, made them want to debate rather than shout at people with different views or showed them that politics is worth engaging with. (Handscombe, 2014a)

Or take the story described in the book and documentary *Life, Animated*. At the age of 3 Ron Suskind's son Owen developed regressive autism and fell mute. Owen's only solace seemed to be watching Disney animated movies over and over again. The family learned to harness Owen's affinity for these films to communicate with him using the dialogue from the films. And the myriad of Disney animated characters and the lessons they taught not only helped Owen talk again, they also helped him grow emotionally, make friends, and learn how to find a place in the world (Suskind, 2014).

UBIQUITOUS POPULAR CULTURE

Research shows that people spend the majority of their free time watching TV and movies—most often stories rather than nonfiction. In fact, according to Nielsen (2017), from April to June 2017, Americans spent around 4½ hours per day watching live or time-shifted TV alone. This preference for voraciously consuming stories exists across sex, race, class, and cultural boundaries. It's perhaps the great democratizer.

Despite the fact that we spend so much time with popular culture stories, however, fans are still sometimes stereotyped as losers and weirdoes who get too involved in fantasy (Jenson, 1992; Sandvoss, 2005; Schimmel, Harrington, & Bielby, 2007). Further, popular stories are often degraded as frivolous, stupid, and even dangerous (Zubernis & Larsen, 2012).

In a sketch on *Saturday Night Live*, William Shatner, synonymous with the fictional Captain Kirk, famously derided *Star Trek* fans by telling them to "get a life" and move out of their parents' basements. Of course, lovers of all things *Star Trek* could be considered the epitome of all fan bases, having personally rescued *Star Trek: The Original Series* from cancellation in the late 1960s. Fans expressed hurt and anger at the nerd-shaming, and Shatner later made up for it in a big way by writing the book *Get a Life*, in which he fully explored how much the love and commitment of the *Star Trek* fan community had changed his life. In the book, Shatner describes the sheer joy of being received all over the planet (Federation!?) as Captain Kirk, and the honor of being a central figure in people's lives, all stemming from the love of character and story.

At the same time, as a society, we don't always like to admit that we spend time "watching TV." Perhaps this is because we are often told that watching television is passive and lazy. No one wants to be called a "couch potato." While the experience doesn't always look very glamorous or seem very productive, this book takes another perspective entirely on the great American past time: drinking in stories (you thought it was baseball?).

Isn't it strange that we spend so much of our time doing something that we are often in denial of or, at least, don't fully understand as a culture? Well, that's where we come in. We are lucky enough to get to study these questions as psychologists and to pass on our nerdy book learning to you! We want to share with you what social scientists have learned about the place popular culture stories have in our lives. We believe this research is exciting, fascinating, and edifying, and we hope you will too.

Furthermore, a lot of the latest psychological research on the impact of stories in our lives seems to be shifting toward our more positive perspective too. Much of the new research being published in the field on popular culture fans and audiences, their motivations, and their activities approaches story consumption as a normal and accepted part of life (e.g., Groene & Hettinger, 2015; Taylor, 2015; Tsay-Vogel & Sanders, 2015). In fact, research has indicated that fandom, particularly fandom for complex drama, may be largely about the search for meaning, the clarification of values, and the quest to hone our social skills and understanding.

As people who have benefited from our association with stories ourselves, we are encouraged by this shifted point of view. Cynthia is a sci-fi/fantasy buff with a long-standing love of *Buffy the Vampire Slayer*, *Supernatural*, and most things superheroic, while Karen is an anglophile who once took a *Downton Abby* tour of England as well as a huge *Star Trek* fan. As a result of our own experiences, we embrace other lovers of popular culture stories and truly appreciate the fulfillment that comes from experiencing a favorite movie or television show—and discussing it with others. There are so many popular franchises out there that it's impossible to talk about or even mention them all. Rather than even attempt it, we will focus most on stories that have demonstrated a large fan following or concentrate on those that have been around for a while. Keeping in mind that readers can't have watched or read everything, we have attempted—as much as possible—to keep our discussion of each property self-explanatory. Meanwhile, if you are a relative youngster, try to keep the exclamation "These stories are old!" down to a dull roar. They're not old; they're classics, and, yes, there's a difference (can you tell that one of us is the mother of two teenagers?). Also, be forewarned, to talk about what audiences get out of films and TV, we are going to drop some spoilers here and there. If you sense one coming and want to avoid it, please avert your eyes and move on.

Really, there is a reason for sticking largely to classics or to stories and franchises that seem poised to become classics. We're confident that in the future, *Star Wars* and *Rebel Without a Cause*, Hitchcock and Charlie Chaplin, Shakespeare and Jane Austen will continue to resonate with audiences. In contrast, the people of 2050 will probably not be watching *Punky Brewster* or *Square Pegs*, unless they're fans of 1980s fashions. We are betting that *Breaking Bad* and *Game of Thrones* will stick around in the public consciousness, and we dearly hope that *Keeping Up With the Kardashians* won't, unless it's as a cautionary tale.

Naturally, part of being someone who loves pop culture stories is disagreeing about the value of various films, shows, and books. Individual tastes vary. It's not our place to argue what the most valuable stories are, beyond researching the stats on audiences and reporting anecdotes from real people who say that stories made a difference in their lives. Stories are pertinent to different people at different times in their lives. It's okay if one person feels vaguely homicidal whenever *Modern Family* comes on TV, while another counts it as one of her all-time favorites. It's not about settling once and for all what's the best story (*Star Wars* vs. *Star Trek*, anyone? Or DC vs. Marvel?) but about understanding what we value about stories.

We have each watched every episode of *Mad Men* as part of a research team studying fan reactions to the show. Karen was emotionally attached to the main character, Don Draper, getting his stuff together. Cynthia kind of wished he would just fall off of a building, as in the show's award-winning introductory animation, and she still gets annoyed if she thinks about him. What we're here to discuss is the psychology behind those reactions. In the words of singer-songwriter John Mayer (2013), "You love who you love. You can't make yourself stop dreaming who you're dreaming of."

In addition, before we move on, so that we don't trip over our words, let's agree on a simplification. In this book, we are writing about stories we love. This includes film, television, video, audio, books and other print materials, and any other forms of narrative that exists. To streamline our writing, we won't name every medium each time we talk about story—a practice that would make this book cumbersome to read. We ask you to trade in a bit of precision in language for greater ease in reading. Just know that we'll take the liberty of being casual, so when we say "books" and "read," or "television" and "watch," or we mention stories in general that, with noted exceptions, it's often not the story's medium that matters as much as the fact that it's a story.

In fact, today transmedia storytelling is common. Transmedia means that, for instance, a person can watch *Doctor Who* on television, read

Doctor Who books, magazines, or fan fiction, buy a doll of her favorite Doctor, dress as her favorite character at a fan convention, listen to a Whovian podcast, and get bonus videos on her phone. So, when speaking of *Doctor Who*, it's not clear whether we should call it a show, a franchise, or something else. What is clear is that *Doctor Who* is a cultural touchstone and a story world with characters who've had personal relevance for generations of people. And those are the ideas we focus on here.

EXPLORING OTHER WORLDS AND PEOPLE THROUGH STORY

Research on what happens when we consume fictional narratives has often focused on the concepts: identification and transportation (Silver & Slater, in press). Let's begin by discussing transportation. Now, this isn't the typical kind of transportation (like planes, trains, and automobiles). It's more of a metaphorical transportation. Melanie Green and her mentor Timothy Brock said that being transported means getting lost in a story (Green & Block, 2000; Green, Block, & Kaufman, 2004). Being transported means traveling to another place—the story world. When we are transported, we loosen our connection to ourselves and our surroundings and are immersed or engaged in the plot, settings, and characters that make up the story world.

So, when we are transported into a story, we engage in this kind of paradoxical process of exploring the self while simultaneously becoming someone else for a while through identification. In our work, we have called this process "dual empathy." While it seems complex, in a way it's actually quite simple—as we watch or read we can switch perspectives from our own point of view to the point of view of the character and back again. We imagine that dual empathy is something that you have experienced often when taking in a story. Imagine you are watching your favorite TV show and it reminds you of a childhood memory, arousing the feelings you felt when the remembered event happened when you were younger. Indeed, research shows that stories can prompt memories from our own lives to come to the surface (Larsen & Seilman, 1988; McDonald, Sarge, Lin, Collier, & Potocki, 2015). Next, you take the perspective of a favorite character. Through that connection you feel new feelings and experience new situations. These are the two parts of dual empathy—exploring the self and extending yourself into different characters and situations to explore what it feels like to be someone else.

Taking the perspective of a character is typically what media scholars mean when we talk about "identification." On the one hand, "to identify with" is a familiar everyday concept. We use it to mean we "relate to" someone or something. But researchers need to rigorously define their terms, so in 2001, scholar Jonathan Cohen called on researchers to more precisely articulate what they meant when they studied identification. Cohen traced the history of the concept, noting that it could signify that we "forget ourselves and become the other" (p. 247), but we can also think of it as sharing another person's perspective.

Cohen (2001) went beyond these options to offer his own definition of identification as "a process that consists of increasing loss of self-awareness and its temporary replacement with heightened emotional and cognitive connections with a character" (p.251). For example, when we watch Hitchcock's *Rear Window*, we may forget ourselves for a while and adopt the perspective of the main character Jeff Jeffries, a photographer in a wheelchair trying to catch a killer. Our heart races when we realize that the killer is coming to our apartment and that the wheelchair means we are at his mercy!

Or when we witness Luke Skywalker struggle to rise above his humble beginnings to become a Jedi in the original *Star Wars* trilogy, we may feel that we ourselves are learning to use the Force. When Luke succeeds in his training, so do we—a victory that can feel valuable and important. Or perhaps we take on the mindset of one of the survivors of the zombie apocalypse while we're watching *The Walking Dead* and find ourselves desperately fighting for survival against the zombie hordes. The survivors' goal to find shelter, food, and safety becomes *our* goal, and we may become breathless as we struggle to get past the encroaching zombie herd to a safer space. We vicariously experience the fear and thrill of these situations through our identification with these different characters.

When we identify with a character in a story, we use our imaginations. This can help us learn what the character's story has to teach us. We may even imitate or emulate characters with whom we identify. Maybe you found yourself on an adventure, and you felt for a short time like the star of a timeless quest? Maybe it was Indiana Jones or James Bond, or maybe it was Shuri from *Black Panther* or Rey from *Star Wars*. Over time, some of the things we learn from characters that we deploy in our real lives may become a part of ourselves. And these characteristics help form our identity.

Scholars Kaufman and Libby (2012) expanded on the idea of identification with a character in a story. They described "the imaginative process of spontaneously assuming the identity of a character in a narrative and simulating that character's thoughts, emotions, behaviors, goals, and traits as if they were one's own" (p. 1) as "experience-taking." Experience-taking is using our imaginations to "feel through" another person (Dill-Shackleford, Vinney, & Hopper-Losenicky, 2016). And, according to Kaufman and Libby's research, the more you are deeply engrossed with a story, the less accessible your self-concept is to you.

Karen (Dill-Shackleford, 2016) has compared this viewer–character connection to the human–avatar connection depicted in James Cameron's *Avatar*. In that film, a medical machine connects the consciousness of a human, Jake Sully, with that of a hybrid avatar, who looks like the Na'vi—a large, blue race who inhabit the planet Pandora. Through this connection, Jake feels what the avatar feels; indeed, Jake becomes this new entity—this merger of one mind and another body. In that same way, we become a hybrid, a merger of ourselves and the character we take on. For example, when we are deep into *Star Trek: Deep Space Nine*, we might feel as if we *are* Captain Benjamin Sisko, tossing his souvenir baseball into the air or unexpectedly accepting his role as "the emissary," a religious figure to a planet full of people. When we bond with Captain Sisko like this, our own self-concept becomes remote for a time. And the more we become the Captain, temporarily, the less access we have to our own self-concepts. For a time, we feel like him instead of ourselves.

Another way we may connect with fictional characters, but maintain our sense of self, is by engaging in a parasocial interactions (PSIs) with them. PSIs are one-sided interactions with a character that take place while we're consuming different kinds of media, including everything from movies and books to morning radio shows and the evening news (Horton & Wohl, 1956). Viewers and readers know PSIs aren't real, but they still experience them as if they were real-life, face-to-face social interactions. When we continue to think about a character outside of a specific viewing situation, we may start to establish a parasocial relationship (PSR) with that character (Giles, 2010). Like PSIs, PSRs are one-sided, but people react to them as though they were real-life social relationships (Giles, 2002). As we'll discuss, we think it's a bit more complicated than being entirely one-sided. More on that shortly.

Although we know the characters we encounter in fictional stories aren't real, we often develop an intimacy and even a friendship-like bond with them (Cohen, 2001; Mellmann, 2002). For example, many viewers may have felt like the seventh friend when they watched the sitcom *Friends*. They enjoyed spending time with the main characters Monica, Chandler, Ross, Rachel, Phoebe, and Joey, and watching them felt like hanging out with their own friends. Some viewers may have found themselves thinking about the characters' stories even when they weren't watching them. Perhaps one viewer wondered how Monica might handle a tough career decision, while another considered how Chandler might prepare for an important social event.

Keren Eyal and Jonathan Cohen (2006) studied college students' attachment to the characters on *Friends* and also their distress when *Friends* ended its broadcast run. This distress at the dissolution of a relationship with a beloved story character is called parasocial breakup. Parasocial breakup can be caused by a show ending, like *Friends* did; by a character leaving a show, like Steve Carell's character Michael Scott on the American version of *The Office*; by something happening to an actor in real life, like when actor Cory Monteith died unexpectedly forcing his character to also unexpectedly die on his show, *Glee*; or when a viewer decides they no longer wish to watch the show on which a character appears.

When it went off the air, *Friends* was so popular that only 6% of the students in Eyal and Cohen's study hadn't seen the show (a revelation that removed these participants from the analysis). The remaining students told the researchers how strongly they were attached to their favorite *Friends* character, the most popular choice being Rachel. Eyal and Cohen discovered that fans did feel distress at the prospect of the show coming to an end because it would take away the time participants spent with their favorite characters every week. Participants' sense of loss followed the same patterns of loss found in face-to-face relationships, but the emotions were generally less intense. The researchers noted that fans experienced lots of pleasure and satisfaction spending time with *Friends*, and like in real life when a friend moves away, it was sad to think about these characters leaving. Fortunately for us, thanks to DVDs and streaming services, we can now binge watch *Friends* any time. In fact, just recently some good friends of Karen's told her that their teenaged sons spent their holiday break binge watching *Friends* from beginning to end and laughing uproariously the whole time. Despite the pain that can accompany the ending of a beloved show, there's definitely joy in seeing your kids or other people you care about catch up on a show that you also love.

In a recent study, Michael Slater, David Ewoldsen, and Kelsey Woods (2017) took the parasocial concept even further by distinguishing between PSRs with the characters from a story (PSR-C) and PSRs with actors or other real-life people, often referred to as personae (PSR-P). For example, Cynthia likes to say she has an intense PSR with the character Dean Winchester from the show *Supernatural*. She's watched every episode of the series, many multiple times, and she relates to Dean's struggles as an older sibling and someone who wants to do the right thing but isn't always sure how. And even though he's fictional, she feels like he's part of her extended social circle. On the other hand, she tries to avoid information on Jensen Ackles, the actor who plays him, so she doesn't contaminate or compromise her understanding of Dean.

In contrast, Karen feels she has a PSR with William Shatner, the actor who played Captain Kirk on the original *Star Trek*. The closest Karen has ever been to William Shatner was watching him in person at an event in Charlotte, North Carolina, where he appeared to discuss the film *The Wrath of Khan* and share anecdotes from his career. Prior to that, she read two of his autobiographies: *Get a Life* and *Leonard: My Fifty-Year Friendship with a Remarkable Man*. (Yes, *Leonard* was about Leonard Nimoy, but, as the subtitle implies, it was really more the story of both Shatner and Nimoy's lives and their work together.) She's seen all the episodes of *Star Trek: The Original Series* and all of the *Star Trek* movies. She watched *Shatner's Raw Nerve* (and loved it!). By the way—and this is *super* important for science—Karen also counts 1960s William Shatner on her personal list of most beautiful men who've ever lived. We can tell you that Karen definitely talks to her friends as if she knows William Shatner and can guess his reactions to things (e.g., "Bill wouldn't like that, would he?" or "Bill really did love Leonard"). And many of her friends do the same. When Karen saw William Shatner in person, he was 87 years old. She'd been a fan for decades, watching him on multiple shows and films. Karen was struck by how recognizable Shatner's voice was to her. Having read a number of his books and seen multiple interviews with him, his life story was familiar. She realized that at the time she saw him in person, he was more like a beloved uncle to her than anything. Karen's real-life uncles are also charming storytellers, and listening to William Shatner felt a lot like listening to one of her uncles tell stories. She wondered if there was such a great difference, after all.

Taking another angle on our relationships with characters and public figures, Slater, Ewoldsen, and Woods (2017) distinguish between PSRs and what they refer to as retrospective imaginative involvement (RII). Unlike PSRs, where one imagines interacting with the characters or actors socially, during RII, people imagine characters outside the story situation but not as a part of their personal social world. Sometimes they'll imagine they are interacting with the character in a different setting than their story world; other times they imagine they themselves are the character either while remembering the story or in scenarios outside the story world. Regardless of whether its PSI, PSR-C, RII, or identification, there are many ways our imaginations enable us to engage with fictional characters. Table 1.1 defines all the different ways we can connect to characters.

TABLE 1.1   MULTIPLE WAYS AUDIENCE MEMBERS CONNECT WITH FICTIONAL STORY CHARACTERS

Method of Connection	Description
Identification	Adopting the perspective of a character in a story and vicariously experience story events through the character.
Parasocial interactions	An imagined interaction with a media figure such as a character or other personality that happens while actively viewing or reading a story. Parasocial means one-sided—only the audience member experiences the interaction.
Parasocial relationship (PSR)	An imagined relationship with a media figure that extends beyond the viewing situation.
PSR–character	A PSR with the character; character continues to exist between viewings; for example, speaking about Sherlock Holmes with other fans as if Holmes is a real person).
PSR–personae	A PSR with the personae (i.e., personalities); personae includes actors, newscasters, anthropomorphized puppets. For example, speaking about William Shatner with your friends as if he were one of your friends ("Well, Bill won't like that").
Parasocial breakup	When a PSR with a media figure comes to an end, either because their TV show ends, their character leaves the show, something happens to the media figure, or the media consumer stops engaging with the media figure.
Retrospective imaginative involvement	"To engage in one's mental world with the story characters after viewing or reading" (Slater et al., 2017, p. 5); for example, imagining the story character in new situations not present in the text or imagining interacting with the character as yourself or another character.

SOURCES: Cohen (2001), Giles (2002), Horton and Wohl (1956), and Slater et al. (2017).

Movies, television, and other forms of fiction often encourage intimacy between characters and their viewers because *viewers often know more about fictional characters than they do even their closest friends* (Mar & Oatley, 2008). Think about it: We watch characters in the most intimate parts of their lives and see their unguarded responses to their experiences. The depth and breadth of what we observe enhances our feelings of closeness, leading us to develop a genuine affection for our favorite characters.

While this may sound odd, it's actually a normal result of our ingrained social natures, which prizes and prioritizes building successful relationships with others. Intimacy breeds attachment. Due to the nature of a good story, in fictional worlds we have the opportunity to see the personal side of the characters' lives: their hopes, fears, and secrets. Again, this is often a perspective that is more intimate than the perspective we get on people in our everyday lives. Small wonder, then, that we feel close to these characters.

While we know some may feel a little defensive at the idea that researchers are studying your relationships with your favorite characters and personalities, we want to make sure you understand that we aren't making fun of these practices. As our previous examples show, these are practices we engage in ourselves without shame. So, if anyone makes fun of these practices, then they're making fun of us too. But we argue that relationships like this are healthy and satisfying for us.

Besides, how different is it to talk about Sherlock Holmes as if he were a real person that we are trying to understand than it is to talk about the Queen of England in the same way? They are both personalities that we've read about and watched on the screen, but with whom most of us will never have a personal relationship. Is our understanding of a character like Katniss Everdeen from *The Hunger Games* that different from our understanding of a historical figure like Joan of Arc? They are both legends who inspire. Each of them is an icon that evokes the idea of a young woman who is a warrior figure and a leader. None of us will ever run through the woods with Katniss Everdeen or with Joan of Arc, and yet they each advance our thinking about a particular set of ideas and values in similar ways. Yes, there are differences between historical figures and story characters. But there are great similarities in how we use their stories in our real lives.

The relationships we forge with characters can make a story feel more significant. Due to the intimate nature of experiencing a PSI or identifying with a story's characters, when we experience these responses, we may feel the story has greater personal relevance for us. This, in turn, will enhance our transportation into the story (Bartsch & Oliver, 2011). Together, then, these responses can create an especially meaningful entertainment experience—an experience that leaves a lasting impression.

It's important to note too that identification, PSIs, and other responses we have to stories are not isolated experiences. We often have multiple exposures to characters, and these exposures are often emotional.

Another essential factor in the psychology of narrative is that it is a dynamic process. One experience gives way to a different one, and then another. For example, you might watch or read Jane Austen's *Pride and Prejudice* and, at one point, identify with the protagonist, Miss Elizabeth Bennet, while engaging in an exciting PSI with her suitor, Mr. Darcy. In the next moment, you might instead identify with Mr. Darcy, while having a PSI with Lizzie. You might alternate between these perspectives with one or the other through the back and forth of their courtship. Perhaps you empathize with Darcy because you too had a marriage proposal rejected or said something you thought was fair, only to realize later that you were being offensive.

Next, you might unplug from these characters. One moment Lizzie was your avatar; the next moment you find yourself thinking about the actress who plays her, her costume, the production of the film, or Jane Austen's reasons for writing the plot as she did. At times, you might even be bumped out of your engagement with the narrative entirely by some demanding stimulus that takes you out of the story world and back into what presses you in our own.

Many have imagined or felt what Elizabeth Bennet was feeling when Darcy (see Figure 1.2) gazed adoringly upon her or imagined ourselves

Figure 1.2 Colin Firth as Mr. Darcy in the BBC/A&E production of *Pride and Prejudice* (Langton, 1995).

engaging in our own relationship with him. Or we may have wished for the two to end up in each other's arms. Then our emotions might shift into thinking how handsome Colin Firth is in the role (Karen!). If you jump out to yet another level of engagement, you'll even feel connected to the other people who love the story.

Now, this is where some will start to say that this means that people who get deeply engrossed and invested in stories are crazy (e.g., people who have interviewed us about our research). "What?" They say, "You've lost yourself in a story and forgotten who you are?" "You've bonded with a fictional character, and now you think you are friends?" Honestly, though, we've wondered, since when did feeling like you were a character in a story and forgetting yourself for a while or forming a bond with someone as your get to know them, even if they're fictional, become a serious pathology? Any psychologist can tell you that most human experiences fall somewhere on a normal curve, and this includes a continuum from health to pathology. Identification, experience-taking, or parasocial experiences can be abnormal and unhealthy. But *most* of it falls under the "that's normal" part of the normal curve. Actually, it's not only normal, but it can also be quite healthy.

POP CULTURE STORIES: WHAT'S IN IT FOR US?

> And Max, the king of all wild things, was lonely and wanted to be where someone loved him best of all.
> —Maurice Sendak, *Where the Wild Things Are*

When we were children, our parents read us story books and encouraged us to imagine ourselves as someone else off on a new adventure. What's the point of *Where the Wild Things Are* without imagining that you are Max, who is sent to his room for being too wild and takes off on his own adventure? We imagine we are Max sailing off to meet the Wild Things. At the end of the adventure, we return with him to the known space of our own rooms.

> And [he] sailed back over a year
> and in and out of weeks
> and through a day
> and into the night of his very own room
> where he found his supper waiting for him
> and it was still hot
> —Maurice Sendak, *Where the Wild Things Are*

Really, we don't need to explain this experience to anyone. Most of us has had it and know what it means. It's just that some of us forget as adults that going off on an adventure as someone else from the comfort of our own rooms is a very, very good idea. It doesn't make much sense to tell kids that stories are "supposed to be good for you" but chastise adults for liking their stories "a little too much."

LIFE-CHANGING STORIES

Stories are important to us. In fact, there are many stories about how popular fiction has changed the course of someone's life. For example, writer Mark Luckie (2015) shared his story about how one of his favorite shows changed his choice of college. Mark, an African American, was a strong student and thought he had a good chance of being accepted to a traditional university. But he knew that he would be in the minority at those institutions and wasn't sure about wanting to continue to be "the other" during his education. Mark became a fan of the 1980s television series *A Different World*, set in the fictional Hillman University, which was an example of an HBCU (historically Black colleges and universities). Although Hillman was arguably different from its real-life counterparts in some ways, Mark found enough in this story world to help him imagine the benefits of an HBCU to his life.

Similarly, our friend and colleague, Monique, is an African American university administrator. Earlier in her career, colleagues asked her candidly how she thought she was able to buck the stereotypes and move quickly up the ladder in academia. Monique replied that she thought her education helped her a lot. She said that she went to a private school for girls called Eastland. The school had a diverse population including Jo, a tomboy and rebel with a sharp tongue; Blair, a rich girl with a lot of dates and an interest in her looks; Tootie, an African American girl with braces who roller-skated through the halls; Tootie's best friend Natalie, who was kind, funny, and full-figured; and Mrs. Garrett, who kept them all on the right track.

Now, anyone who was a teen in the 1980s will immediately recognize that Monique was referring to the show *The Facts of Life*. Monique describes her experience with the show like this:

> While I . . . identified with Tootie, given our racial similarity, I attained confidence from Natalie's wit and strong self-image as a fuller figured teenager. Jo consistently reminded me that insidious

attacks on girl's femininity are all too common, and that we can (and perhaps should) develop some of our most endearing friendships with "dainty" girls who, similar to Blair, seem to have it all—but . . . those of us labeled "tomboys," most often by adults, can be constrained from embracing their wild flower girl power. (Monique Snowden, personal communication, August, 2018)

Something that a story like this offers those who are transported into it is witnessing multiple personalities in the same situation dealing with problems. As Monique put it, she saw her "classmates" at Eastland and imagined herself "working out life's challenges independently and collectively, with our multifaceted selves" (Monique Snowden, personal communication, August, 2018). Stories like this are so common, but at the same time, if you ask us if television or movies changed our lives, we aren't always aware that this was the case—or at least we aren't willing to admit it. Sometimes this is because we are unconscious of how stories impact us (Kaufman & Libby, 2012).

Buffy the Vampire Slayer is another iconic story world that was intriguing to many viewers. The story resonated with legions of fans, which is why it is still beloved today, 20 years later. On the 18th anniversary of *Buffy*, *The Atlantic* contributor Sophie Gilbert (2015) said that one thing *Buffy* did for young women and girls is acknowledge their struggles by portraying them as metaphorical battles against supernatural monsters and thereby showing that they could be overcome. Often stories that stand the test of time are less about their surface appearance and more about their deeper meaning. They speak to universal human experiences that touch us viscerally.

For example, Jason Flores described how *Buffy* helped him fight his battle with depression. Flores (2016) writes,

> *Buffy* gave me an opportunity to both enjoy the entertainment and get to know myself through my reactions and thoughts on what I was seeing—and I started to love the person I discovered. What started as entertainment became a means of survival. What started

as a means of survival became a guide to thriving in life. It gave me what I needed, when I needed it, and has since become the biggest factor in my moral, emotional, political, and spiritual compass. (¶12)

There are so many examples, from simple to profound, of people being touched by favorite characters and stories. In our research, one *Mad Men* fan told us that when faced with challenges at work, she would ask herself, "What would Don Draper do?" (Dill-Shackleford, Vinney, Hogg, & Hopper-Losenicky, 2016). We imagine as you are reading this, you may well have your own version of this: "What would (my favorite character) do?" One of us (who shall remain nameless) once listed her religion on Facebook as "What Would Scooby Doo?" That, by the way, was a tongue-in-cheek comment, although this author is a serious *Scooby Doo* fan. (You must admit, Scooby lives by the golden rule—except when it comes to snacks.)

While working on a project, one of us interviewed a *Doctor Who* superfan, asking him how comfortable he was with the fact that the actor who plays the Doctor changes every few years. She asked because she wondered how *Doctor Who* fans managed to stay engaged with the show as it transitioned from a given actor's portrayal of the character, which they may have become attached to. The superfan responded that when the Doctor "regenerates" (the word that's used in the story for the character's transition to another body), it inspired him to think about major changes in his own life. He figured that if the Doctor could go through multiple regenerations, then he could go through life transitions such as moving, marrying, divorcing, and changing jobs. The Doctor's journey meant adaptability and survival to him, which inspired him to do the same.

SIMULATION AND IMAGINATION

People have always turned to stories to understand who they are and what makes life worth living (Isbouts & Ohler, 2013). Fictional stories are especially good at showing us different aspects of the human experience because they simplify and distill events down to their essentials. In other words, stories focus only on the most fundamental and important parts of life. This causes the events in a story to be more coherent and comprehensible than the same set of experiences would be in real life (Mar & Oatley, 2008; Oatley, 1999a, 1999b). As a result, fiction is like a cognitive and emotional simulation of real-life experiences (Djikic, Oatley, Zoeterman, & Peterson, 2009; Oatley, 1999a, 1999b). Running a story simulation in our minds enables us to explore our emotions, mentally rehearse possible actions, consider our values, engage in social interactions, and access many other parts of the human experience that we might not otherwise have access to in our everyday lives.

We think the idea of fiction as simulation particularly helps us understand why we love to watch and read stories. But perhaps some may find the term "simulation" a bit cold and mechanical. If that metaphor doesn't do it for you, then may we suggest using the language of imagination. Fiction helps us imagine ourselves experiencing the most compelling, dramatic, or comic situations in life. Stories are often about the bits of life we are most drawn to understand and to "get right" or at least get better at in our own lives.

For instance, *Mad Men* fans, in their blogs and comments, often longed for, even begged for, the philandering, lost, and generally messed-up character Don Draper to treat his current woman right (Dill-Shackleford et al., 2016). Viewers watch the consequences of his cheating on himself and his family. As we connect with his character and with those he is cheating on, we feel the punishment of his transgressions, the regret, the downward spiraling of his life. We use our imaginations to think about how his life could be different if he got it together. We take on his goals as our own, as well as identifying with the women in his life and wanting things to be better for them. We imagine how things will turn out if he does finally get his act together, or if he never does. So, whether you want to call it simulation or imagination, it amounts to the same thing. Maybe our imagination is the simulation generator inside our heads.

Recent research documents that we do indeed let our imaginations pursue the questions about what characters might do in the future. We play with the people, feelings, and situations in our own minds (Slater et al., 2017).

There's a theory that one reason we find it so gratifying to imagine we're someone else is that being ourselves is emotionally taxing. Just being a human being all day long is a lot of work. It takes energy to maintain our personal identity. Life is threatening sometimes, and being an individual can be confining and stressful. When we want to escape our identity for a while, we may choose to take in a story so we can live vicariously as a "desired" self (Slater et al., 2014).

It follows, then, that one thing fiction does for us is give us other people to be and other worlds to inhabit so we can escape from the strains of our own lives. For example, when we watch Spider-Man, Black Widow, Batman, or Superman, one of the main gratifications is imagining that we, ourselves, are that superhero. We vicariously experience being powerful, in control, admired, and sometimes also brave and capable of making the world a better place.

Another reason we want to experience the world through another person's eyes is because it expands our own experience. Slater, Johnson, Cohen, Camello, and Ewoldsen (2014) call this basic idea "temporarily expanding the boundaries of the self," noting that when we identify with a fictional character, we can "feel the feelings and think the thoughts of another—a degree of intimacy that is not possible in the living social world" (p. 443). This is what happens during a deep connection or engagement with a character. Using stories to expand the boundaries of self may be adaptive for us as social creatures because we get to imagine "what if" this kind of situation happened to us. How would we feel? What would we do? If you watched the miniseries *Roots*, you were probably imagining what it was like to be a slave in America during that period in history. You likely felt the injustice of slavery and empathized with the characters. If you watched the reboot of the popular series *Battlestar Galactica*, you had the opportunity to imagine what it would be like if your planet was attacked, many world leaders perished, and you needed to find a new home.

FICTION: IT'S PERSONAL

Research on our responses to stories suggest that who we are and what we know are at the forefront of our interactions with fiction. As we mentioned earlier, fiction often triggers our own memories, which researchers refer to as autobiographical memories. In early research on this topic, scholars Steen Larsen and Uffe Seilman (1988) found that reading fiction generated more memories of experiences in which the reader actively participated than ones they heard about second hand. These researchers suggested that when fictional stories triggered such memories, individuals would feel the stories were especially pertinent and meaningful to them.

More recently, scholars found that watching television shows and movies sparked autobiographical memories in viewers' minds (McDonald et al., 2015). While these memories were only elicited about 10% of the time, this percentage is far greater than the percentage of autobiographical memories researchers have found we experience in other parts of our lives. In our daily lives, autobiographical memories may spring to mind anywhere from a mere once a week to five or six times a day. Based on those figures, the fact that viewing television and movies has been shown to elicit memories up to six times in 1 hour speaks to how personal the experience of watching a narrative that resonates with us can be.

Furthermore, although we know we aren't watching "real" events when we watch a fictional story, our emotional reactions are as spontaneous and unfiltered as they would be in a real-life social situation (Mellmann, 2002). While the emotions and memories we have when we read or watch fiction are the result of our reactions to the story, they are also personal to each of us (Oatley, 1999a, 1999b). Each of our responses and interpretations are different and specific to our circumstances (Larsen & Seilman, 1988; Oatley, 1999a). We each pay attention to different things while reading or watching. So even though we may see the same movie or TV show or read the same book, in some ways every experience we have with fiction is unique to the individual.

People may find their favorite stories resonate with them for any number of reasons. And they may find the entertainment that they love the most even helps them grapple with their individual issues and uncertainties. For example, the *Mad Men* fans we mentioned earlier often used the show to reflect on their lives (Dill-Shackleford, Hopper-Losenicky, Vinney, Swain, & Hogg, 2015). Fans regularly brought up their personal experiences and related them to those of the characters, using the show as a means through which they could reevaluate their own memories and reassess their values and beliefs.

The personal nature of fiction gives people the opportunity to make sense of their emotions and memories by exploring them within the context of their favorite story, away from any real-life obstacles that might prevent them from doing so (Mar & Oatley, 2008; Oatley, 1999a). Challenging emotional experiences in our own lives are frequently accompanied by anxiety because we know the effects of those experiences will be ongoing and we'll continue to have to deal with them. However, research by Thalia Goldstein (2009) has shown that when we watch television and movies that depict similarly challenging emotional experiences, while we still feel the same emotions we would in real life, we do so without anxiety. We know the emotions and events we encounter in fiction won't affect our real lives once the story is over so we don't feel the need to protect ourselves from them (Keen, 2006). As a result, stories offer us the freedom to cry, scream, or get angry within the safety of the fictional situation. Stories also offer opportunities for growth as we carry the emotional experiences from our encounters with them into other parts of our lives and apply what we've learned (Keen, 2006; Mar & Oatley, 2008).

In this vein, a group of European scholars (Menninghaus et al., 2017) exploring the psychology of aesthetics proposed that all forms of art—from music to painting to theater—provide a way for us to open ourselves up to and be moved by portrayals of difficulty, suffering and conflict. They called this the distancing-embracing model, and it explains why we can actually enjoy the negative emotions we experience when we consume art. According to the model, art keeps consumers at a safe distance from the suffering it depicts but is simultaneously attention-getting, emotionally involving, and memorable. So, while we feel the emotions art conveys, the distance it offers provides us with power and control, allowing us to feel safe to experience those emotions,

Let's say you are watching a movie where an interesting and likeable character is in trouble and needs help. As we've mentioned elsewhere, what often happens when you connect with a character is that you take on their goals and motives. You want what they want. Maybe you want an end to oppression, abuse, prejudice, or just poor treatment. If you had seen a similar story on the news, you may have reacted by shutting down because the people suffering were too close to you and you felt powerless to help them. The film, on the other hand, may actually be a more effective way to help people deal with real-world issues because it offers this comfortable distance and is therefore less likely to trigger an emotional shut down.

Melanie Green and Kaitlin Fitzgerald (2017) point out that journalists sometimes try to inspire their audience to help others in need by sharing stories of suffering. As the distancing-embracing model proposes, the problem is that exposure to human suffering can be too much, causing those exposed to tune out. So, people who want to create empathy and social change can end up turning people off instead. This tendency to shut down when we encounter an emotionally charged news story is perhaps an especially relevant problem today given the emotion-laden media messages that seem to constantly arise in this fraught era of political conflict.

Fortunately, recent research demonstrates that there are ways to get around the problem of emotional overwhelm. In one study, Mina Tsay-Vogel and K. Maja Krakowiak (2016) had participants watch a reality show that showed experts transforming people's lives. Shows like *Queer Eye*, *Supernanny*, and *Undercover Boss* fall into this category. The researchers found that when people watched a lifestyle transforming show instead of a game reality show like *Survivor* or *The Amazing Race*, they were more likely to reflect on the story and feel moved. Moreover, these viewers were more likely to say that the show motivated them to help others.

In a different study, Melanie Green and Kaitlin Fitzgerald (2017) exposed research participants to narratives about people in traumatic situations such as hurricanes and tornados. They varied the way the stories ended: either with an uplifting or a negative conclusion. For example, when reading a story about a storm victim, the ending was either restorative (the victim ended up with his dream job) or nonrestorative (the victim lost his job due to PTSD). Results showed that those who read the happy ending were more likely to volunteer to work for disaster relief. In this study, the researchers didn't specify to participants whether the story they read was fact or fiction.

In another study, however, participants were told that a story about a female student who had to deal with sexism from her physics professor was either fictional or nonfictional. Those who thought the story was fictional were more sympathetic to the girl and were more aware of the bias directed at her by the professor. This effect was even stronger when participants read a first-person version of the story. The researchers posited that knowing a story is fictional could increase people's ability to take in a story without putting up their emotional walls because it provides the distance people needed to regulate and manage their emotions (Green, Kaufman, Fitzgerald, Freeman, & Flanagan, 2017).

Furthermore, in an experiment, participants were asked to recall a film they found especially meaningful. The researchers found that when participants said they felt touched, inspired, moved, or other meaningful emotions while they watched, they were more likely to also say the film gave them the desire to live a more moral and meaningful life (Oliver, Hartmann, & Wooley, 2012). So, when viewers watch movies that depict moral beauty and prosocial behavior, it may motivate them to engage in these behaviors themselves. So, contrary to a popularly held believe, watching movies is not always a meaningless experience or all about wasting time. It can make a difference to the viewer and to those whose lives the movie touches.

There are other ways that stories play a role in changing what we think and feel. According to research, stories can even alter our beliefs about our own personalities. Maja Djikic and Keith Oatley (2014) argue that there are three ways fictional stories help us develop our understanding of our own personalities. First, fiction simulates social interactions including our ability to observe the way other people work and how they think. That makes sense, given that our own social interactions require more of us than does watching interactions on a screen. When we're in a conversation, we think about how to reply, whereas when watching a conversation, we see it from a less defensive and more relaxed perspective. Second, stories can change us internally, which can lead, long term, to personality shifts. Third, stories help us understand others' points of view and give us an opportunity to feel what they feel, which can prompt change. In other words, personality changes in response to fiction don't happen because the story persuaded us, but because our experience with fiction allows us to indirectly confront who we are and who we'd like to be.

Recent research has shown that reading fiction can lead to personality shifts, at least temporarily. For example, in one study (Djikic et al., 2009), participants completed a popular personality inventory that measured five key personality traits as well as a measure of emotions. Then they either read Chekhov's *The Lady With the Toy Dog* or a documentary-style version of the narrative. Those who had read the fictional story showed changes in personality traits afterwards, although the traits that changed varied with the person.

In addition, to changing the self, the vicarious experiences we have through stories help us understand others better and develop greater empathy by enhancing what is called "theory of mind." Theory of mind basically involves our ability to simulate another person's perspective—knowing that the person has desires, motives, and a perspective that's all their own. Theory of mind enables us to ascribe an individual's external behavior to his or her internal thoughts, feelings, and motives and helps us relate to others and navigate social interactions (Mellmann, 2002; Zunshine, 2008). While our assessments of people's mental states aren't always correct, this ability is automatically activated whenever we encounter another person—including people we meet in stories.

So, watching and reading stories helps us strengthen our theory of mind skills. For example, Raymond Mar, Keith Oatley, and Jordan Peterson (2009) found that people who read fiction, compared to nonfiction, demonstrated greater empathy, which was positively associated with a person's ability to get lost in a story. Further, the people who read fiction perceived themselves as having more social support than nonfiction readers. Similarly, Jessica Black and Jennifer Barnes (2015) had participants watch either an award-winning television drama like *The West Wing*, *The Good Wife*, or *Lost* or a television documentary. Those who watched the fictional drama did better on a test of theory of mind than those who watched the documentary.

The importance of the fact that meeting characters through fiction helps us develop theory of mind cannot to be understated, especially when we think about how bookworms or popular culture fans are sometimes stereotyped as having lesser social skills. It turns out we may actually be developing our social skills during these experiences. When watching *Beauty and the Beast*, for example, why do we cry when the Beast lies expiring in Belle's arms? Why do we laugh and feel exhilarated when we watch Doc Brown joyously cheer when Marty uses the DeLorean to travel *Back to the Future*? Theory of mind and the empathy that develops because of it are mechanisms by which we can understand how each of these characters (the Beast, Belle, Doc Brown) feels. We experience those feelings *through* them. And we experience our own feelings as people who has developed feelings *for* them. As mentioned before, this dual empathy (Dill-Shackleford et al., 2016) involves us simultaneously feeling from the inside out and from the outside in. This enables us to better understand ourselves and to connect with those around us. We'll examine this further in the next chapter and further discuss the psychology behind how we use popular culture stories to make meaning in our lives.

REFERENCES

Adams, E. (2014). *Murder in the mystery suite*. New York, NY: Penguin.

Bartsch, A., & Oliver, M. B. (2011). Making sense of entertainment: On the interplay of emotion and cognition in entertainment experience. *Journal of Media Psychology*, 23(1), 12–17. doi:10.1027/1864-1105/a000026

Black, J., & Barnes, J. L. (2015). Fiction and social cognition: The effect of viewing award-winning television dramas on theory of mind. *Psychology of Aesthetics, Creativity, and the Arts*, 9(4), 423–429. https://doi.org/10.1037/aca0000031

Cohen, J. (2001). Defining identification: A theoretical look at the identification of audiences with media characters. *Mass Communication & Society, 4*(3), 245–264.

Dill-Shackleford, K. E. (2016). *How fantasy becomes reality: Information and entertainment media in everyday life* (2nd ed.). New York, NY: Oxford University Press.

Dill-Shackleford, K. E., Hopper-Losenicky, K., Vinney, C., Swain, L. F., & Hogg, J. L. (2015). Mad men fans speak via social media: What fan voices reveal about the social construction of reality via dramatic fiction. *Journal of Fandom Studies, 3*(2), 151–170. http://doi.org/10.1386/jfs.3.2.151_1

Dill-Shackleford, K. E., Vinney, C., Hogg, J. L., & Hopper-Losenicky, K. (2016). *Mad men unzipped: Fans on sex, love, and the sixties on TV* (1st ed.). Iowa City, IA: University of Iowa Press.

Dill-Shackleford, K. E., Vinney, C., & Hopper-Losenicky, K. (2016). Connecting the dots between fantasy and reality: The social psychology of our engagement with fictional narrative and its functional value. *Social and Personality Psychology Compass, 10*(11), 634–646. http://doi.org/10.1111/spc3.12274

Djikic, M., & Oatley, K. (2014). The Art in Fiction: From Indirect Communication to Changes of the Self. *Psychology of Aesthetics, Creativity, and the Arts, 8*(4), 498–505.

Djikic, M., Oatley, K., Zoeterman, S., & Peterson, J. B. (2009). On being moved by art: How reading fiction transforms the self. *Creativity Research Journal, 21*(1), 24–29. http://doi.org/10.1080/10400410802633392

Eyal, K., & Cohen, J. (2006). When good *Friends* say goodbye: A parasocial breakup study. *Journal of Broadcasting & Electronic Media, 50*(3), 502–523.

Flores, J. (2016, October). 5 lessons Buffy taught me that helped me survive depression. *Everyday Feminism Magazine*. Retrieved from http://everydayfeminism.com/2016/10/buffy-helped-me-survive-depression/

Gaiman, N. (2011). Afterward. In A. Palmer, J. Webley, & C. von Buhler, *Evelyn Evelyn: A tragic tale in two tomes*. Milwaukie, OR: Dark Horse Books.

Gilbert, S. (2015, March). At 18, Buffy the Vampire Slayer is still revolutionary. *The Atlantic*.

Giles, D. C. (2002). Parasocial interaction: A review of the literature and a model for future research. *Media Psychology, 4*, 279–305.

Giles, D., & Maltby, J. (2006). Praying at the altar of the stars. *Psychologist, 19*(2), 82–85.

Goldstein, T. R. (2009). The pleasure of unadulterated sadness: Experiencing sorrow in fiction, nonfiction, and "in person." *Psychology of Aesthetics, Creativity, and the Arts, 3*(4), 232–237. doi:10.1037/a0015343

Green, M. C., & Brock, T. C. (2000). The role of transportation in the persuasiveness of public narratives. *Journal of Personality and Social Psychology, 79*(5), 701–721. http://doi.org/10.1037//0022-3514.79.5.701

Green, M. C., Brock, T. C., & Kaufman, G. F. (2004). Understanding media enjoyment: The role of transportation into narrative worlds. *Communication Theory, 14*(4), 311–327.

Green, M. C., & Fitzgerald, K. (2017). Fiction as a bridge to action. *Brain and Behavioral Sciences, 40*, 29–30. https://doi.org/doi:10.1017/S0140525X17001716

Green, M. C., Kaufman, G., Fitzgerald, K. S., Freeman, G., & Flanagan, M. (2017). *Using narratives to raise awareness of stereotype threat in STEM*. Unpublished manuscript, University of Buffalo, Buffalo, NY.

Groene, S. L., & Hettinger, V. E. (2015, April 20). Are you "fan" enough? The role of identity in media fandoms. *Psychology of Popular Media Culture*. Advance online publication. http://dx.doi.org/10.1037/ppm0000080

Handscombe, C. (2014a, September 19). I'm the biggest *West Wing* fan you'll ever meet. *Washington Post*.

Handscombe, C. (Ed.). (2014b). *Walk with us: How the* West Wing *changed our lives*. Washington, DC: CH Books.

Holley, D. (2006, September 7). How *Star Trek* changed my life. *BBC News*.

Horton, D., & Wohl, R. R. (1956). Mass communication and parasocial interaction: Observations on intimacy at a distance. *Psychiatry, 19*, 215–229.

Isbouts, J.-P., & Ohler, J. (2013). Storytelling and Media: In K. E. Dill-Shackleford (Ed.), *Oxford Handbook of Media Psychology*. Oxford University Press. https://doi.org/10.1093/oxfordhb/9780195398809.013.0002

Jenson, J. (1992). Fandom as pathology: The consequences of characterization. In L. A. Lewis (Ed.), *The adoring audience: Fan culture and popular media* (pp. 9–29). New York, NY: Routledge.

Kaufman, G. F., & Libby, L. K. (2012). Changing beliefs and behavior through experience-taking. *Journal of Personality and Social Psychology, 103*(1), 1–19. http://doi.org/10.1037/a0027525

Keen, S. (2006). A theory of narrative empathy. *Narrative, 14*(3), 207–236.

Larsen, S. F., & Seilman, U. (1988). Personal remindings while reading literature. *Text, 8*(4), 411–429.

Luckie, M. (2015, October 26). I went to a Black college because of "A Different World." *Buzzfeed News*. Retrieved from https://www.buzzfeed.com/marksluckie/i-went-to-an-hbcu-because-of-a-different-world?utm_term=.chyJQrPW6#.jloymdz15

Maltby, J., Day, L., McCutcheon, L. E., Houran, J., & Ashe, D. (2006). Extreme celebrity worship, fantasy proneness and dissociation: Developing the measurement and understanding of celebrity worship within a clinical personality context. *Personality and Individual Differences, 40*, 273–283. doi: 10.1016/j.paid.2005.07.004

Mar, R. A., & Oatley, K. (2008). The function of fiction is the abstraction and simulation of social experience. *Perspectives on Psychological Science, 3*(3), 173–192. http://doi.org/10.1111/j.1745-6924.2008.00073.x

Mar, R. A., Oatley, K., & Peterson, J. B. (2009). Exploring the link between reading fiction and empathy: Ruling out individual differences and examining outcomes. *Communications, 34*(4), 407–428. http://doi.org/10.1515/COMM.2009.025

McCutcheon, L. E., Lange, R., & Houran, J. (2002). Conceptualization and measurement of celebrity worship. *British Journal of Psychology, 93*, 67–87.

McDonald, D. G., Sarge, M. A., Lin, S-F., Collier, J. G., & Potocki, B. (2015). A role for the self: Media content as triggers for involuntary autobiographical memories. *Communication Research, 42*(1), 3–29. doi:10.1177/0093650212464771

Mellmann, K. (2002). E-motion: Being moved by fiction and media? Notes on fictional worlds, virtual contacts, and the reality of emotions. *PsyArt: An Online Journal for the Psychological Study of the Arts*. Retrieved from http://www.psyartjournal.com/article/show/mellmann-e_motion_being_moved_by_fiction_and_medi

Menninghaus, W., Wagner, V., Hanich, J., Wassiliwizky, E., Jacobsen, T., & Koelsch, S. (2017). The distancing-embracing model of the enjoyment of negative emotions in art reception. *Behavioral and Brain Sciences, 40*, e347. https://doi.org/10.1017/S0140525X17000309

Nielsen Company. (2017). *The total audience report: Q2 2017*. Retrieved from http://www.nielsen.com/content/dam/corporate/us/en/reports-downloads/2017-reports/total-audience-report-q2-2017.pdf

Oatley, K. (1999a). Why fiction may be twice as true as fact: Fiction as cognitive and emotional stimulation. *Review of General Psychology, 3*(2), 101–117.

Oatley, K. (1999b). Meeting of minds: Dialogue, sympathy, and identification in reading fiction. *Poetics, 26*, 439–454.

Oliver, M. B., Hartmann, T., & Woolley, J. K. (2012). Elevation in response to entertainment portrayals of moral virtue. *Human Communication Research, 38*, 360–378. https://doi.org/10.1111/j.1468-2958.2012.01427.x

Tsay-Vogel, M., & Krakowiak, K. M. (2016). Inspirational reality TV: The prosocial effects of lifestyle transforming reality programs on elevation and altruism. *Journal of Broadcasting & Electronic Media, 60*(4), 567–586. https://doi.org/10:1080/08838151.2016.1234474

Sandvoss, C. (2005). *Fans: The mirror of consumption*. Cambridge, UK: Polity Press.

Schimmel, K. S., Harrington, C. L., & Bielby, D. D. (2007). Keep your fans to yourself: The disjuncture between sport studies' and pop culture studies' perspectives on fandom. *Sport in Society, 10*(4), 580–600. doi: 10.1080/17430430701388764

Silver, N., & Slater, M. D. (in press). A safe space for self-expansion: Attachment style and motivation to engage and interact with the story world. *Journal of Social and Personal Relationships*.

Slater, M. D., Ewoldsen, D. R., & Woods, K. W. (2017). Extending Conceptualization and Measurement of Narrative Engagement After-the-Fact: Parasocial Relationship and Imaginative Retrospective Involvement. *Media Psychology*. https://doi.org/ DOI: 10.1080/15213269.2017.1328313

Slater, M. D., Johnson, B. K., Cohen, J., Comello, M. L. G., & Ewoldsen, D. R. (2014). Temporarily expanding the boundaries of the self: Motivations for entering the story world and implications for narrative effects. *Journal of Communication, 64*(3), 439–455. https://doi.org/10.1111/jcom.12100

Suskind, R. (2014, March 7). Reaching my autistic son through Disney. *New York Times Magazine*. Retrieved from https://www.nytimes.com/2014/03/09/magazine/reaching-my-autistic-son-through-disney.html

Taylor, L. D. (2015). Investigating fans of fictional texts: Fan identity salience, empathy, and transportation. *Psychology of Popular Media Culture, 4*(3), 172–187. doi:10.1037/ppm0000028

Tsay-Vogel, M., & Sanders, M. S. (2015). Fandom and the Search for Meaning : Examining Fandom and the Search for Meaning : Examining Communal. *Psychology of Popular Media Culture*.

Zubernis, L., & Larsen, K. (Eds.). (2012). *Fandom at the crossroads: Celebration, shame and fan/producer relationships*. Newcastle upon Tyne, UK: Cambridge Scholars Publishing.

Zunshine, L. (2008). Theory of mind and fictions of embodied transparency. *Narrative, 16*(1), 6.

2

It Matters

Finding Meaning in Stories

You walk down the street, thinking dark thoughts and questioning your faith in humanity. You're having a bad day. Then you see someone in a coffee shop wearing a *Doctor Who* T-shirt and your mood shifts. "Aha!" you think, "a kindred spirit!" You strike up a conversation with your new friend, asking each other "Who's your favorite Doctor?" and sharing inside jokes, like saying "*Allons-y*" and threatening to "exterminate" your barista. Your mood is lifted. Suddenly the world is brighter. Through your love a favorite story you've made a connection, remembered the good times you've had with *Doctor Who*, and make some new ones with your fellow fan.

> Sometimes a feeling is all we humans have to go on.
> —Captain Kirk (William Shatner), *Star Trek: The Original Series*, Season 1, Episode 23 ("Top 10 Best," n.d.)

Finding Truth in Fiction. Karen E. Shackleford and Cynthia Vinney, Oxford University Press (2020).
© Oxford University Press.
DOI: 10.1093/oso/9780190643607.001.0001

Great stories make us *feel something*. We feel like a time lord or a savior of the human race, like anything is possible. Or we get that feeling that *Doctor Who* or *The Matrix* helped us understand some universal truths, which is one reason we are so attached to them in the first place. If you're like us, when you're lost in a favorite story world, there are moments when you are flooded with emotions. You feel that tingle in the back of your neck and that fullness in your heart telling you, "Pay attention! This is important."

Maybe you remember all the times Rory Gilmore and Lane Kim had each other's backs on *Gilmore Girls*, and it makes you think about the deeper meaning of love and friendship. Maybe your life sometimes reminds you of the moment when *Thelma and Louise* drove off a cliff together holding hands. We share the fictional stories that have meaning to us with others who also understand what it means to have a "Rory and Lane moment" or a "Thelma and Louise moment." We like knowing that other people will understand when we reference well-known fiction, like if we refer to a middle-aged seductress as a "Mrs. Robinson," based on the character of that name from *The Graduate*, or commenting that we "have a case of the Mondays" like they do in *Office Space*. Cynthia and her husband like to joke that one of the best ways to calm their spazzy terrier, Cordelia (a name that is also a pop culture reference!), is to treat her like baby Simba and "Circle of Life" her, holding her aloft like at the beginning of *The Lion King*. Our shared story experiences not only give us a shorthand when we communicate with each other, but something we can bond over and enjoy together.

OUR SHARED STORY EXPERIENCES

Our shared investment in stories also gives us a platform for understanding the common emotions we've experienced in response to a specific story. For example, nearly 20 years after *Titanic* sailed across the screen with Kate and Leo on deck, fans who watched the actors talk and hug at the Golden Globes in 2016 tweeted, "Does anyone else see Leo and Kate together now and feel relief from the emotional trauma of *Titanic*?" (Nededog, 2016). The feelings expressed in this tweet are actually backed by a growing body of research. We do indeed feel trauma or joy along with our favorite story characters, and it turns out that the emotional experience itself can be part of the psychological process of self-discovery and even personal growth and change (Djikic, Oately, Zoeterman, & Peterson, 2009). Research also tells us that one of the things deep emotional experiences do is to burn things into our brains. Another fan tweeted: "Kate and Leo won tonight. It's still real to me dammit" (Nededog, 2016). Some would tease or even mock fans for caring about the resolution to the emotional journey of a fictional story, but we wouldn't. *Titanic* touched millions of people, and Kate Winslet and Leonardo DiCaprio were our avatars for that experience. Of course, when we see them together again, it conjures up the emotionally gripping adventures the movie enabled us to share together.

Through our shared love of stories, we connect with others who are drawn to the same story moments, lessons, and worlds as we are. If you assembled a room full of people who grew up around the same time in Western culture, you could prompt the room to fondly remember a nearly endless array of iconic scenes from the stories we have in common. You could yell out, as if you were playing a game, "Okay, do you remember when E.T. made Elliott's bike fly across the sky?" "And do you remember when Ripley wore the exoskeleton to beat back the alien queen?" "Indiana Jones running from a giant boulder?" And so on. We make meaning through both vicarious experiences and through sharing those experiences with others.

We all know what it feels like to be an excited fan, just wanting to celebrate that story we love with other people. Comedian Chris Farley did a skit called the Chris Farley Show on *Saturday Night Live* that sums up the giddy experience of wanting to connect through our favorite stories well ("The Chris Farley Show," 1991). He portrays as the quintessential awkward fan talking with a big star, as seen in Figure 2.1. Chris is pumped up, yet bumbling, as he asks the stars he's speaking with if they "remember" something big from their career. For example, in one episode, Farley asks actor Jeff Daniels if he remembers a scene from his film

Figure 2.1 *The Chris Farley Show*: Always a big fan, Chris asks actor Jeff Daniels if he remembers the time when Melanie Griffith tied him to a bed in *Something Wild* and then throws out his catchphrase, "That was awesome!"

Something Wild where Melanie Griffith ties him to a bed. Then Farley, unable to contain his excitement, asks Daniels if he's seen *Die Hard*, a movie he wasn't even in. "Remember when [Bruce Willis] had to cross all of that broken glass without his shoes on and there was nothing that he could do about it so he just walked on all the broken glass with his bare feet? Did you like that?" asks Farley. "Yes," says Daniels. "Yeah I did too. That was awesome!"

As fans, we can take a little kidding about our potential to be awkward or shy around the stars and creators that produce the memorable experiences that fill our imaginations. We hope that if we were ever lucky enough to have our own talk show, we'd be a bit cooler than Farley, though. Joking aside, Farley's enthusiasm reminds us how much we love to relive exciting moments from our favorite stories, how we grapple with the ideas they present us, and talk about them when we have the chance. Just like the situations we experience in our own lives, or the stories our friends tell us about their experiences, using a story as a means to figure out what we feel and think about things is healthy and adaptive.

FINDING MEANING

Let's explore some ideas we've shared through our connection with popular culture. When we think of films that many of our readers are likely to have seen at least once, and perhaps many times, one that comes to mind is Frank Capra's 1946 film *It's a Wonderful Life*, starring James Steward and Donna Reed. *It's a Wonderful Life* is an American classic, beloved by many. Nominated for five Oscars, the American Film Institute (n.d.) ranks the film at number 20 on its list of "100 Greatest American Films of All Time." Likewise, it's currently ranked as the 24th best film of all times by users of the Internet Movie Database and has the distinction of being the oldest film on that list.

Why do we keep watching *It's a Wonderful Life* year after year no matter our age, gender, or other attributes? Why is it so highly rated by experts and everyday people? The answer to those questions tell us something about how we make meaning from story and why certain stories resonate deeply with individuals across our culture. The answers suggest that our connection with stories helps us resolve personal issues and clarify values, goals, and issues. To remind you of some of the film's quintessential moments, see Table 2.1.

In our search for meaning via *It's a Wonderful Life*, we can reflect back on one of the main ideas touched upon earlier—the relevance of the story to our understanding of ourselves. Films, especially those that are recognized as cultural touchstones, are both shared with others who know and love the story as we do and, at the same time, highly personally meaning.

If we think about the plot of *It's a Wonderful Life*, we can see why the story's messages resonates. As you probably recall, in the film George Bailey marries the love of his life. He dreams of traveling the world with her and leaving behind the small town where they were raised. Instead, he feels stuck in the town running the family business. When a disaster strikes the business, George wishes he had never been born. But his guardian angel, Clarence, makes him realize that his life has meaning because it enriches all the people around him.

TABLE 2.1. FAVORITE QUOTES FROM FRANK CAPRA'S *IT'S A WONDERFUL LIFE*

"I'm shakin' the dust of this crummy little town off my feet and I'm gonna see the world. Italy, Greece, the Parthenon, the Colosseum. Then, I'm comin' back here to go to college and see what they know. And then I'm gonna build things." —George Bailey

"What is it you want, Mary? What do you want? You want the moon? Just say the word and I'll throw a lasso around it and pull it down. Hey. That's a pretty good idea. I'll give you the moon, Mary." —George Bailey

"You've been given a great gift, George: A chance to see what the world would be like without you." —Clarence, George's guardian angel

"Remember, George: no man is a failure who has friends." —Clarence, George's guardian angel

"A toast to my big brother George: The richest man in town." —Harry Bailey

---

When we connect with George Bailey while watching the film, we go back and forth between sharing his experience and realizing how what he's learning is what we need to learn too. In the words of David Allan, writer of CNN's The Wisdom Project, "we are all George Bailey. We have dreams unrealized. We are stressed by daily life. We don't fully appreciate what we have, or by what we've managed to accomplish despite our obstacles" (Allan, 2016). Allan reminds us of the angel Clarence's remarks to George, "Each man's life touches so many other lives. When he isn't around, he leaves an awful hole." *It's a Wonderful Life* feels good to a lot of us because it affirms core values such as the notion that a life well lived is one that serves others and that friends and loved ones, not money, are what make a person rich. It's comforting to think that it is not material wealth or outward success that ultimately matter, but rather it is our value to other people.

Another part of what captures our empathy is George Bailey's experience of trial and redemption. We are attracted to those story arcs where the hero gets precariously close to losing something important but is snatched back from the edge of oblivion just in the nick of time. Figure 2.2 shows the scene where George is at his lowest point, contemplating suicide on a snowy bridge. Psychologist Dan McAdams, author of the book *The Redemptive*

Figure 2.2 A meaningful moment in *It's a Wonderful Life*, when George Bailey (Jimmy Stewart) stands on a dark, snowy bridge wondering if he's more useful to his family dead than alive. We can think of this moment if a similar thought ever crosses our own minds and remember that George's life turned around, and so will ours.

Self (McAdams, 2013), has documented our shared love of telling our own personal redemption stories in his research and how much these kinds of stories are reproduced in our culture. Because of this shared attraction to and familiarity with redemption stories, when we watch George Bailey's life unfold, we easily experience it with him. His story reminds us of our own, and we root for him as we would for ourselves. Ultimately, *It's a Wonderful Life* allows us to celebrate and affirm someone else's life while celebrating and affirming our own. As George gains insight about the meaning of life, so do we. This is why the story attracts us so strongly.

Something for Everyone

Of course, there is no book, show, or film that is universally loved and regarded. That would be impossible. There are stories that are widely loved or appreciated and that continue to garner an audience year after year, but there will never be a complete consensus on a single story. Take Frank Capra's work as an example. Capra directed films such as *It Happened One Night* (1934), *You Can't Take It with You* (1938), and *Mr. Smith Goes to Washington* (1939). He won multiple Academy Awards and a lifetime achievement award from the American Film Institute. However, some criticized him for being too idealistic, even sappy. Some critics dismissed his films as Capra-corn, because they felt they were so corny.

But one person's Capra-corn is another's cornucopia. Consider the following study: Markus Appel, Michael Slater, and Mary Beth Oliver (2019) investigated how personality factors play a role in our interpretation of meaningful films. They examined the responses of a certain personality type, known as the Dark Triad, to movies that deal with the human condition and the what makes life valuable. The Dark Triad consists of three personality characteristics: Machiavellianism, narcissism, and psychopathy. These individuals are self-promoting and lack empathy for others. So even when they felt touched, moved, and inspired by a meaningful film, they also thought it was inauthentic and corny. The researchers think this means that while people like this can still be moved by films with these characteristics, they put up defenses against these feelings by rejecting the movies. Obviously, what's going on with these individuals isn't limited to their stated opinions about the films, but this study does predict that they'll respond negatively to films for which others openly express affection. Still, the point is that each of us has something we are drawn to, something we can find meaning in. While we don't have to agree on what those stories are, we should acknowledge that there's something out there for just about everyone.

Furthermore, even if people like the same story, it won't affect everyone in the same way. For example, in *It's a Wonderful Life*, we're told that every time a bell rings, an angel gets his wings. Some of us will reject that idea, even make fun of it as too sappy. Others will embrace it, with some taking it so far as saying an angel just got his wings when they notice a bell ring. Others will take it as metaphor for something else. There are many ways to react to this one idea. Still, in general, many people identify with the core values of the film and take away their own personal understanding of it.

Anne Bartsch, a communication scholar at the University of Leipzig in Germany, has explored the meaning we derive from stories. In a 2012 study, Bartsch argues that watching movies and television can fulfill psychosocial needs, including feeling emotions and self-reflection. Bartsch (2012) says that entertainment satisfies "individuals' search for deeper insight, meaning, and purpose in life" (p. 273). She found that there are seven kinds of gratifications that viewers experience when they engage with a movie or TV show. These are (a) fun, (b) thrill, (c) empathic sadness, (d) contemplative emotional experiences, (e) emotional engagement with characters, (f) social sharing of emotions, and (g) vicarious release of emotions. These gratifications show that we like to feel with and for fictional characters, even if the emotions are ones we think of as negative, like sadness (empathic sadness and emotional engagement with characters). And we like emotional experiences that make us think (contemplative emotional experiences).

Anne Bartsch and Penn State University's Mary Beth Oliver have conducted a great deal of research together, along with their colleagues, on the cognitive and emotional factors that are key to the psychological experience of consuming a story (Oliver & Bartsch, 2011; Bartsch & Oliver, 2011). Their work is based on the uses and gratifications approach to media, which claims that people actively select the media they consume based on their specific wants and needs (Rubin, 1993). In other words, people make conscious choices when it comes to what they watch and read, and their awareness of their desires and the experience a story can provide drives those choices. Sometimes what we want or need is fun or thrills. For example, if we come home from a hard day at work feeling depressed, we might put on a television sitcom like *Will and Grace* or *The Big Bang Theory* to distract us from our problems and make ourselves laugh. This desire to consume fare that increases positive emotions while decreasing or distracting from negative ones is called hedonic motivation (Bartsch & Hartmann, 2017; Oliver & Raney, 2011). Other times, however, we want something more. Maybe we're feeling contemplative and wish to explore what it means to be alive, with a little action thrown in, so we cue up a science fiction thriller, like the classic *Blade Runner*. This desire to find meaning and insight in a story is called eudaimonic motivation (Oliver & Raney, 2011). People who are more likely to be eudaimonically motivated to take in a story usually have personalities that lend themselves toward thinking, being self-reflective, and seeking meaning in life. When people watch or read meaningful entertainment, their response to the story is referred to as "appreciation." Appreciation is an experience that involves mixed emotions, such as the sensation that something is moving, combined with the perception that the story is meaningful and the desire to contemplate the thoughts and feelings it inspired (Oliver & Bartsch, 2010).

Now, we know that no one really sits down to watch a movie or read a book saying, "And now to work on my psychosocial needs!" (Well, we know some nerdy researchers who would—okay, *we* might!) Besides, we don't always know what we might learn or appreciate in a story. Sometimes we find deep meaning in what we thought was going to be merely comic relief. And sometimes what we think will be meaningful is anything but. When we do watch and read meaningful stories, however, these experiences of appreciation can enhance our well-being over time because they help us think through what we value and what we want. And we have data to back that statement up!

The two of us, along with Courtney Plante and Anne Bartsch, (Vinney, Dill-Shackleford, Plante, & Bartsch, 2019) set out to document the various experiences that film and television fans have and to relate those experiences to health. While common wisdom, both from media researchers and society in general, has it that consuming popular culture is mostly a frivolous diversion people take part in for enjoyment, we believed something deeper might be happening. We believed that people who loved popular culture often had experiences of deep meaning with their favorite stories.

In our research began by asking 210 mostly American popular culture fans questions in seven areas of fan experience: enthusiasm; enjoyment; appreciation; self-definition; and personal, social, and participatory fan experiences. Participants were asked to name a specific TV show or movie of which they considered themselves a fan and answer our questions about that particular story. We then performed a statistical analysis that told us which of these concepts tended to go together and what items on our survey were the strongest.

Next, we developed a short survey that measured three facets of fan experience: enthusiasm for one's fan object, appreciation of one's fan object, and social interaction with others who share an interest in one's fan object. Enthusiasm was measured by items like, "How much do you love [your favorite television show or movie]?" Note that the phrase "your favorite show or movie" was replaced by the name of the show or film that participants identified as their favorite. In other words, if they said they were a fan of *Firefly*, the sentence read, "How much do you love *Firefly*?" An example of an appreciation question is, "*Firefly* helps me think about the things I value." And a social interaction item was, "I have friends who are also fans of *Firefly*."

We then asked another set of participants, this one made up of 201 fans from the United Kingdom, to complete our short survey along with a well-being scale. What we found was that overall well-being was significantly positively related to these fan experiences. In other words, our data indicate that the bigger fan you are of a specific piece of popular culture, the greater your well-being. The more enthusiasm you have for your favorite story, the more you talk with other people about it, and the more you find meaning and insight in it, the healthier you are.

Similarly, Cynthia completed a study of *Buffy the Vampire Slayer* fans where she asked them about their experiences as fans and about how much emotional and cognitive meaning they derived from the show (Vinney, 2016). Her results showed that people who strongly identified as *Buffy* fans felt the show was more meaningful, reflected more on the show, and experienced more poignant, moving emotions in response to it. Further, being a bigger fan led to more thoughts about the self, which led to an increased sense that the show was meaningful. Cynthia's findings suggest that our connections with the stories that resonate with us can be deeply personal. These meaningful experiences with popular media stories are important because they offer us opportunities to learn and grow. Such stories enable us to consider our values, offer strategies to deal with hardships, and decide what's important to us, ultimately, enhancing our well-being and leaving us psychologically healthier and happier.

Furthermore, media researchers Mina Tsay-Vogel and Meghan Sanders (2017) found that Harry Potter fans who sought meaning in the entertainment they consumed used were more likely to feel like they were a member of the fan community and were more likely to communicate with other fans. In addition, fan community membership enhanced a number of these fans' experiences with the franchise, such as gaining appreciation for the stories, enjoying the stories more, and gaining more knowledge from the experience. Taking these recent findings together, we can easily start to see how our associations with popular fiction can be good for us. This stands in sharp contrast to the stereotype of popular culture lovers as sad, lonely losers. Instead, fans are active and vibrant thinkers and socializers.

Gaining Insight and Learning Lessons

We all likely have a character from a story that we sometimes imagine ourselves being or who we think about when we're trying to figure out what we want to do or whom we want to be. We like to live vicariously through them and maybe think about how we can be more like them. Maybe these characters help us sort out what risks we are willing to take in life and which aren't worthwhile to us. Stories help us consider all of those possibilities and infinitely more.

When we find deep wisdom in a story, we perk up and pay more attention to it. As we watch the glowing screen or turn the final page, perhaps with tears streaming down our faces, we take the time to think that we are glad we encountered this story; we feel renewed or changed by it. To some degree, we may feel we can carry the ideas from the story into our own lives and use them as a guide for living, as a cautionary tale, or as a reaffirmation of what matters. We appreciate the opportunity to explore and clarify our values, including the big questions in life. And we are drawn to stories that inspire us to become a better version of ourselves.

Many of us have had these moving experiences with stories ourselves. Perhaps you are a fan of a particular franchise and you've talked with

TABLE 2.2. SPIRITUAL AND EMOTIONAL LIFE LESSONS FROM *HARRY POTTER*

1. Be open to love.
2. Don't judge someone based on the past.
3. All knowledge is power.
4. Never underestimate someone.
5. Sometimes it's okay to give up.
6. Learn to let go and move forward.
7. Beware of pompous people.
8. Stay true to your nerdy friends.
9. Realize your family is more important than you think.
10. Speak your pain.
11. Don't fear death because love is stronger than death.

Adapted from Huang (2018) and Sheahen (2008).

friends about the insights on life the story revealed to you. While there is often still a stigma associated with the assertion that we can learn something important from popular culture, we know, and you may well know too, that you aren't alone in gaining insights and honing your understanding of life through popular culture stories.

There are so many examples of people sharing how much a story meant to them. To see just some of these, take a look at Tables 2.2 and 2.3. For example, Huang (2018) and Sheahen (2008) shared some core spiritual and emotional ideas they discovered in the Harry Potter series (see Table 2.2). For instance, they caution against underestimating anyone. This is a reference to the way Voldemort underestimated and dismissed Harry's abilities as a wizard (Huang, 2018). And, actually, that concept is a reminder of our shared love for stories about the underdog. For whatever reason someone is considered an unlikely hero, be they young, small, weak, or otherwise, we root for them to achieve ultimate victory. As Unitarian Universalist minister Deborah Cayer (2017) said,

TABLE 2.3. LIFE LESSONS FROM *FORREST GUMP*

1. You'll never know what you're capable of until you try.
2. To have good friends, be a good friend.
3. Pay attention.
4. Do what you love, no matter what.
5. Stay positive and focused.
6. It's great to give back.
7. Expect the unexpected and be open minded.

Adapted from Messer (2014).

I believe it's possible to reconstitute [the] world, because that's the plot line of just about every folk story, and every sacred story we humans tell. We're Frodo and Sam [from *Lord of the Rings*]; we're little and the world's evils are large. Even though we shake and cry, we stick together and encourage each other, and when we see a tiny opportunity we seize it. (¶6)

The lessons we draw from fiction enable us to actively use the stories we love as a vehicle for personal transformation. As we detailed in the previous chapter, people acknowledge that stories have helped them change their lives. As Djikic et al. (2009) put it, "for avid book readers, books were powerful instigators of self-change" (p. 24). Whether we knowingly select a story that fits our current emotional and social needs or whether we stumble upon it, we might find something there that we need to know, something we can adapt and assimilate into our own lives.

Sometimes while reading or watching a story, the emotions flood over us, and we get a feeling of clarity and comprehension—that we understand something like never before. Maybe while watching *Veronica Mars* or *Rocky*, you felt you witnessed how important it was for a character to stand up themselves and face their fears. So later, when a challenging situation happened in your life, you thought of that story moment and it inspired you to face your fears as well.

In a fascinating study, researchers in the United Kingdom (Alderson-Day, Bernini, & Fernyhough, 2017) investigated how readers experience fictional characters both during and after reading. One participant related:

> I become so engrossed in a novel that the characters become real to me. I know that they are not real, but they *feel* real. It is as vivid as watching the characters in a film on TV where the screen is my mind's eye. In fact, if I can't hear the characters' voices, I find it impossible to carry on reading the novel because it is the vivid experience of characters' voices (or sometimes the author's "voice") that I want when I read a novel. (Alderson-Day et al., 2017, p. 104)

These researchers found that 70% of readers "hear" the voices of characters as they read. Nineteen percent of readers also had what the researchers termed an "experiential crossing," or vividly experiencing the character in a nonreading, real-life context. This might involve the reader hearing the voice of the character or experiencing the character's response to or perspective on a situation when they're not reading. These readers constructed a "mindscape" or consciousness for the character that they could experience outside of reading.

We are guessing that if you are a fan of a story and its characters, the experiences detailed by the participants in this research are nothing new to you. Speaking for ourselves, we have imagined how a favorite character might think and feel during experiences we've had in our own lives. As a personal example, Karen is a fan of *Parks and Recreation*, a comedy mockumentary in which, in uncomfortable moments, characters glance at the camera as if to say, "Can you believe this?" Looking into the camera and "looking" at the viewer like this is called "breaking the fourth wall." During her own awkward moments, Karen sometimes imagines she is being filmed like the *Parks and Rec* characters and that there is an audience out there sharing in the awkwardness. This is similar to thinking about how one of those characters would react to her life's awkward moments.

So, breaking the fourth wall is a way for a character to bring the audience into the story. Likewise, having an experiential crossing is a way for the viewer or reader to bring the character into their world. Both breaking the fourth wall and having an experiential crossing are ways to increase the merging of the story and its audience. Experiences like this enable us to experience the story and its characters on a very intimate level. From there, it's not a far leap to see how we might take what we learn from the characters and apply it in our own lives.

For example, research has shown that reading selections from the Harry Potter series helps kids develop less biased attitudes toward stigmatized groups like immigrants. In one study (Vezzali, Stathi, Giovannini, Capozza, & Trifiletti, 2014), a researcher read excerpts to Italian fifth-graders about prejudice from the series where one of the main characters, Hermione Granger, is called what amounts to a wizarding world racial slur ("mudblood") by Draco Malfoy, a peer who regularly insults and harms Harry and his friends. The chosen text also involves the emotional reactions of the key characters: Hermione's shame and her friends' anger at the insults. We think this study was particularly smart in that the researchers chose a story about childhood friendship and realistic childhood conflict, which likely is something these elementary school children could relate to. And, indeed, the children who identified with Harry Potter improved their attitudes about immigrants, becoming more accepting of this out-group. We'll provide more details on this study in Chapter 8 of this volume.

Now, someone out there might scoff and say that the problems of wizards and witches who have magical powers are irrelevant to the lives of real children. Presumably these lovely Italian children will not be facing off against a legendary villain in an epic to-the-death wand fight. (The proper term for the person who pointed this out would be "a smart aleck," or in *Harry Potter* parlance, "a right git.") But avoiding a wand battle with an epic villain doesn't mean you avoid being exposed to prejudice. Harry and his friends model antiprejudice values, something readers, including these Italian kids, learn from. And by seeing characters they love hurting when they are discriminated against or being accepting of those that are different, readers' contact with these characters causes them to consider their perspectives on people who are unlike themselves. If they like Harry

Potter and his friends, they effectively get to see what it's like to overcome prejudice through the eyes of these characters, an experience that helps shape or reshape their values to better align with those expressed in Harry Potter. Of course, this is something storytellers have done forever—addressing real-life prejudice by writing a story where fictional out-groups stand in for real-world groups, enabling people to examine this issue while keeping real-world problems at a safe distance.

Our children watch *Sesame Street*, where they encounter Muppets with everyday problems (or MEPs—just kidding! There's not an acronym for that). Kermit the Frog is famous for singing about how it's not easy being green. Of course, talking about being green moves the discussion to a comfortable distance from real-world discrimination related to skin color. But parents know that not only can it be hard to be green, it can be hard to be black or brown, or to have a disability, or to be a part of a nonmajority religion. Kids may not be able to articulate it, but they implicitly understand this principle and apply it. And the parents are less likely to argue with Kermit's difficulties being green because they don't have preconceived notions about what it means to be this particular color.

The Line Between History and Fiction

Neuroscientist Norman Holland (2009a) says that when we immerse ourselves in a story, we enter what Csikszentmihalyi (1998) called a flow state, where we lose our connection to our sense of self and our environment. Instead, we strongly connect to the character and the character's environment. We stop thinking about reality, and we vicariously experience the character's feelings. Similarly, Holland (2009b) argues that when we first enter a story, we open ourselves up and automatically accept it. Later, we engage in effortful processing to decide if we want to reject some elements of the story. For example, we may accept that in Sherlock Holmes's Victorian London, certain historical artifacts, like hansom cabs, were real, but that Holmes himself was not.

How do we decide where to draw the line? There is much in fiction that is based on fact and much that comes from the author's (or director's or producer's) imagination. There are some fictional characters who seem to lend themselves to confusion. It's harder to tell whether the character is based on history or is entirely fictional. Sherlock Holmes is one such example. In fact, Massie (2014) the recently took on this subject in a *London Telegraph* article titled, "It's Elementary: Of Course, Sherlock Holmes Was Real," and went on to say that "as the most famous Englishman of the 19th century is honored at the Museum of London, let's not pretend he was a fictional character."

Massie (2014) argued that Holmes's London is "the London of our historical imagination" and that there is, in fact, a plaque at 221B Baker Street to mark the famous address associated with Holmes. When 221B Baker Street is arguably more famous than 10 Downing Street where the prime minister resides, it's clear that it's not always easy to tell the difference between history and imagination.

And, as children, we may learn about Sherlock Holmes and Professor Moriarty in much the same way we learn about Jesse James and the Pinkerton Detective Agency, which ultimately hunted down Jesse James. Then again, Holmes is much more famous than the Pinkertons.

One thing that's key about Holmes is his ability to see details and extrapolate from them. He's famous for describing how he got from clues to conclusions as being "elementary, my dear Watson." Many other detective duos have been based on Holmes and Watson. For example, Shawn Spencer and Burton "Gus" Guster on TV's *Psych* is a Holmes and Watson story. In the goofy and irreverent *Psych*, Shawn (James Roday) was trained by his cop father Henry (Corbin Bernsen) to notice clues and solve crimes. Meanwhile, childhood bestie Gus (Dulé Hill, also known for playing Charlie on the *West Wing*) acts as his Watson, supplying some of the more down-to-earth facts needed in the case, as well as providing humor. Fans and the curious can find out more in *Psych's Guide to Crime Fighting for the Totally Unqualified* (Spencer & Guster, 2013), which is "authored" by the character Shawn Spencer with contributions by Burton Guster (aka "Gus"). Some digging will reveal Chad Gilovich as the real author of the book. But attributing authorship to *Psych*'s characters is another example that leads to reality and imagination blending in our minds.

After watching *The DaVinci Code*, which mixes historical fact with imagination and speculation, isn't it sometimes unclear which parts were story and which parts were history?

Is Paul Bunyan real? How about Jonny Appleseed? Some are said to be based on historical figures; some are legend. Let's face it, when a president became famous for his role on a reality TV show where he fired employees and that same president often fires his own staff members, the line between fact and fiction seems hopelessly entangled.

Sharing Stories

While our responses and reactions to stories can be highly personal, popular culture isn't only consumed by one person in private. Even from a young age, we understand that people everywhere are watching or reading the same stories that we are. Children understand, for example, that their peers may have seen *The LEGO Batman Movie* and that children across the world may also have seen it. In many cases, if a story is popular enough, we don't even have to see or read it to have a general knowledge of the characters and storylines, be it Darth Vader from *Star Wars* or the story of Dorothy's trip to the land of Oz in *The Wizard of Oz*. What we can infer, then, that one thing we have in common with many people is a common love and understanding of a given story. When a child goes to a local store and sees other children buying a T-shirt or a toy version of *Guardian of the Galaxy*'s Groot, it conveys the message that their peers also endorse and appreciate Groot's story. In this case, it's a simple message: People have seen Groot and like him, just like I do. Just saying the words, "I am Groot"—the character's single line of dialogue from the film—can convey meaning to other people who know and like Groot and offer an opportunity for social connection.

So, catchphrases from movies or TV shows often reflect bits of shared experience. And we can apply them in our own lives to express ourselves and convey our affiliation with a given story. If the catchphrase is well-placed, other don't even have to know where it comes from to enjoy hearing it. But for those who do know the source of the quote, it makes a shared social experience that much more meaningful. For example, a well-known TV catchphrase from the show *Arrested Development* is "I've made a huge mistake." Wired magazine's practical guide to the catchphrases of *Arrested Development* suggests using "I've made a huge mistake" either when you really have made one or when you want to joke about a little mistake, as in:

"Speaker 1: *Wait—was that half-and-half or non-dairy creamer?'*
Speaker 2: I've made a huge mistake." (Edidin, 2013)

We talked earlier about the difference between hedonic (pleasurable) and eudaimonic (meaningful) entertainment. "I've made a huge mistake," as a catchphrase could certainly just evoke a simple pleasurable experience. But this particular phrase has the potential to evoke more, including the mixed experience of pleasure and meaning for the viewer. An *Arrested Development* viewer will have seen this phrase presented in a variety of contexts, some silly and some moving. For example, the saying connects to another *Arrested Development* catchphrase, "There's always money in the banana stand." When business mogul George Bluth Sr. is in jail for his shady activities, he hints to his son Michael, now running the family business, where he can find some money. George insists, "There's always money in the banana stand." Sadly, Michael interprets this to mean that he can make money running the family's banana-stand business. However, George Sr. was trying to tell Michael that money was quite literally hidden inside the banana-stand building. It's only after Michael burns down the banana stand to express some of his pent-up emotions that he learns he's "made a huge mistake" and set fire to $250,000 in cash. This plotline is funny. It's absurd. On one level, it's just a joke. But on another level, it can remind us of the absurdity of life, bad decisions, and how easily we can misunderstand each other. And when we use this catchphrase in our own lives, especially in the presence of others who understand our reference, we can make a connection with another person while also tacitly bringing up all the humor and poignancy associated with this single line.

Similarly, in a much-loved episode of *Star Trek: The Next Generation*, one of the main characters, Captain Jean-Luc Picard (Patrick Stewart) is stranded on an alien planet in a dangerous situation. He is having trouble communicating with an alien leader because the leader speaks only in metaphor, for instance, repeating the phrase, "Darmok and Jalad at Tanagra." Picard realizes that this phrase is a metaphor for working together to defeat a common enemy. Fans of the show who love this moment therefore can say to each other, "Darmok and Jalad at Tanagra" as a way of saying, "We need to work together." Figure 2.3 shows a Darmok-inspired T-shirt Karen purchased for her husband on Etsy that commemorates this meaningful idea.

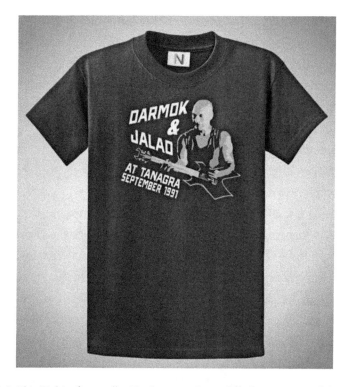

Figure 2.3 This T-shirt from seller Nerdvana on Etsy celebrates a meaningful message on *Star Trek: The Next Generation* that sometimes the answer is for two people from different perspectives to work together for the common good.

Getting the Message

That brings us to another topic: a story's ability to evoke meaning in a viewer or reader is not limited to genres that are classically associated with learning and growth, like serious dramas. Naturally, when we sit down to watch *Schindler's List* or *Citizen Kane*, we understand that we will be taken on an emotional journey, and we may come away feeling that we have been poignantly reminded of what's important in life. But growth can spring from a story experience not explicitly designed or marketed as serious art or entertainment-education.

One of the elemental features of storytelling is that it is inherently social. There are some inherent social messages folded into a popular movie, TV show, or book that we don't often think about. We know that the show was written, acted, directed, and produced by real people. We know that a television network, film studio, or other business entity agreed to produce and air the show or print the book. The point is that any popular culture narrative has been approved by multiple people before it makes it to us. What that adds up to is that the story is socially sanctioned, at least to some degree. If there is a value or a message expressed in the story, there is a sense of legitimacy behind it.

We'll give you a personal example of this. When Karen was a girl, she remembers watching the show *Three's Company* with her brother and sister. *Three's Company* is a comedy about roommates who, to get the landlord to agree to let a man live with two women, give the excuse that the male roommate is gay (remember, this was the 1970s). So, the show presents scenes where male roommate, Jack, who is not gay, interacts with his attractive, female roommates for laughs. Nine-year-old Karen remembers the show made her wonder things like: When people are in their 20s, do they live in apartments with their friends? Do adults think anything about sex is funny? Do adults think being gay is funny? Am I going to work in a flower shop (like roommate Janet) when I grow up? Karen was assuming that the adults who make TV shows were basing them on how real adults understand the world. Of course, as an adult she knows there are more layers to it than that, although asking such questions is a step toward developing what we call media literacy—understanding the sources of media production and its implications.

In taking meaning from a TV show, then, we might imagine and be impacted by the characters as if they were real people. After all, even if the characters are fictional, there are real people behind them. So this means, for instance, that if little Karen witnessed the characters on *Three's Company* laughing every time Jack's being gay was mentioned (which reflected our immaturity with the topic and our discomfort with sexuality as a culture at the time), she would ponder if in real-life people think being gay is funny. While we can't really see things as we did when we were 9, our 9-year-old selves would have some sense of the fact that it takes people to make a television show and that these people are communicating through their show that they think that being gay is funny. And that's really the bottom line: when a story expresses specific values, it implies that there are many people who hold those values. This is important when one is using a story as a vehicle to figure out how the world works and what it all means.

In fact, a recent study suggests that it is a basic human tendency to look to stories to understand societal norms and values. A group of researchers led by anthropologist Daniel Smith examined stories told by a hunter-gatherer population in the Philippines called the Agta (Smith et al., 2017). According to these scholars, "hunter-gatherer societies have strong oral storytelling traditions dictating social behavior" (p. 2). The Agta stories are no exception to this observation. A majority of the stories told by the Agta elders were about social behavior, including communicating social norms and behavioral expectations. Agta mostly survive by foraging so their stories conveyed messages that would help in this endeavor by championing values like cooperation and sexual and social equality. The researchers even found that Agta camps with more skilled storytellers exhibited higher levels of cooperation. Furthermore, the Agta said they'd prefer to live in camps with skilled storytellers, more than they wanted to live with talented foragers, and skilled storytellers had more children than others in the population. Taken together, these findings demonstrate how valuable storytelling is in conveying social norms and coordinating social behavior, and the rewards that come with being someone who is able to effectively communicate these things through stories.

Storytelling in Western cultures through movies and television is certainly more technologically sophisticated and involves many more people than the oral tradition of the Agta. But our movies and TV shows are no less powerful in conveying norms and values. This is why the question of who believes the messages a story communicates, why they are being communicated, and who might benefit from them become so important to ask of our popular culture stories.

Looking at this from another angle, as adults we may or may not learn more details about the question of how a story is produced and who believes it the perspectives and principles it communicates. For example, when it comes to a movie, we know that there is a writer who writes a script that articulates a story. The story could have been the writer's original idea or may have come from another source. Then actors are hired to act out the script. The actors' representation of their characters comes from their interpretations of their characters' personality, perspectives, and beliefs. Then the director helps shape the story as a whole. For instance, the director can tell an actor how to understand a character's actions or deliver a line of dialogue, adding her own interpretations to the mix. Then there are all kinds of other professionals who add to the story, from those who work on the lighting and costuming to those who compose the musical score and on and on. In the end, myriad people help shape a highly produced movie.

Becoming aware of this fact, enables us to ask ourselves if an idea embedded in the movie is a product of the director, the writer, the actor, or some more nuanced combination of players. For example, if there are a lot of films that tell stories about humans in the dystopian postapocalypse in one year (something that's been trendy for a while now, actually, from movie and TV series like *The Hunger Games* to *The Walking Dead* to *The Handmaid's Tale* to the 2017 surge in interest in novels like *1984*), we might consider how the filmmakers are using their movies to reflect our own troubled times and how society can deal with our own struggles in the here and now.

As audience members, it's natural to feel that the story comes from the actors. We'll discuss the specifics in Chapter 3, but the thing to know for now is that people tend to believe that when a person performs an action, they are doing it out of personal motivation. So, if we're wondering who believes the ideas in a film or TV show, we're likely to come away thinking that the actors who performed the characters' actions and delivered the characters' dialogue does. This is why we see many interviewers on talk shows and at press junkets ask actors about their characters' motivations and what might happen to them next. But it may or may not be true, which is why many actors push back on such questions by suggesting their interviewers ask a story's writers to get insight into its characters. In other words, while the actors embody the characters, they aren't the voice of authority on them. That privilege lies with the writers who choose exactly what the actors will perform as the characters. However, if the film persuades us to believe that the ideas it champions are important, through the talent of the actors and the hard work of the whole behind-the-scenes team, then the film will convince us to internalize some of its perspective in our own lives, changing us in small or large ways. So, whether the universally loved ideas from *It's a Wonderful Life* are there because Frank Capra believed them or Jimmy Stewart did (or both—or neither), what matters to us as viewers is that we walk away having taken the film's message to heart.

Would you like to hang out with an actor like Tom Hanks or Meryl Streep because a film they performed in really spoke to you? Do you believe Tom is like the Tom we see on screen? Or maybe he's actually completely different from his well-known affable characters? How would we know? In the next chapter, we get into the rather complex psychology of separating an actor from the on-screen roles they play. Along the way, we'll talk about how we feel if an actor's private actions betray his lovable persona, an issue that has received a great deal of attention in the last several years.

REFERENCES

Alderson, B., Bernini, M., & Fernyhough, C. (2017). Uncharted features and dynamics of reading: Voices, characters, and crossing of experiences. *Consciousness and Cognition, 49*, 98–109. https://doi.org/10.1016/j.concog.2017.01.003

Allan, D. (2016, December). It's a wonderful lesson. *CNN: The Wisdom Project*. Retrieved from http://www.cnn.com/2015/12/21/health/its-a-wonderful-life-lesson-wisdom-project/index.html

American Film Institute. (2007, May 20). AFI's 100 years, 100 movies. Retrieved from http://www.afi.com/100Years/movies10.aspx

Appel, M., Slater, M. D., & Oliver, M. B. (2019). Repelled by virtue? The dark triad (narcissism, Machiavellianism, psychopathy) and eudaimonic narratives. *Media Psychology, 22*(5), 769–794.

Bartsch, A. (2012). Emotional Gratification in Entertainment Experience. Why Viewers of Movies and Television Series Find it Rewarding to Experience Emotions. *Media Psychology, 15*(3), 267–302. https://doi.org/10.1080/15213269.2012.693811

Bartsch, A., & Hartmann, T. (2017, January 13). The role of cognitive and affective challenge in entertainment experience. *Communication Research, 44*(1), 29–53. https://doi.org/10.1177/0093650214565921

Bartsch, A., & Oliver, M. B. (2011). Making Sense of Entertainment. *Journal of Media Psychology: Theories, Methods, and Applications, 23*(1), 12–17. https://doi.org/10.1027/1864-1105/a000026

Cayer, D. (2017, February). How is it with your heart? Life at Eno River Unitarian Universalist Fellowship. Eno River, NC. Retrieved from http://www.eruuf.org/From-the-Ministers/in-care-february-2017.html

The Chris Farley Show, interview with Jeff Daniels. (1991, October 5). *Saturday Night Live* [video clip]. Retrieved from https://www.nbc.com/saturday-night-live/video/the-chris-farley-show/n10099

Csikszenthihalyi, M. (1998). *Finding Flow*. New York: Basic Books.

Djikic, M., Oatley, K., Zoeterman, S., & Peterson, J. B. (2009). On being moved by art: How reading fiction transforms the self. *Creativity Research Journal, 21*, 24–29. https://doi.org/10.1080/10400410802633392

Edidin, R. (2013, May 23). A practical guide to the catchphrases of *Arrested Development*. *Wired*. Retrieved from https://www.wired.com/2013/05/guide-arrested-development-catchphrases/

Holland, N. N. (2009a). *Literature and the brain*. Gainesville, FL: PSYArt Foundation.

Holland, N. N. (2009b, August 6). Why don't we doubt Spiderman's existence? *Psychology Today*. Retrieved from https://www.psychologytoday.com/us/blog/is-your-brain-culture/200908/why-dont-we-doubt-spider-mans-existence-3

Huang, S. (2018, May). Life lessons from Harry Potter. *Belief.net*. Retrieved from http://www.beliefnet.com/entertainment/movies/harry-potter/09/06/life-lessons-from-harry-potter.aspx

McAdams, D. P. (2013). *The redemptive self: Stories Americans live by* (2nd ed.). New York, NY: Oxford University Press.

Messer, L. (2014, July 6). 7 life lessons from "Forrest Gump" on its 20th anniversary. *ABC News*. Retrieved from http://abcnews.go.com/Entertainment/life-lessons-forrest-gump-20th-anniversary/story?id=24417895

Nededog, J. (2016, January). Leonardo DiCaprio and Kate Winslet had a "Titanic" reunion at the Golden Globes, and fans went nuts. *Business Insider: Entertainment*. Retrieved from http://www.businessinsider.com/leonardo-dicaprio-and-kate-winslet-golden-globes-2016-1

Oliver, M. B., & Bartsch, A. (2010). Appreciation as audience response: Exploring entertainment gratifications beyond hedonism. *Human Communication Research, 36*, 53–81. https://doi.org/10.1111/j.1468-2958.2009.01368.x

Oliver, M. B., & Bartsch, A. (2011). Appreciation of entertainment: The importance of meaningfulness via virtue and wisdom. *Journal of Media Psychology, 23*(1), 29–33. https://doi.org/10.1027/1864-1105/a000029

Oliver, M. B., & Raney, A. A. (2011). Entertainment as pleasurable and meaningful: Identifying hedonic and eudaimonic motivations for entertainment consumption. *Journal of Communication, 61*(5), 984–1004. https://doi.org/10.1111/j.1460-2466.2011.01585.x

Rubin, A. M. (1993). Audience activity and media use. *Communication Monographs, 60*, 98–105.

Sheahen, L. (2008, September). Life lessons from Harry Potter. *Belief.net*. Retrieved from http://www.beliefnet.com/entertainment/2008/09/life-lessons-from-harry-potter.aspx

Smith, D., Schlaepfer, P., Major, K., Dyble, M., Page, A. E., Thompson, J., ... Migliano, A. B. (2017). Cooperation and the evolution of hunter-gatherer storytelling. *Nature Communication, 8*(1853), 1–9. https://doi.org/10.1038/s41467-017-02036-8

Spencer, S., & Guster, B. (2013). *Psych's guide to crime fighting for the totally unqualified*. New York, NY: Grand Central.

Top 10 best *Star Trek* quotes. (n.d). *Top 10 Best*. Retrieved from http://www.top10-best.com/s/top_10_best_star_trek_quotes.html#QHMUzzMB5LwjKQkz.99

Tsay-Vogel, M., & Sanders, M. S. (2017). Fandom and the search for meaning : Examining fandom and the search for meaning: Examining communal. *Psychology of Popular Media Culture, 6*(1), 32–47.

Vezzali, L., Stathi, S., Giovannini, D., Capozza, D., & Trifiletti, E. (2014). The greatest magic of Harry Potter: Reducing prejudice. *Journal of Applied Social Psychology, 45*(2), 105–121. https://doi.org/10.1111/jasp.12279

Vinney, C. J. (2016). *Personal pop culture: An investigation of fans' eudaimonic responses to favorite television* (Doctoral dissertation). Available from ProQuest Dissertations and Theses database. (ProQuest No. 10248081)

Vinney, C., Dill-Shackleford, K., Plante, C. N., & Bartsch, A. (2019). Development and validation of a measure of popular media fan identity and its relationship to well-being. *Psychology of Popular Media Culture, 8*(3), 296–307.

Vinney, C., & Hopper-Losenicky, K. (2017, April). *More than escapism: How popular media helps fans learn, cope, and live*. Paper presented at the Popular Culture Association/American Culture Association annual conference, San Diego, CA.

3

On Actors and Their Roles

The Social Psychology of Narrative Person Perception

> I'm stopped on the street, I'm invited for dinner, I'm hugged by every age. I'm never treated other than [as] a friend. . . . People are unbelievably warm to me, no matter where I am.
>
> —Actor Henry Winkler on being received by fans as Fonzie, the iconic character he portrayed on *Happy Days* (Puckrik, 2011)

Fans of actor Henry Winkler have seen him in a variety of roles over his long, successful career, from his portrayal of Chuck Lumley, the nervous and neurotic late-night morgue employee in the movie *Night Shift*, to his more recent TV roles as Dr. Abe Saperstein, obstetrician and misguided father on *Parks and Recreation*, and Barry Zuckerkorn, the bumbling lawyer on *Arrested Development*. But the role he'll always be most associated with is that of Arthur Fonzarelli (aka, "The Fonz") from the 1970s hit show *Happy Days*. Reading Winkler's words as previously quoted, we get a window into the world of an actor being greeted by fans *as if he were* the same person as the iconic character he portrayed.

In this chapter, we explore how the mind makes sense of a person (the actor) who also acts as if he were another person (the character). Some of the ideas we'll explore include how we understand the identity of actors and their role, and what the craft of acting is all about. Later in the chapter, we will hear from some experts, including actors, acting professors, friends of famous actors, and fans who will help us fill in some details.

In an interview, an anonymous source who worked on the soap opera *Days of Our Lives* told us a story about a fan who had trouble drawing a firm line between a character from the show and the actress who played her. Our source, we'll call him Erik, was in an upscale mall in Los Angeles wearing his *Days of Our Lives* show jacket. A woman approached him, apologetic for disturbing him. She mentioned that she was a long-time fan of *Days* (set in the fictional town of Salem) and particularly of Marlena (Evans, the character played by Deirdra Hall since 1976). After talking for a while, she worked up the nerve to ask him if he knew if there were any vacancies in Marlena's building. Erik explained to her that Marlena's townhouse is a set. She promised not to disturb Marlena if they became neighbors and said that she wouldn't ask, but she thought Marlena's townhouse would be perfect for her. Finally, after the fan wouldn't take no for an answer, Erik came up with a way to dissuade her. He told her that she wouldn't be able to move into Marlena's building. When the fan asked why, Erik replied, "Because. It's in Salem." The fan looked serious and said, "Of course. I can't move to Salem!"

Hearing a "crazy fan story" like this isn't uncommon. The media tend to pick up on particularly egregious examples of fans who seem to be out of touch with reality. Unfortunately, this characterization then gets applied to all fans. In the worst cases, fans are publicly shamed. This is a misguided and simplistic vision of the fan experience that we are here to challenge. Here's another fan story that's more typical of everyday fan behavior. Actor Michael Kelly plays Doug Stamper on *House of Cards*, the acclaimed American political drama series. Bort (2017, ¶1) says, "President Frank Underwood (Kevin Spacey) may be the face of *House of Cards*, but his ruthless, unerringly loyal chief of staff, Doug Stamper, is its soul." Kelly says that fans often ask to take a selfie with him in character, saying "'Can you just do it with the Stamper face and, like, put your hands around my neck like you're choking me?'" Kelly likes to do it because it makes their day (EW Staff, 2016). In this case, the fans show how they can play with the transformation between actor and character.

Psychologists study how we make sense of other people, including how we form a picture of other people's personalities. Because we, the authors of this book, are exploring how an audience makes sense of characters and actors, we are essentially applying what scholars know about these basic psychological processes in real life to the specific case of fictional narratives. To set the stage (if you'll pardon the pun), let's first define our terms.

THE SOCIAL PSYCHOLOGY OF PERSON PERCEPTION

One of the foundational fields of study in social psychology is the analysis of "person perception." Social psychologists who study person perception, also known as social perception, try to understand how we use clues from people's appearance and behavior to form impressions and make social judgments, such as who they are and what we can expect from them. How do you know, for instance, whether Benedict Cumberbatch is fun loving or haughty or both? Is Robert Downey Jr. just like *Iron Man*'s extravagant Tony Stark, or is he actually mild and unassuming?

Whether characters, actors, or people we meet in real life, the processes by which we make such judgments essentially start the same way. When sizing someone new up, we need to quickly decide if they're a friend or a foe. Those who study person perception have found that when meeting someone for the first time we very quickly perform a bottom–up and a top–down analysis (Jolij, 2010). The bottom–up approach involves scanning for clues in the individual's outward appearance and presentation, including facial, bodily, and vocal cues (Brooks & Freeman, 2018). It's like we turn on a computer in our minds and quickly scan the person to assess appearance-related categories (such as sex, age, race, and socioeconomic status), personality traits (e.g., does their facial expression suggests kindness?), emotions (e.g., tired), identity (e.g., suit = businessman), and goals (e.g., seems to be looking for a cup of coffee). In contrast, the top–down approach involves applying our own internal understanding of people to the new individual: our stereotypes, our past experiences, and our assessment of the person's current motives. For example, scanning a stranger may reveal the judgment that he is a seemingly harmless guy looking for the elevator. Ultimately, our conclusion would be that people like this don't pose a threat.

It may seem strange that our primary goal when assessing someone new is determining if they're a threat. For instance, in the previous example, if we determined he looked like he came from the wrong side of the tracks and appeared frantic and anxious, we might judge that his situation and motives made him desperate and, consequently, that he did pose a threat. This is adaptive in the evolutionary sense. We don't consciously decide to assess people; it's something we do automatically as social creatures, so you may not notice this process.

One very important aspect of our relationship with fictional characters is that they can't pose the kind of threat that people we meet face to face do. Because of this, stories give us the opportunity to be more empathically connected to people we either wouldn't normally encounter or would avoid in real life. Think about how movies allow you to get inside the head of some extreme characters, from *Bonnie and Clyde* to *Wolverine*, from *Dexter* to the *Unbreakable Kimmy Schmidt*, and from the bad guys of *Suicide Squad* to the Lyon family on *Empire*. These encounters are opportunities to understand how we would feel if we experienced these character's stories. Experience is a great teacher, even experience gained through imagination, so we shouldn't underestimate the lessons we can learn when we encounter fictional characters.

Other human beings are so important to us as social animals that it's crucial that we try to understand them. This tendency is hard-wired into us; we don't turn it off or on based on whether we're sizing up a person standing in front of us or a person on a screen. Yes, there are differences. Obviously, the person standing in front of us may be in a position to more immediately affect us. But the person on the screen may be more likely to grab our attention due to the way movies and TV shows are crafted.

We know that the person on screen is an actor playing a role, but—fairly or not—the role still gives us an idea of what we can expect from the actor when they appear "as themselves." Fans have access to videos, audio clips, and images of stars' behavior, and with the rise of outlets like TMZ, that access is more immediate and plentiful than in the past. Based on the information we find, we make judgments about actors' motives, personalities, and even their sanity. For example, when Shia LaBeouf first appeared in the *Transformers* movies, like his character he appeared to be a humble, friendly guy. But then his public behavior started becoming erratic. By 2015, *The Telegraph* offered up a timeline of LaBeouf's "most bizarre moments" (Hawkes, 2015). These included attending the Berlin Film Festival premier of his movie *Nymphomaniac* wearing a paper bag over his head that read, "I am not famous anymore," and staging a performance art piece where he ran a pretend marathon around Amsterdam's Stedelijk Museum dressed in purple tights. Some fans might find LeBeouf's behaviors endearing, but many were turned off by it and concerned for the actor's mental health. LaBeouf's sanity or lack thereof, some might argue, should be a private matter among his friends and family. But, when a public figure like an actor behaves in unexpected or unsavory ways, it can cause audiences to respond differently to the characters he portrays or will portray.

Many Roles, One Actor

When an actor plays multiple roles on the same show, it can obscure and confuse our idea of who a character is, and the actor who plays them is. Perhaps our favorite recent example of an actor playing multiple characters comes from the TV show *Orphan Black* in which Tatiana Maslany played a group of clones. Because the show revolved around the clones, Maslany was in practically every scene, often multiple times, but it never feels like that to the audience. Despite the fact that they all look the same, each clone character has such a distinct personality, it's never difficult to determine which one (or ones) Maslany is playing. Of course, part of the audience's ability to distinguish between the clones is due to the different accents in which each character speaks and the various costumes, hairstyles, and make-up each character wears.

But the show's clone conceit would fall flat if, upon meeting a new clone, we as audience members didn't instinctively work with the show to determine how the character sees the world, what she wants from it, and what matters to her. While each clone is played by Maslany, we have no problem delving into their personal perspectives and quirks because of theory of mind, which you'll remember from Chapter 1 is our innate ability to ascribe other people's external behavior to their internal thoughts, feelings, and motives. It's because of theory of mind that viewers come to understand that the character Sarah wants to protect her daughter, that the character Cosima can use her scientific knowledge to figure out how she and her clone sisters came into being, and that the character Alison will fight her hardest to win her suburban neighborhood's election for school trustee. And we have no trouble following the individual characters' storylines, enjoying the divergent traits of each clone, and even choosing a favorite among the various clones. As a result, when viewers watch the show, they can accept that multiple clones occupy *Orphan Black*'s fictional universe.

So, when actors play multiple roles, the story relies on person perception and theory of mind to cause us to believe that one actor is multiple characters. These abilities are so fundamental to us as humans that we have to try harder to wrap our minds around the fact that there is only one person behind the many personalities we see on screen than that we are witnessing multiple, distinct people. This is something that even confused the actors who worked with Maslany on *Orphan Black*. During a panel at the 2017 PaleyFest in Los Angeles, the cast confessed that they would often forget that it was Maslany behind the various clone characters, causing them to respond and speak with her differently than they would if she were playing another clone. Of course, when we developed person perception and theory of mind, television, movies, and even plays as we know them in their current form didn't exist. So, it makes sense that we would react uniquely to anyone we can distinguish as an individual entity, even if we really know better.

Our Attraction to Actors and Characters

At the same time, people we see on screens are different from the ones we see in everyday life. These differences influence how we think and feel about them. One of the most obvious ways that screen actors are different from everyday people is that they're generally more physically attractive. Apologies to all of us "regular people," but Hollywood *is* known as the home of the "beautiful people." If a child is very attractive, people often tell the him "you should be an actor."

Now, acting is (and/or should be) about more than looking good, as we'll see later in this chapter, but we all know looks are a big part of how actors get selected for major film and television roles. The reason goes back to basic human nature. Beautiful people have high mate value, which is their value as a potential romantic partner. As evolutionary biologists would tell us, mating and reproduction are our most pressing imperatives and beauty is a sign of reproductive fitness. That is, we believe we are more likely to produce fit and able children with an attractive partner. So, when confronted with such a "valuable" other, our response is automatic.

Our tendency to revere attractive people was parodied by the TV comedy *30 Rock*. In a role very different from that of *Mad Men*'s Don Draper, Jon Hamm plays the very attractive, but completely incompetent Dr. Drew Baird. Tina Fey's character, Liz Lemon, notices how differently Drew is treated. He is terrible at almost everything but thinks he's amazing at everything. And no one corrects his perceptions; they just let him get what he wants. Of course, this is satirical, but it's based on something true: We tend to believe attractive people are more competent and capable than those who are less attractive, even if we have no evidence to support this belief. This phenomenon has been called, "What is beautiful is good," or the physical attractiveness stereotype (for a discussion, see Brand, Bonatsos, D'Orazio, & Deshong, 2012).

How many scenes from film and television are burned into our brains because of the extreme beauty of the actors? Here are some that we recall: a muscular Will Smith in the shower in *iRobot*, Ursula Andress on the beach in a white bikini in the James Bond film *From Russia with Love*, Audrey Hepburn in black evening gown and pearls in *Breakfast at Tiffany's*, an open-shirted Harrison Ford in the first *Indiana Jones* movie, Chris Hemsworth with his shirt off in *Thor*, and Charlize Theron kicking ass in *Atomic Blonde*. Evolutionary biologists would tell us that mating and reproduction are our most pressing imperatives and that beauty is a sign of reproductive fitness. No one has to explain why the images of these actors are unforgettable.

Human attraction is also one of the classic areas of study in social psychology. Although we all say we want a mate with a great sense of humor or high intelligence, physical beauty is one of the keys to interpersonal attraction. In fact, many studies document that, when it comes to the early stages of a potential relationship, physical attraction is the one and only factor that predicts whether two people will want to pursue a relationship with each other. For example, psychologists sent college students on arranged dates. Each student was previously rated by multiple people on their level of physical attractiveness. Despite a host of other factors that could have drawn the study participants together on their dates, such as similar interests, when students were asked if they wanted to see their "date" again, the one and only factor that made a difference in their decision was the date's physical attractiveness (Walster, Aronson, & Abrahams, 1966).

How does physical beauty compare with other traits that could attract people to each other? The concept of mate value has been studied for years and researchers have discovered a number of things that play into our attraction to actors. As the previously reviewed study suggests, physical attractiveness plays an important role in mate value. While it is more important in initial meetings, it also continues to play a role long term.

There are gender differences in mate value as well. Classic evolutionary psychology says heterosexual men prefer women who are younger and more physically attractive, while heterosexual women tend to value wealth and status in men. The theory is that these inclinations relate to gender differences in producing and caring for children: Men can produce more offspring than women, women physically give birth and must be healthy to do so, and men's resources will help the child grow and thrive (Sheldon, 2007). Of course, this may seem rather antiquated now, but many scholars believe that our evolutionary predilections are ingrained in us, no matter how much they no longer apply to our modern circumstances. So, we still value physical beauty, even if we no longer value it for its role in helping us produce and raise children.

Further, to whom we are attracted does go beyond looks and power. Newer research suggests that we also have an eye for something deeper. Sheldon (2007) showed unattached college students some singles ads and asked them to rate which of the people in the ads they'd most like to date. He manipulated the ads to feature what we'll call for simplicity's sake, three "shallow" and three "deep" values. (He called them "extrinsic" and "intrinsic.") The shallow values were wealth, status/fame, and looks. The deep values were emotional intimacy, personal growth, and helping others. Sheldon found that the college students were more attracted to the potential mates' deep values than their shallow values. Women were more attracted to deep values than men, with the exception that women placed more importance on a partner who values financial success than men did.

We cannot underestimate the power of these tendencies when it comes to actors and the characters they play. We are attracted to good looks, especially initially. So, the physical beauty of an actor can help draw us into a story. In addition, we've talked about how stories tend to distill and clarify social relationships and problems and how magnetically attracted we are to all things social. Actors playing roles are more than just highly attractive in a shallow, outward sense. Through the characters they embody, they also act out values to which we're highly attracted. We want to be with people who value emotional intimacy, personal growth, and helping others. And many television and movie characters demonstrate at least one of these characteristics.

Take a moment to think of some memorable scenes you've seen on screen. Think of scenes that have stuck with you, that are there buried somewhere in the back of your mind. Think of characters appearing in scenes that, to you, bring together all of these highly attractive features. Maybe it's something that made you cry, or made you feel transcendent, or made you think, "This is important." Go ahead, we'll wait!

Okay, now we'll describe such a scene for you and interpret it in the light of the psychological research we've just been discussing. This scene is from the BBC series *Broadchurch*, starring David Tennant and Olivia Colman. (Warning: Spoilers ahead!) Broadchurch tells the story of an English seaside community where an 11-year-old boy, Danny Latimer, has been murdered. The circumstances are gut-wrenching for multiple members of the Broadchurch community, including the lead detectives in the case. The murderer confesses and is brought to trail but is found innocent. Just when we think vigilante justice is next on the agenda, the people most affected by the murder band together and exile the criminal, taking the high road instead of the low. The final scenes of the season show the characters we've grown to care about staying strong together to put the situation as right as they can, despite the fact they can't bring Danny back. It's a beautiful story about human weakness and strength, struggle and survival.

We recount this story because we think it epitomizes those deeper values that attract us to mates and friends and also to media characters and personalities: personal growth, emotional intimacy, and the desire to help others. The TV show also features some beautiful men and women. Naturally, we would be drawn to all of this. And if we got into the story told by Broadchurch, it would seem highly valuable and interesting to us.

We hope by now it's easy to see why the actors, the characters, and the events of a story like this become burned on our brain. From the outside, it may seem simplistic to say, "Oh, I'm a fan of *Broadchurch*!" or "I love David Tennant and Olivia Colman!" But what those statement really mean is that we're declaring ourselves a fan of the values we glean from the story, including human growth and intimacy, and our desire to have those things in our lives. We also enjoy the experience of connecting with people who are very compelling, both physically and psychologically, which prompts us to declare ourselves fans of the actors. As a rule, when people form an emotional attachment to a movie or TV show and its characters, there's probably something substantive triggering that reaction.

Of course, it can be difficult for us to express why a story means something to us. Have you ever tried to get a friend to watch your favorite show? We don't always realize that what we're trying to say is that the people we connect to in stories aren't just expressing their values; they're expressing our values too. So, the characters in movies and television aren't just speaking for themselves; they're speaking for us too. And when we try to share that with someone else, we're actually trying to share a part of ourselves. That's what we're really saying when we blurt out, "I love *Game of Thrones!*" or get excited because we see another *Avengers* fan in the crowd. One of our hopes in writing this book is that we help each other find the words to better understand and explain those experiences.

THE PERCEPTUAL PROBLEM POSED BY ACTORS PLAYING ROLES

Let's look more deeply into how the audience perceives actors and the roles they play. In Chapter 1 we discussed, at some length, the ways we relate to those individuals we encounter on the screen. Recall that scholars Slater, Ewoldsen, and Woods (2018) separated the concept of parasocial relationships into two separate constructs they called parasocial relationship–personae (PSR-P), which describes our connection to a persona or media "personality" such as an actor or talk show host, and parasocial relationship–character (PSR-C), which describes our connection to a fictional character. These concepts point to the fact that when we take in a film or TV show there are two different people the viewer can relate to, even though they occupy one body: the character and the actor.

The Actor/Role Identity Problem

Actors and the roles they play present a special problem in social perception. This problem arises whenever two targets of social perception appear physically identical, but have (at least) two separate identities.

Because the actor/role perceptual problem involves appearance and identity issues, we think a way to explain it better is to use the special case of identical twins. If you think about it, identical twins pose a special problem for the social perceiver as well. Normally, when we look at an individual, we identify them by their physical appearance. Their looks tell us "who" they are. Except that in the case of identical twins, their appearance *doesn't* tell us their identity. In a way, they are a body with a secret identity. You could think of an actor as a person with multiple identities.

Twin Actors

To help make our point, it'll be helpful to consider twins and their identities more deeply. We'll use some specific famous twins as examples.

JONATHAN AND DREW: TWINS WITH DIFFERENTIATED IDENTITIES

We'll start with one set of well-known identical twin actors: Jonathan and Drew Scott. The Scott twins are known as "the property brothers," after the reality TV show that made them famous. While Jonathan and Drew Scott were looking for work as actors, they each had a backup career plan. Drew became a real estate agent, and Jonathan became a building contractor. Their Hollywood aspirations and their "Plan B" careers merged in their show, *The Property Brothers*, a home remodeling show where the real estate agent and the builder work with a couple to find and remodel a home.

The Scott brothers and their handlers were wise to the identity dilemma. The show goes out of its way to individualize the brothers. One strategy that helps viewers know "who's who" is the different costumes the brothers wear: Drew is always seen in the fashionable suit of a business mogul, while Jonathan appears in the jeans and boots of a working

Figure 3.1 Karen showing off her garden gnomes depicting identical twins Jonathan and Drew Scott, stars of the reality TV show, *The Property Brothers*. The figures show the distinct wardrobes and accessories the twins sport on the show: Jonathan's contractor gear (L) and Drew's realtor look (R).

contractor (see Figure 3.1). In addition, Drew meets with clients in his office, while Jonathan is seen in their new living room bashing down a (hopefully nonload-bearing) wall with a sledge hammer.

So, the twins are two physically identical people, with two distinct characterizations: the realtor and the builder. When one twin walks into a room, no one needs to ask, "Who are you?" Their appearance and behavior wordlessly communicate that information. From a social perception perspective, by playing two distinct "characters" the show has essentially solved the identity problem for us.

Mary Kate and Ashley: Twins With Undifferentiated Identities

Mary-Kate and Ashley Olsen became TV stars when they were infants. In the 1990s, the twins shared the role of Michelle Tanner on the sitcom *Full*

House. TV producers like to hire twins for children's roles because kids are only supposed to work part-time. But only two people who look alike can share the same role, so only young twins can each work half a day and still end up putting in a full day's work playing one character. (For you Mary Kate and Ashley fans, we know that they're actually fraternal twins. Still, they look enough alike to play identical twins on television, so we think the example works.)

Mary-Kate and Ashley went on to co-star in their own television series, *The Adventures of Mary-Kate and Ashley* (see Figure 3.2), as well as several movies and music videos. As adults, the twins are known as business moguls as co-owners of a number of successful fashion companies. They have also been on Forbes's list of wealthiest celebrities for years.

Although they undoubtedly have distinct personalities in their private lives, the Olsen twins have largely been identified with the same public persona throughout their lives. As babies, the audience knew them both as "Michelle Tanner." Then they were "one of the Olsen twins," who sang, danced, and acted side by side. Now, as adult businesswomen, they share a very similar identity as wealthy, successful fashionistas.

Many of us are aware of the Olsen twins, but don't differentiate between the two of them. In fact, in an interview on *Ellen*, the twins reported that they each get asked, "Are you Mary-Kate and Ashley?" or "Are you the Ashley twins?" to which they respond, "I'm one of them." Ellen played the game, "Me or Her?" with them, in which she asked them questions such as "Which one is messier?" They each had a paddle reading "Me" on one side and "Her" on the other. The twins appeared to be unable to differentiate between themselves on a number of the questions. In fact, Mary-Kate said she had asked for a paddle that read "Both." (For whole interview, see "Mary-Kate or Ashley," 2014.)

Confusing Actors and Their Roles

These twin examples also speak the issues we face when we see an actor who is well known for playing a particular role. To better understand the actor/role identity issue, let's play a game called *Who is it?*

In the game, you walk into a room and find one twin seated at a table. Your job is to guess the identity of the twin. Let's imagine that you see one of the Scott twins. In the game, all mundane clues (style of dress, hairdo)

Figure 3.2 The Olsen twins: Scenes from *The Adventures of Mary-Kate and Ashley*.

have been removed, so that nothing gives it away. You know the situation you're in: You see a body, and you know that the mind inside this body either belongs to Jonathan or Drew. You may not know who it is, but you do know that it is either one or the other. You have a 50–50 shot of getting it right.

Now imagine that you walk into the room, and a man who looks like William Shatner is seated at the table. Who is he? *Star Trek* fans know both the actor, William Shatner, and the character, Captain Kirk. With

Drew and Jonathan, you knew it was one of them. If they were dressed in their "costumes," you'd be able to say which one. With the Olsen twins, when presented with one, you might never be able to figure it out on your own. But you'd know you were looking at one of the Olsen twins. With Shatner/Kirk, it's harder to say what you know for certain. Do you know that both Shatner and Kirk are "in there somewhere"? Or do you believe that the man you see is only William Shatner? If so, then who or where is Captain Kirk?

On one level, you may well argue that these are foolish questions. We know that this man was born William Shatner and that he portrayed a number of roles and that Captain Kirk was one of them. Captain Kirk is not real, and so it is absurd to ask who or where he is. He is nowhere. We get that this line of reasoning is, in its way, flawless.

On the other hand, to say that Captain Kirk doesn't exist anywhere is a bridge too far for us, and for many *Star Trek* fans. (Did we really say a "bridge" too far, as in the bridge of the Enterprise!?) Yes, we know that Shatner is an actor who portrayed Kirk, and yet that doesn't really do justice to the experiences that viewers have had in the world of *Star Trek*. If you walk into a *Star Trek* convention or attend a meeting of a *Star Trek* fan group, the idea of Captain Kirk is there in all of the minds of the fans who are present. He is discussed as if he were a real person, just as William Shatner is discussed as a real person. The pop culture icon of Captain Kirk is there in fans' collective consciousness., is it fair to say that Captain Kirk doesn't exist anywhere? Karen can tell you that Shatner/Kirk definitely exist in her consciousness, mostly appearing as the young and shirtless version pictured in Figure 3.3.

Many of us have imagination enough to also believe that Chris Pine is the young Captain Kirk. Likewise, we have memories of a person named Mr. Spock, who might look like both Leonard Nimoy or Zachary Quinto. Because this is science fiction, Nimoy's "old" Spock and Quinto's "new" Spock even meet and have a relationship in the new Star Trek movies. Of course, some have very strong opinions about who the "real" Kirk or Spock is, adding to the complexity. But that's the beauty of imagination,

Figure 3.3 Is this William Shatner? Or is it Captain Kirk? The answer involves understanding where a character lives in relation to the actor. This is a dual identity or multiple identity problem in perceptual psychology.

isn't it? Things that aren't possible in the real world become possible in our imaginations.

Acting is an art. That art does nothing less than bring people to life. If an actor and the team who created a character (the writer, director, etc.) are talented enough, the new person, born of a creative endeavor, can becomes as real and maybe as dear to people as their own friends and family. Sometimes even more so.

Returning to the dynamic duo of William Shatner/Captain Kirk, we can examine how people judge the difference between an actor and the characters they play. When people encounter William Shatner/Captain Kirk, they compare the persona or public image of William Shatner with the character Captain Kirk. In the case of Captain Kirk, we merely have to watch *Star Trek* to glean information about him. But to gather information about William Shatner, we have to seek out promotional interviews on television, online, or in the pages of magazines or other publications. When we read or watch an actor being interviewed, we engage in the social perception process we spoke of earlier. We look at William Shatner and ask ourselves what kind of man he is. We look for evidence of his personality (e.g., Is he trustworthy?). We listen to his voice, note his posture and movements, or gauge his responses to the people with whom he interacts. *Star Trek: The Original Series* debuted on September 8, 1966, so some fans have had over 50 years to determine the differences between Shatner and Kirk.

Shatner appeared on the *Colbert Report* in 2012 to talk about his one-man Broadway show *Shatner's World*. When the subject turned to Shatner's being best known for *Star Trek*, Colbert confessed, "I just have to say, man to man, how goddamn beautiful you were on that show. . . . They did not need lights on that show. You glowed. You were a golden God!" ("William Shatner," 2012). When asked whether he knew he was beautiful, Shatner replied, "I did. And I gloried in every moment of it," but, ever the comedian, added, "Why do you use the past tense" ("William Shatner," 2012)?

A few things to mention about this conversation: Notice that Shatner's such a well-known personality that he actually wrote and performed an entire Broadway one-man show about his life, and people came to see it. Fans of Shatner, the personality, have a sense of who he is distinct from Captain Kirk.

What are some things William Shatner is known for? It's safe to say he's known for his quirky sense of humor as seen in his role as the "Priceline negotiator." He is also known for being a bit of a prima donna. There have been accounts over the years in books and interviews that characterize Shatner as a difficult, selfish attention hog who resented his *Star Trek* co-stars taking attention away from him. For example, Shatner himself confessed in his book *Leonard: My Fifty-Year Friendship with a Remarkable Man* (Shatner & Fisher, 2016) that he was jealous of the attention Leonard Nimoy was receiving from fans during the first run of the show. Some of the supporting cast members reportedly held ill feelings for Shatner over the years. For example, when Shatner hosted his own talk show, *Shatner's Raw Nerve*, Walter Koenig, who played Ensign Chekov on the original series, came on and spoke frankly about that rift. The late Leonard Nimoy also appeared on *Raw Nerve*, where the two expressed their friendship for each other. On the other hand, Shatner confessed in his book that Nimoy wasn't speaking with him during the last several months of Nimoy's life.

So, those of us who've observed Shatner's public persona over the years have formed a picture of who he is both from the opinions of people he's worked with over the years as well as his facial expressions, his body language, his style, and his comments during public appearances.

We've also had the opportunity to observe Shatner playing different characters throughout his career. Shatner starred in multiple successful television series, including *TJ Hooker*, *Boston Legal*, and *The Practice*. When we watch an actor in multiple roles, we can look for commonalities in their behavior and emotional expression throughout their performances. If we see similarities between their different characters, we may conclude that the common denominator is the actor's personality. And it gets more complex than that. We may infer, for example, that Shatner we saw on *Star Trek* was very different from the Shatner we saw in *Boston Legal*, but that the Shatner playing Denny Crane on *Boston Legal* is very similar to the Shatner we see in interviews. If so, we decide that Kirk is Kirk, but after *Star Trek*, Shatner simply played himself.

Again, we are not saying that these judgments are correct. And none of this leaves us with any absolutes. Perceptions are not the same as facts. And besides, a philosopher might ask whether we can ever truly know who anyone is, ourselves included.

In the end, our impressions of an actor based on their public persona and the characters they play may help us predict an actor's behavior, but we're not always accurate. For example, we may think that Tom Hanks is a great guy and probably loves babies and puppies. On the other hand, we may think Ralph Fiennes would murder us in our beds if he had half a reason. Therefore, if we hear that Fiennes bullied other actors on the set, it might not surprise us as much as if we learned the same thing about

Hanks. Because we have watched Hanks play heroes and Fiennes play villains, we believe that their off-screen behavior will be consistent with that. In essence, watching them play good or evil convincingly, we come to believe that they have those particular tendencies in them.

Psychology can help us understand more about why this happens. First, because others are so important to our well-being, we pretty much constantly pay attention to and make judgments about their behavior. For example, if we notice our neighbor stealing some aspirin at the drug store, we generate reasons why he might have done this. These reasons are called attributions. We might attribute his stealing to his having kleptomania or to a broken moral compass. These are called personality attributions—we think he did it because he's "that kind of person." If we thought about it longer, we might think about his circumstances and decide he was under pressures external to himself that caused him to steal. Maybe we know he recently lost his job and his wife needs aspirin, then we can attribute the theft of the aspirin to the situation.

The thing is, we often err on the side of guessing that people do things because "that's the way they are." We overestimate the effects of people's personalities on their behavior, and we underestimate the effects of their situations. This phenomenon is called the fundamental attribution error.

When we believe an actor is "just being himself" when playing a character in a film or movie, sometimes we're committing the fundamental attribution error. We're ignoring the situation: He was given a script that dictated his actions. Instead, we think that if he convinces us that he can be mean, it's because he's really mean in his everyday life. In some cases, the better the actor, the more apt we are to think he's just playing himself. Here's an interesting example. When William Shatner appeared in the *Saturday Night Live* sketch where he told his fans to "get a life," he was saying words that were written by SNL writers ("Trekkies," 1986). The writers could have had him say anything. But that's not how the sketch is explained. When we talk about that sketch, we say that Shatner was responsible for the words he said. Now, we could say that by appearing in this sketch he was endorsing the SNL writers' perspective on his fans, even if he didn't write the actual words, but either way, as the actor, he got the blame. As audience members by attributing what he says in the sketch to him and ignoring the circumstances, we are making the fundamental attribution error.

This is much like a classic study in social psychology known as the "Castro speech study" (Jones & Harris, 1967). In the 1970s, when Fidel Castro was often in the news, college students were given either a pro-Castro or an anti-Castro speech to read aloud. Their speeches were videotaped and then played for other college students who did not know the speakers. This second set of students were told that the speakers had been assigned to the speech they recited. But when the students who listened to the speeches were asked what they thought the speaker's real attitude toward Castro was, the listeners overwhelmingly said that the speaker believed what he or she was saying. In the language of psychology, we say this is because people think the behavior corresponds to the person, also called correspondence bias (which is very similar to the fundamental attribution error). So, even though we know the students were assigned to the speeches they read, we believe they wouldn't say the things they did if they didn't mean them.

Of course, when it comes to actors and roles, sometimes we don't make the fundamental attribution error. Sometimes we can separate the actor from the role and recognize that a man who plays a villain on screen may be a loving husband and father in real life who spends his free time watching kitten videos on YouTube.

Ultimately, our desire to determine if people are good or bad may be less about the evidence and more about our human desire to understand people by casting them in roles—to make these good/bad distinctions—that prompts our judgments. Many of us are not comfortable with uncertainty or complexity. We want to put people in boxes. We want to know if they're a villain or hero, so we can know what to expect and simplify our interactions with them. Even producers and casting agents may succumb to typecasting because they make the fundamental attribution error. They may think that a person who has successfully played a villain is just that sort of person and, therefore, unable to play the hero.

SIDEBAR

How the Role Touches the Actor

Actor Jaleel White is known for playing the uber-nerdy character Steve Urkel on the sitcom *Family Matters*. Steve was a skinny teen who wore his pants pulled way too high and oversized nerdy glasses. He was in love with the girl next door, "the lovely Laura" Winslow who was the object of his awkward and relentless overtures. Over the course of the series, Steve, being a genius scientist, built a special booth that transformed him into a super-cool version of himself, known as "Stefan." When Stefan showed up for the very first time, speaking in his dulcet voice and unleashing his suave moves on Laura, the live audience roared. Years later, White told CNN what that moment meant to him: "To this day, I've never heard a roar like that. . . .That was a seminal moment in my adolescence" (CNN, 2017). That moment might have happened to Stefan, the character, but it also happened to White. White was going through puberty at the time and appreciated an audience reacting to him—to *his* body, *his* voice—like that. It makes you wonder if an actor can ever completely separate others' reactions to himself and to the characters he plays.

In this case, Jaleel got to play two very different characters, the sweet geek and the smooth Romeo (see Figure 3.4). As a result, he experienced two very different audience responses. How many of us get to try on different roles and immediately see how a live audience reacts to them? While we all present a picture of ourselves to the outside world, only actors are able to play with these perceptions professionally. And our propensity to unabashedly express our opinions about actors and the roles they play gives actors an insight that few of us rarely get into who they are and who they could be. As a result, just as we are able to learn from the vicarious experience of taking on a character's perspective while watching or reading a story, actors are able to learn from their experiences portraying a character. For example, Jaleel White's

Figure 3.4 The nerdy Steve Urkel (L) and the suave Stefan (R), both played by actor Jaleel White. Being Steve and Stefan had an effect on Jaleel's life.

portrayal of Steve Urkel offered some life lessons to him about love. In Jaleel's words, "We can't control who we love, and nobody symbolizes that better than Steve Urkel" (CNN, 2017).

Inside the Actor's Studio

In our quest to understand how we make sense of actors and roles, we interviewed two people who know the art of acting deeply. First, we spoke with Dennis McLernon, professor of theater and head of performance at the University of Alabama at Birmingham. McLernon has earned national recognition for his teaching, directing, and acting from the Kennedy Center American College Theatre Festival (2007, 2008, and 2010, respectively; "Dennis McLernon," n.d.).

We also interviewed an actor who has appeared on stage and screen, lived in Hollywood for decades, and has spent quite a bit of time around well-known actors. In addition, this individual has been a counselor in Hollywood for years and has interacted with celebrities in that capacity too. You'll remember our Hollywood source from our earlier *Days of Our Lives* discussion, whom we refer to by the pseudonym, "Erik."

We asked our experts to help us understand how actors create characters. We began by asking our sources to define what acting means to them personally. Dennis said that acting "is a fearless and courageous acceptance of the fictitious circumstances of a character and having this courageous need and urgency to engage in those circumstances without judgment. And allow those circumstances to affect us. As if they were our own. In a way that has incredible importance" (personal communication, 2017).

When asked whether playing a character long term could influence the actor's personality and style, Erik said, "I absolutely would believe and be confident that whatever mannerisms, whatever things, whatever lines I think that they do . . . that the lines become blurred between their on-camera or on-stage and off-stage persona if someone has played something for that long, I think that it's just a natural and common adaptation" (personal communication, 2017).

Dennis's description of acting includes the idea that the character is allowed to take over the actor, and Erik's comments explain how a long-term role can work its way into the actor's personality and style. These two observations are relevant to an identity theory originated by Daryl Bem (1972) known as self-perception theory. This theory states that we sometimes form an impression of ourselves in the same way we form an impression of another person; namely, we look at what we appear to be like and assume that's what we are like. So, if you notice that you yell a lot and frequently become unglued in response to the slightest adversity, you might conclude that that you are an angry, unhinged, or overwrought type of person.

Using Dennis's description, imagine that you are David Suchet, who is known for playing the role of Agatha Christie's great detective Hercule

Poirot for many years. You allow the personality of Poirot to overtake you to show the audience what he's like. Following Erik's comments, it may be that over time you take on some of Poirot's mannerisms in your own life. In his book *Poirot and Me*, Suchet (2013) notes that he read every character description of Poirot Agatha Christie provided in her novels and, from those, formed a list of 93 "character notes," which he included in the book (pp. 291–295). Among them were, number 4: "wears pointed, tight, very skinny patent leather shoes"; number 13: "conceited professionally—but not as a person"; number 22: "very particular over his appearance"; number 39: "relies on his 'little grey cells'"; and number 93: "will wipe dirty seats or benches with his handkerchief before sitting down." Suchet mentioned that he saw Poirot's little habits seeping into his real life at times. He says, like Poirot, he is also fastidious, although he doesn't need his breakfast eggs to be absolutely symmetrical as Poirot does. (The eccentricities of Poirot are so important to his character that Kenneth Branaugh's recent remake of the film *Murder on the Orient Express* began by highlighting Poirot's quirks.)

David Suchet tells a charming story in his book about taking a break in costume while on set in the town of Hastings, England. An older lady walked by him on the street and greeted him, "Hello, Monsieur Poirot," then after a pause, asked, "There hasn't been any trouble, has there? I mean, there hasn't been a murder or anything?" Suchet responded in character as Poirot, assuring the lady that he was in Hastings for "*Mes vacances*, [vacation] madame. I am on holiday" (Suchet, 2013, p. 170).

It is fun to hear about a fan who has this fictional detective so engrained in her psyche that she is not surprised to find him roaming the streets of her town in search of suspects. I mean, what would you do if you arrived on the roof of a building and saw Spiderman there? (After all, where else would you find him?) But the point here is that Suchet was so familiar with his character that he was able to maintain Poirot's persona to respond to this woman, engaging in a little improvisation while meeting her expectations. This is the art of acting: embodying a character so thoroughly that it's hard to tell where the line between the real person and the role lies.

The Kominsky Method

Here's a perspective from another professional, or actually, a set of professionals. Chuck Lorre wrote and produced the first episode of the *Kominsky Method*, a show about a famous acting coach named Sandy Kominsky (played by Michael Douglas) and the people in his life. The Kominsky method is an approach to acting, a fictionalized cousin of the Stanislavski method, in which actors try to feel and behave as if they were the character.

In the first scene of the show, Sandy Kominsky addresses the aspiring actors in his class, explaining what acting is:

> I just want to take a moment to talk about our craft: acting. So, what is acting? I mean, when an actor acts, what is he, or she, or they actually doing? Well, on one level, the answer is simple: they are making believe; they are pretending. But, on a much deeper level, we need to ask ourselves, what is really happening? . . . I want you to listen carefully: What's really happening is that the actor is playing God. Because, after all, what does God do? God creates. (Lorre, 2018)

As fate would have it, at just about the time Sandy Kominsky was giving this speech, scientists were demonstrating that he was right about how actors create characters. Steven Brown, Peter Crockett, and Ye Yuan (2018) at McMaster University in Ontario, Canada, provided new and exciting evidence about what is happening in the method actor's brain when they create characters. Brown et al. say that the ultimate goal of the Stanislavski method of acting is to portray the character's experience "as if it were happening to" the actor (p. 3).

Using an ingenious research design, the team tested actors who had studied the roles of Romeo and Juliet from the method acting perspective. They then put the actors inside brain scanning machines to undergo functional magnetic resonance imaging. Then they asked the actors to answer questions from four perspectives. They answered as (a) themselves in their own voice ("the self"), (b) as a close friend ("the other"), (c) as the character they were portraying (Romeo or Juliet), and finally (d) as themselves, but with a British accent. The resulting brain patterns suggested that creating a role is distinct from being oneself or thinking through the perspective of another. It appears to be more like creating a second self. Interestingly, using an accent was the next closest thing to playing a character. What this study demonstrated is that creating a character is more like creating a second self than like seeing something through another person's eyes. We love it when heavy-duty science such as brain scans can confirm what artists have been saying for a long time: True method acting is creating another part of yourself.

In the next chapter, we'll discuss why we comprehend stories and how we construct them in our minds. We'll examine the different ways we assess reality in fiction. Really, the distinction between story and character is a false one. The person can't be fully divorced from the situation, just as the character can't be fully divorced from the context of the story. So, next, we'll continue our exploration of how we make sense of characters and the story situations they find themselves in.

REFERENCES

Beach, L. R., Bissell, B. L., & Wise, J. A. (2016). *A new theory of mind: The theory of narrative thought*. Newcastle Upon Tyne, England: Cambridge Scholars.

Bem, D. J. (1972). Self-perception theory. *Advances in Experimental Social Psychology, 6*, 1–162. https://doi.org/10.1016/S0065-2601(08)60024-6

Bort, R. (2017, May 29). "House of Cards": Michael Kelly on playing Doug Stamper, the Trump effect. *Newsweek: Culture*. Retrieved from http://www.newsweek.com/michael-kelly-house-cards-interview-614359

Brand, R. J., Bonatsos, A., D'Orazio, R., & Deshong, H. (2012). What is beautiful is good, even online: Correlations between photo attractiveness and text attractiveness in men's online dating profiles. *Computers in Human Behavior, 28*(1), 166–170. https://doi.org/10.1016/j.chb.2011.08.023

Brooks, J. A., & Freeman, J. B. (2018). Psychology and neuroscience of person perception. In J. T. Wixted (Ed.), *Handbook of experimental psychology and cognitive neuroscience* (4th ed., Chapter 13, pp. 429–464). New York, NY: Wiley.

Brown, S., Cockett, P., & Yuan, Y. (2018). The neuroscience of Romeo and Juliet: An fMRI study of acting. *Royal Society Open Science, 6*(3). https://doi.org/10.1098/rsos.181908

CNN. (2017, June 29). The lovestruck genius of Steve Urkel. *CNN: The Nineties.* Retrieved from http://www.cnn.com/videos/cnnmoney/2017/06/29/steve-urkel-nineties-orig-mc.cnn/video/playlists/90s-nineties/

Trekkies [Video clip]. (1986, December 20). *Saturday Night Live.* Retrieved from https://www.nbc.com/saturday-night-live/video/trekkies/n9511

Dennis McLernon. (n.d.). *University of Alabama at Birmingham, College of Arts and Sciences, Department of Theatre.* Retrieved from https://www.uab.edu/cas/theatre/people/faculty/dennismclernon

EW Staff. (2016, April 8). Fandemonium: Celebs share their craziest fan stories. *Entertainment Weekly.* Retrieved from http://ew.com/gallery/crazy-fan-stories/michael-kelly-house-of-cards

Hawkes, R. (2015, June 30). Shia LaBeouf's most bizarre moments: A timeline. *The Telegraph.* Retrieved from http://www.telegraph.co.uk/culture/film/10936223/Shia-LaBeouf-where-did-it-all-go-wrong.html

Jolij, J. (2010). One-tenth of a second to make a first impression: Early visual evoked potentials correlate with perceived trustworthiness of faces. *International Journal of Psychophysiology, 77*(3), 207.

Jones, E. E., & Harris, V. A. (1967). The attribution of attitudes. *Journal of Experimental Social Psychology, 3,* 1–24.

Lorre, C. (Dir.). (2018). An actor avoids from the Kominsky method [Television series episode]. In C. Lorre, A. Higgins, & M. Douglas (Executive Producers), *The Kominsky method* (Season 1, Episode 1). Los Angeles, CA: Netflix.

Mary-Kay or Ashley? [Video clip/Interview]. (2014, April 14). *The Ellen Show.* Retrieved from https://www.youtube.com/watch?v=APshm-9gPgI

Puckrik, K. (2011, September 27). Henry Winkler: The Fonz was everything I wanted to be. *The Guardian.*

Shatner, W., & Fisher, D. (2016). *Leonard: My fifty-year friendship with a remarkable man.* New York, NY: Thomas Dunne Books, St. Martin's Press.

Sheldon, K. M. (2007). Gender differences in preferences for singles ads that proclaim extrinsic versus intrinsic values. *Sex Roles, 57*(1–2), 119–129. https://doi.org/10.1007/s11199-007-9215-3

Slater, M. D., Ewoldsen, D. R., & Woods, K. W. (2018). Extending conceptualization and measurement of narrative engagement after-the-fact: Parasocial relationship and imaginative retrospective involvement. *Media Psychology, 21*(3), 329–351. https://doi.org/10.1080/15213269.2017.1328313

Suchet, D. (2013). *Poirot and me*. London, England: Headline.
Walster, E., Aronson, V., & Abrahams, D. (1966). Importance of physical attractiveness in dating behavior. *Journal of Personality and Social Psychology, 4*(5), 508–516.
William Shatner [Video clip]. (2012, February 29). *The Colbert Report*. Retrieved from http://www.cc.com/video-clips/puth71/the-colbert-report-william-shatner

4
Mental Models of Fiction

The Mechanics of Getting Lost in a Story

Of course it is happening inside your head, Harry, but why on Earth should that mean that it is not real?

—Albus Dumbledore in
Harry Potter and the Deathly Hallows

Think about your favorite story. What makes it your favorite? Do you enjoy spending time with the characters? Maybe you relate to the hard choices and righteous bravery of *The Hunger Games*' Katniss Everdeen or you adore the exuberance of Will Farrell's overgrown *Elf*. Do you love escaping into the story's setting? Perhaps the world of *Avatar* is so fully realized that when you watch the movie you feel like you've traveled to a distant, previously unknown planet. Do you feel breathless and exhilarated as you experience the story's different plot points? Maybe the suspense of Alfred Hitchcock's *Vertigo* still gives you a thrill no matter how many times you watch it or you can't wait to see what new mayhem comes from the Upside Down on *Stranger Things*. Can you quote lines from the story verbatim, reliving it in your mind as you do? Perhaps you find yourself reciting dialogue from *The Princess Bride* whenever an appropriate opportunity

Finding Truth in Fiction. Karen E. Shackleford and Cynthia Vinney, Oxford University Press (2020).
© Oxford University Press.
DOI: 10.1093/oso/9780190643607.001.0001

presents itself—and, let's face it, an opportunity always presents itself ("As you wish," "Inconceivable!"; "Mawiage, that bwessed awangement. That dweam within a dweam"; "Have fun stormin' the castle"; "Hello. My name is Inigo Montoya. You killed my father. Prepare to die!" We could go on.)

Of course, you know your favorite story is fiction, so why do you become so absorbed in it? Why do you react to it with all the emotion and interest you might if your best friend or your spouse was telling you about the most compelling experience they'd ever had? What does your mind do while it's watching or reading a fictional story that allows you to become so immersed and involved, even with the knowledge that what you're seeing, hearing, or reading isn't real?

MENTAL MODELS

The key to our ability to get lost in a story is our skill at constructing representations in our minds called mental models. Mental models are not only pertinent to stories. We create mental models to represent many parts of our external reality (Busselle & Bilandzic, 2008). These models guide how we comprehend and perceive all kinds of things in our lives and help us understand, relate, and respond to the world around us.

For example, imagine you are opening up a website you've never seen before to shop for a book by your favorite author. What do you do first? How do you decide how to find what you're looking for? We know you likely open up new websites all the time and just start browsing. It feels instinctive, like you're not thinking about the mechanics of it at all. But really as you navigate a new website, you automatically start to form a mental model of how to use and interact with it in your head. Maybe you look through the navigation options on the top of the page or you try to find the search box. Either way, in your mind, you're creating a mental structure that tells you how this website can be used and how the different parts of the website work together. When you get to the page with the book you're looking for, you may expect to see pricing information, user reviews, and a description of the book. Perhaps the page offers something you didn't expect like an aggregate rating for the book from critics. Your mind will note the information available and the order in which it appears. This will help you determine how to use the information and the pattern of information you can expect to see when you go to new product pages on the site. By creating a mental representation of the information available on each kind of web page on the site, you will understand the different things you can accomplish on it and how to do so successfully.

In other words, the mental model you build in your mind of the website helps you anticipate what to expect from it and makes your experience smooth and easy every time you use it. Even though you don't have an actual map of the website as you browse through it, your experience with it helps you build one internally. You can use that map in your mind to easily click through the site and complete the tasks you came there for. Also, if you come back to the website later, you'll have an even easier time. The site will be familiar so you'll know exactly what to expect and anticipate as you click its different links. This will make your visit that much more efficient, effortless, and satisfying.

Without a mental model, however, on each new web page you'd have to try to figure out what to do and how to accomplish your goals from scratch. So, the mental models you carry with you help you predict what will happen and how (Hawkins, 2007), not just on websites but for everything from the different ways you can drive from point A to point B in your hometown to what to expect and how you'll behave when you attend a rock concert to understanding the network of relationships between the different members of your family. Right now, can you visualize the layout of your elementary school or your childhood home? Those are mental models. Because a model is a representation, it may not be completely accurate. In fact, we may go back to our childhood school and notice that a few things are different. Likely, it looks smaller in person than it did in our minds because the eyes we used to see it through were closer to the floor. But generally speaking, mental models make your journey through the world smoother by giving you a way to take mental shortcuts, reducing the number of things you need to figure out about the world around you on a regular basis.

To relate this to movies, television shows, and books, we think you'll find that you have a number of mental models that represent facets of story worlds too. Actually, in a way, those worlds exist most fully in the minds of those of us who love stories. Hollywood has been called the Dream Factory because it constructs a kind of dream world in our minds. And it takes a dreamer to have a dream.

As an example of some of the mental models you use when interacting with a story, take a look at our mental models quiz (see Table 4.1). We selected some shows that many people are familiar with. If one of your favorites isn't on the list, write your own quiz and send it to us! Whether or not you know these particular answers, the point of the quiz is to get you to think about the way you use mental models even when you're watching a TV show.

As you can see from our mental models quiz, mental models help us understand many things, from how to navigate a room to the relationships between people, whether in real life or in fiction. Of course, in the case of our mental models of story worlds from movies and TV, the settings we are intimately familiar with are actually an illusion created by a team of talented professionals. For example, if you go to Universal Studios Hollywood and take the studio tour, at one point you'll drive down Wisteria Lane, the place where the main characters from the TV drama *Desperate Housewives* lived. On the show, the exteriors of these houses led seamlessly to their interiors, but in reality, the actors shot those interior scenes on a soundstage unconnected to the exterior Wisteria Lane set the Universal Studios tour tram drives through.

Fans of the show may have mental models of the homes of the characters Susan, Lynette, Bree, and Gabrielle from their front porches to their kitchens to their bedrooms. But for the actors who played them, these places were several individual sets complete with space for cameras and crews that viewers never saw. Naturally, many of us understand this is true, although many of us haven't given it much thought. But when our mental models of a story world are compromised it can be a strange, even jarring, experience. At the same time, it can also be fun and enlightening. After all, thinking about our mental models of story settings like this helps

TABLE 4.1.   MENTAL MODELS OF STORY WORLDS

These questions are designed to help you access your mental models of specific story worlds. Pick a story world that you know from these TV shows and see if you can visualize the answers. To check your answers, you can Google images from the shows.

Favorite Sets:

1. *The Office*: As you enter the office, where are Jim and Dwight's desks? Where does the accounting department sit? Where is the conference room in relation to the rest of the office? Describe the reception desk.
2. *The Brady Bunch*: What color were the walls in the Brady girls' bedroom? What color was the Brady boys' bedroom furniture? If you were sitting on the Brady's sofa in the living room, in what direction would you walk to get to Mr. Brady's study?
3. *Sherlock Holmes*: Can you describe the furniture placement in 221B Baker Street? What color are the chairs? Where does Mrs. Hudson live, relative to Sherlock's flat?

Relationships

1. *The X-Files*: Who is Mulder and Scully's boss at the FBI? When did Mulder's sister disappear? What is the name of Mulder and Scully's son and what happened to him?
2. *Mad Men*: Who are Roger Sterling's wives? How many children does he have? What are their names? How many of Don Draper's secretaries can you name? Can you list all of the women that Don Draper slept with?
3. *Game of Thrones*: Whose house is led by Lord Eddard Stark? How many children does he have and what are their names? Who is Jon Snow, and who is his mother?

---

us realize how our minds work to put together the information provided by a movie or film to create a complete picture in our mind's eye. When we encounter the exterior of a house, for instance, we apply our mental model of the broad category "house" to understand what we're seeing and how it works. So, when we see Susan's home on *Desperate Housewives*, (see Figure 4.1), our minds work with the show to use the visuals of the parts of the house

Figure 4.1 During Universal Studios Hollywood's Studio Tour, trams drive down Wisteria Lane, the street where the characters from *Desperate Housewives* lived. But while these look like real houses, they were only used for the exterior scenes. Interior scenes were shot elsewhere.
Source: https://www.universalstudioshollywood.com/things-to-do/rides-and-attractions/the-world-famous-studio-tour/

we're shown to turn it into a whole, complete with continuous exteriors and interiors, just like any other house. We process all the information we encounter this way. We unconsciously use our mental representations of the way things work to comprehend new information so we can understand it more quickly. This allows us to more easily interact with the world and each other.

What Makes Up Our Mental Models?

The building blocks of our mental models are the schemas and scripts we've developed from a lifetime of interacting with the world (Busselle & Bilandzic, 2008; Graesser, Olde, & Klettke, 2002). A schema is a mental structure that helps us categorize and organize the information we encounter every day. Schemas set our expectations for people and situations.

There are different kinds of schemas, including role schemas (What is a waitress like?), self-schemas (What am I like?), and a variety of social schemas (What makes a good friend?). Meanwhile, a script is a basic outline for an interaction that may take place. In other words, a script is an event schema—a set of expectations for a situation (What happens in a fast food restaurant?) or ritual (What happens at a wedding?). A script is a lot like a script for a play, film, or TV show—it gives us a step-by-step idea of how an event will unfold

For example, we have a person schema, or mental set of expectations, for what makes a good mother. We may think of a good mother as nurturing and affectionate, as kind and gentle, and as concerned with the welfare of her children. In the context of film and television, many mother characters fit this schema, such as Marion Cunningham from *Happy Days*, Marge Simpson from *The Simpsons*, Lorelai Gilmore from *Gilmore Girls*, Tami Taylor from *Friday Night Lights*, and Donna Reed from *It's a Wonderful Life*. By the way, these are also called "prototypes," as in "Tami Taylor is the prototypical good mother."

On the other hand, some movie and TV moms don't match our good mother schema. For instance, Peg Bundy from *Married with Children* seems like the antithesis of this schema because she doesn't cook, is rude to her children, and often puts her own needs above theirs. Peg Bundy violates our schema of what makes a good mother. Likewise, there are characters that fit the schema of "good teacher," such as Robin Williams's character in *Dead Poet's Society*, whereas Walter White in *Breaking Bad* is the polar opposite.

Why does it matter? Well, for one thing, once we know whether a person fits a schema, we can predict how they might behave. There's a theory called expectancy violation theory that says that if someone violates our expectations in a positive direction, then we give them even more credit for their behavior. If, for instance, we don't think a Black man has equal opportunities to succeed in business, then when he does, we rate him as even more competent than a similar White man because he has exceeded our expectations (Bettencourt, Dill, Greathouse, Charlton, & Mulholland, 1997).

Scripts act in a similar way. For example, we have a script for "honeymoon." On the iconic TV show *The Brady Bunch*, a blonde woman with three blonde girls marries a brunette man with three brown-haired boys. On their honeymoon, the parents start to miss the children and decide to pick them up and bring them along on the honeymoon. (If memory serves, they also pick up the housekeeper and the dog.) We can safely say that *The Brady Bunch* pilot, therefore, violates our script for "honeymoon." In this case and many others, violations of our schemas and scripts can be humorous.

The much-loved sitcom *Frasier* showcases the antics of Frasier Crane, a stuck-up, but endearing psychiatrist in Seattle, and his brother Niles, an equally stuck-up, but endearing psychiatrist in Seattle. Frasier and Niles are snobby about everything from dinner parties and wardrobes to bath products and kitchen items. Meanwhile, their father, Martin Crane, and Frasier's radio producer, Roz Doyle, are the brothers' foils. Whereas Frasier and Niles love the opera and fine wine, Martin and Roz like sports and beer. Many episodes explore the difference between the snobby (or refined?) versus the down-to-earth (or pedestrian?) idea of things like parties and what constitutes a good time. This gives audience members the opportunity to ask themselves what their script for a great party is. Who do they agree with, Frasier or Martin? As we go deeper, we might decide that one script really isn't better than the other, because it's not about whether wine or beer is served; it's the people at a party that make it special.

As you might have guessed, mental models, and the schemas and scripts that create them, can help us, but they can also get us into trouble. One problem happens when these mental shortcuts cause us to ignore or discount information, resulting in stereotypes that can be hard to overcome. While our mental models improve our interactions with the world in many ways, they also blind us in some ways. Because of our reliance on our mental models, we focus on information that confirms our understanding of the world and overlook information that might change it. And since we use our mental models all the time, both consciously and unconsciously, it can be very hard for us to incorporate information that doesn't sync up with them. That's why our stereotypes can become so insidious and hard to change.

MENTAL MODELS OF FICTION

> Come with me and you'll be
> In a world of pure imagination
> Take a look and you'll see into your imagination.
> —"Pure Imagination" from *Willy Wonka & the Chocolate Factory*

Schemas, scripts, and stereotypes also help us comprehend stories. When we're reading or watching a story, we construct multiple kinds of mental models that enable us to understand it. These mental models become deeper and more complex as we get deeper into the story. The mental model that scholars most often point to as essential to story comprehension is the situation model (Busselle & Bilandzic 2008; Graesser et al., 2002; Zwaan, Magliano, & Graesser, 1995).

The situation model is, as its name suggests, the mental representation we construct of the situation depicted in a story. As psychologist Arthur Graesser and his colleagues explain, when we watch or read a story, in our minds we assemble a representation

> of what the text is about. The situation model for a story is a microworld with characters who perform actions in pursuit of goals, events that present obstacles to goals, conflicts between characters, emotional reactions of characters, spatial settings, the style and procedure of actions, objects, properties of objects, traits of characters, and mental states of characters. (Graesser et al., 2002, pp. 230–231)

The situation model is constantly revised and updated as the story lets us in on new information while we read or watch. And new story information is incorporated in light of older information we've already encountered. A situation model for a story is constructed successfully when a reader or viewer can easily integrate new plot points and character information as it appears in the story. On the other hand, it might be impossible to construct a coherent situation model if the new information is difficult to integrate because, for example, it contradicts earlier parts of the story (Busselle & Bilandzic, 2008).

Continuity

Research on story comprehension has shown that audiences monitor multiple dimensions of continuity to construct a situation model. In particular, Rolf Zwaan et al. (1995) showed that readers monitor three dimensions of continuity while reading a story. First, readers monitor temporal continuity, which is the kind of continuity that occurs when current story information takes place within the same timeframe as previous story information. Second, readers monitor causal continuity, which occurs when current story information is directly caused by or follows from previous story information. Finally, readers monitor spatial continuity, which occurs when current story information takes place in the same setting as previous story information.

Over two experiments, Zwaan et al. (1995) found that temporal and causal discontinuities, but not situational discontinuities, interfere with story comprehension when readers take in a story for the first time. In other words, during the first encounter with a story, shifts in time and events without a direct causal relationship made it more difficult to understand the story. Meanwhile, when rereading a story, spatial discontinuities interfere with comprehension. For instance, one of the stories participants read was Edgar Allan Poe's *The Tell-Tale Heart*, a short story where a man describes how he murders and dismembers an old man. The story is told from a first-person perspective, and it can be challenging to follow the narrator as he confesses to his crime. When study participants initially read this story, their reading speed would slow down as they tried to follow the shifts in time between events—such as the time between the murder and when the police arrive as well as the direct causal relationships between events, such as how it might be possible for the narrator to hear the sounds he hears, including the beating of the old man's heart. Then, when reading the story for a second time, readers would slow down to understand shifts in the story's spatial setting, such as when the narrator conceals the body in the old man's chambers and then goes somewhere else to let the police inside. Thus, while readers are likely to pay the most attention to temporal and causal continuity when first reading a text, once they are familiar with this information, especially the causes for the events of the story, they then focus their attention on information they missed, such as the story's spatial settings, during a second reading.

In the end, readers construct multitiered mental models as they read that can include temporal (When did this happen?), causal (Why did this happen?), and spatial (Where did this happen?) components that help them comprehend a story. And it's likely that audiences monitor similar story continuities and construct similar multifaceted situation models when they watch movies and television and even when they play video games or listen to music with a narrative.

Generally speaking, most stories have a linear structure where one event causes another. So, later scenes follow earlier ones in the time frame of the story and the settings remain consistent. But some storytellers choose to play with continuity. Some of the devices storytellers use to break continuity—like flashbacks and flashforwards—are so common that we follow them easily. However, some stories use more complicated story structures to create puzzles of continuity. To comprehend the narrative, audiences must piece these puzzles together as they watch or read the story.

For example, in Quentin Tarantino's *Pulp Fiction*, the viewer encounters multiple temporal and causal discontinuities. The movie begins and ends on the same scene, but in between the story jumps forward and back in time showing viewers both how the plot got to that first scene and what happens afterwards. It's up to each individual viewer to construct a timeline of events and the reasons for them in his or her mind while watching, something that must be done scene by scene as more story information is acquired and the viewer determines where each scene belongs in the narrative so that it makes sense.

Similarly, Christopher Nolan's *Memento* keeps viewers guessing, much like the film's main character, as they try to figure out what's happening in the story and why. It isn't until the end of the film, however, that the temporal discontinuity baked into the movie's narrative becomes clear. The plot is presented—spoiler alert!—in reverse chronological order, and it is only once viewers grasp this that an understanding of the story's causal continuity snaps into place.

In cases like these, the stories' discontinuities aren't a bug; they're a feature. These movies and other stories like them unfold like mysteries, providing clues to their secrets here and there as the viewer gets deeper into the narrative. Each piece of story information contributes to the mental model being formed, and many viewers find it rewarding to take the discontinuous information the story presents and reconstruct the story in their minds with a linear timeline and cause-and-effect logic. One of the reasons people enjoy this may be that when stories present unexpected or discontinuous information, it provides an opportunity for audience members to think creatively.

In an experiment, psychologists William Wenzel and Richard Gerrig (2015) showed that when people listened to stories with both expected and unexpected outcomes, the stories prompted creative thoughts, although the thoughts were of a different quality for each kind of story. In the case of the stories with expected outcomes, listeners' thoughts were more certain and positive, and they were more likely to think about themselves. On the other hand, stories with unexpected outcomes led listeners to have more uncertain and negative thoughts and to have more emotional reactions.

While the stories tested in this experiment were short and simple, these findings likely also apply to longer, more complicated stories as well. So, when we take in a story with a lot of discontinuity, such as the previously mentioned movies, we may experience a great deal of uncertainty as we attempt to build a coherent situation model of the story. Even though this makes us feel off-kilter, at the same time, the process of building a situation model out of the story information presented engages us creatively, enabling us to consider what the discontinuities mean and where they could eventually fit in the model we're constructing in our minds.

Part of the fun of putting together the story for some people may be this opportunity for creative speculation. Think of a TV show like *Lost*. While the main story explored the lives of the survivors of a plane crash on a strange island, viewers quickly became used to, and anticipated, the flashbacks to different characters' lives prior to being stranded on the island. The flashbacks gave the audience information that helped them better contextualize the different characters' actions in the storyline on the island, while answering the questions presented by certain mysteries and opening up other mysteries too. In addition, constant questions about the island itself came up (Why is there a polar bear running around? Are people really being attacked by a smoke monster? Who is this French woman speaking over the walkie-talkie? Whaaa?). Taken together, the flashbacks and causal discontinuities gave audiences an opportunity to use their creativity to develop theories about what was really happening on the island and what different characters might be thinking or planning.

When the story switched to flashforwards a few seasons into the show's run, the audience quickly adjusted to this new temporal discontinuity and embraced the chance to fill in more blanks. In the final season of the show, however, when the nonisland scenes could not easily be explained as either flashbacks or forwards, the audience was confused and uncertain through the whole season, unsure what information these scenes that had previously given context to the story as a whole were now providing. This led some viewers to great feats of creative speculation, and fan theories abounded. But, for many, the final explanation during the series finale was a let-down, leaving many questions unanswered and failing to excuse all the discontinuities and unexpected plot points that had come before. This is a risk that is always inherent in any high-wire storytelling that seeks to stoke audience interest by using discontinuities or unexpected plot points. But if story discontinuities don't become too overwhelming or leave too many loose ends, many stories that employ this kind of storytelling will ultimately still be coherent and understandable.

At the same time, however, individual differences in creativity will cause people to respond to discontinuities and unexpected plot points in different ways. Some readers and viewers will ignore these story features and just continue to read or watch the story without dedicating any thought to them. Others may become more or less creatively engaged by the mysteries presented by various story features. In some cases, this creative engagement can lead to elaborate theories about the story and its characters, as it did for many *Lost* fans. In other cases, it can lead to more limited creative speculation regarding the immediate outcomes of the plot or the fate of the characters as one reads or watches the story. As Wenzel and Gerrig (2015) note, because of these different creative responses, people's experiences with the same story may actually be quite different.

Filling in the Gaps With Schemas

As previously mentioned, viewers and readers actually bring a lot of themselves to building a situation model for a story. While creative engagement draws us in and encourages speculation, actual story comprehension is dependent on our pre-existing schemas, scripts, and stereotypes. Stories don't address every element of their plots explicitly. Instead, it is up to us as individual viewers or readers to infer some things so we can fully flesh out the narrative in our minds. Our existing schemas, scripts, and stereotypes help us fill in these blanks, just like we do when we encounter new information in real life (Busselle & Bilandzic 2008; Graesser et al., 2002). In addition to the schemas and scripts we use regularly to understand both real life and stories, when we encounter a story, a schema that is specifically dedicated to our knowledge of what stories are is also activated, at least initially. Because of this story schema, we expect a story to conform to certain expectations (Busselle & Bilandzic, 2008). For example, we expect that a story will contain a narrative that features a beginning, middle, and end, that a story will introduce and resolve a conflict, and that stories will have temporal, causal, and situational continuity.

Furthermore, we use our schemas for different narrative genres as a framework for contextualizing and understanding the story events and characters. Each genre has specific conventional features, and our knowledge of these features guides our expectations for stories that fall into each given genre. For example, in a romantic comedy, like *When Harry Met Sally* or *Pretty Woman*, we expect to see two people meet cute and fall in love by the end of the story. In a science fiction story, we won't bat an eye at fantastic or impossible events, like aliens trying to take over Earth, as in *War of the Worlds*, or a cyborg traveling back in time from the future, as in the *Terminator* franchise. And in an action movie, like *Die Hard* or *John Wick*, we expect to see good guys and bad guys square off in epic fight scenes. Knowing the genre of a specific story helps us anticipate the kind of narrative we will be reading or watching and also helps guide our attention to and understanding of important plot and character details (Busselle & Bilandzic 2008; Graesser et al., 2002).

Story World and Character Models

In their model of narrative comprehension and engagement, Rick Busselle and Helena Bilandzic (2008) propose two additional mental models. These models—the story world model and character model—work with the situation model to form a complete understanding of a story. First, the story world model represents "the setting and all that setting implies: place, time period, and general contemporary state of affairs" (p. 259). The story world model includes the logic of the story, such as the rules that dictate what is and isn't possible in the world of the narrative. Once constructed, this mental model is unlikely to change much. Instead, it creates a framework through which we can understand the story.

If the different parts of the story create a coherent whole, we probably won't be overly aware of the story model we've constructed or the rules we expect to govern the story world. But if those rules are violated, we're likely to become hyperaware of the compromised logic of the story. For example, the movie *Blade* centers on vampires who follow many of the conventional rules of these well-known fantasy creatures: In particular, they drink blood and are allergic to sunlight, so they can't go out during the day. Yet the vampires find a way around the former rule when they realize if they put on enough sunblock, they're able to venture out in broad daylight without consequence. Some viewers were able to incorporate this curveball into their story world model and continue to enjoy the movie. For Cynthia and viewers like her, however, this rule violation disrupted the logic of the story, preventing her from incorporating it into her story world model and from being able to continue to take the movie seriously.

In addition, character models are developed for each important character in a story. Initially, when characters are first presented, character models rely on stereotypes. The outward appearance and actions of a character will call to mind our ideas about what people who look and act like each character are like. For example, when we first meet Ed Harris's character, the Man in Black, in the HBO show *Westworld* (who you can check out in Figure 4.2), we quickly determine through his appearance and behavior that he is a character in the mold of many of the villains

Figure 4.2 Ed Harris plays the Man in Black on HBO's *Westworld*. Initially the character comes across as a one-dimensional black-hat villain, but as the show's first season unfolds, we learn more about him and how he came to be the character we know.

we've encountered in Westerns—a black-hatted cowboy whose intentions are evil.

As we observe more of what a character says and does, however, and consequently learn more about a them, our model evolves. Theory of mind plays a key role here. As we mentioned earlier, theory of mind allows us to understand other people's mental states, perspectives, and goals, including those of fictional characters. All our observations about a character, including the inferences we've made based on theory of mind, combine to create a model of who the character is. And that model enables us to incorporate new character information as it comes up. It is in this way that we develop mental models of characters as individuals with their own internal logic. So, in the case of the Man in Black, as the episodes of *Westworld* unfold, we discover more about who he is and his world view. Then, in the final episodes of the show's first season, we become privy to the character's background and begin to understand how he developed into the villain the viewer knows. While we may not condone the character's behavior, our knowledge of him is much deeper than it was at first, causing him to become much more than a one-dimensional villain.

Like the story world model, character models are often more static than the situation model, which is constantly evolving with the story. On other hand, it can be incredibly difficult to get to know certain characters even when a story provides a substantial amount of information about them. In the TV show, *Mr. Robot*, for example, we are introduced in the first season to both the story's narrator, Elliot, a computer hacker, and the character Mr. Robot, the head of a hacker collective with plans to change the world. As we learn about both characters, we create character models for them. However, by the end of the season, we discover that neither Elliot nor Mr. Robot are who we thought they were. Elliot is not a reliable narrator, and because of this twist, we have to reconsider and revise our models for these characters. In the series' subsequent seasons, we are more skeptical of Elliot's narration, something we incorporate into our character model for him, which also impacts how we incorporate the new story information Elliot provides into our situation model of the ongoing narrative.

Of course, the medium through which we take in a story will also have an impact on the mental models we build. Audio-visual media like film, television, and online videos allow us to see and hear what story worlds and their characters look and sound like and to see the events that take place in the story. Audiobooks and podcasts provide audio information that let us hear interpretations or recordings of different characters' voices, but the audience must conjure up an image of the story's setting and the way the characters look, move, and interact in their minds. Comics and graphic novels provide a sequence of images and written words, but we must fill in the blanks left between panels as well as the verbal and audio soundscape of the story. Finally, literary books and novels are dependent on the written word to convey characters, events, and the settings of the story. In this case. we rely on our imagination to define the look, feel, tone, and everything else about the story.

Although various media give us different kinds of audio and visual information, that information likely isn't transferred directly into the mental models we construct of a story. Instead, the audio and visual information offered by different media provide cues that assist in mental model creation. Scholar Karin Kukkonen (2013) points out that such information probably operates "more like blueprints than photo-ready copies" (p. 159). In other words, our mental models aren't a facsimile of the information presented in a story. Our mental models are built from the information we find most salient as we're reading or viewing. So when we construct mental models for a story, accuracy isn't our primary concern. Our goal is to interpret and represent the story in a way that helps us best comprehend and make sense of it.

Further, different people bring varying levels of interest and ability to the production of mental models. If readers or viewers are unable or unwilling to create the mental models needed to make a story make sense in their minds, they won't become fully engaged by the story. But when the complexity of a story matches the abilities of a reader or viewer to produce the mental models needed to understand it and the reader or viewer is interested in taking on this challenge, the individual can become completely engaged. Constructing and refining situation, story world, and character models can be an absorbing process that promotes total focus on and transportation into the narrative, leading to an enjoyable experience in which we can truly get lost in a story (Busselle & Bilandzic, 2008).

WHAT IS REAL ANYWAY?

> There is no life I know
> To compare with pure imagination
> Living there, you'll be free, if you truly wish to be
> —"Pure Imagination" from
> *Willy Wonka & the Chocolate Factory*

Another thing that contributes to the successful construction of mental models of a story is how "real" the narrative seems to the viewer or reader. When we think of what's real, we often think about reality as we experience it in the real world. Not surprisingly, then, one of the most popular definitions of perceived realism in stories in early research on the topic was stories that accurately and factually represent reality (Hall, 2003; Potter, 1988). This definition worked for some fictional stories in some genres but lacked nuance. Given many people's love of superhero films, supernatural stories, or other fantastical narratives, it's clear that fictional stories don't have to exactly simulate the real world for us to feel a narrative is realistic as we're reading or watching it. The plot, world, and characters a story presents just have to have a consistent logic. This logic and what is considered real is dependent on different things in different genres. Many scholars recognize that perceptions of realism should be broken down into multiple dimensions and have offered various ways to do this.

For example, communication scholar Alice Hall (2003) conducted a series of focus groups to explore how people defined realistic and unrealistic TV shows and movies. From these focus groups, she developed six separate categories for evaluating media realism. First, for many people, plausibility, or whether or not a story portrayed something that could potentially happen in real life, helped them judge realism. Some study participants took this notion a step further and based their realism judgments on typicality, or the extent to which not only an event in a story could happen, but whether it is a common occurrence for a majority of people. Many also pointed to factuality, or the accurate portrayal of a real event or individual, as a way of evaluating realism.

While all three of these realism judgments rely on comparisons with the real world to some extent, the other three conceptualizations Hall (2003) found relied on different standards, including narrative absorption and emotional investment in the story. First, involvement, or the audience's ability to become caught up in the story and its characters, relied on participants' emotional responses to a story to determine its realism. Narrative consistency, or the internal coherence of a story, including a lack of discontinuities that take one out of the story was also brought up as a way to evaluate realism. Finally, people mentioned perceptual persuasiveness, or how convincing the visual representation of the story was separate from the content of the story, as a means for making realism judgments.

Hall's (2003) various concepts of media realism demonstrate the complexity of people's perceptions of what's "real" in stories. Moreover, depending on the genre of the story we're watching or reading, we may be more or less likely to utilize these different concepts to judge the realism of the narrative. For narratives that claim to be based on a true story, factuality may be the most important factor when judging realism. So, our knowledge of the real-life history of World War II or America's founding fathers may be the sources we use to evaluate a film like *Schindler's List* or a musical like *Hamilton*. On the other hand, we may base our judgments of the realism of science fiction and fantasy stories, such as those of superheroes like Superman, Batman, Wonder Woman, and Spider-Man, on our emotional involvement in the story or the narrative's consistency. As Hall points out, different story features shape each realism category and different audience members likely emphasize or pay attention to different elements of a story when judging realism.

In their model of narrative comprehension, Busselle and Bilandzic (2008) present a simplified framework for grouping judgments of story realism. Instead of six categories, they specify just two categories into which these judgments fall: external realism and narrative realism. External realism is the degree to which the story accurately mirrors the real world. Narrative realism, on the other hand, is the degree to which the story is consistent, logical, and coherent within its specific fictional context. Busselle and Bilandzic posit that we actually won't even make realism judgments while watching or reading a story unless some part of the story is inconsistent with our existing schemas, scripts, or stereotypes. If this happens, we'll probably evaluate the story negatively because the otherwise smooth process of constructing mental models for the story will be interrupted. Such interruptions effectively throw up mental red flags that cause us to scrutinize the part of the story that gave us pause. So, if Don Draper suddenly showed up with a brand-new laptop in the 1960s-set TV show *Mad Men*, we would immediately question the story's realism. Unless the story can explain the reason for the anachronism, we'll quickly disengage from it.

Yet, as we've mentioned, we tend to judge the realism of a narrative partially on our understandings and expectations of the genre of the story we're watching or reading. Moreover, we're able to imagine how various events might happen, regardless of the authenticity of the events themselves—a judgment that should strongly contribute to perceptions of realism (Shapiro, Barriga, & Beren, 2010). Thus, our realism evaluations may be more influenced by "some sort of commonsense plausibility criterion" (Busselle & Bilandzic, 2008, p. 270) that is specific to the context of the story than by the verisimilitude of the story. If new story information is inconsistent with what has already been established in the situation, story world, or character models we have constructed and, consequently, can't be comfortably incorporated into these models, the story will be evaluated as unrealistic. For example, if Meredith Grey from *Grey's Anatomy* abruptly decided to quit being a surgeon to become a full-time mom, viewers would likely judge this plot development as highly unrealistic. This is because fans of the show know from over a decade of character development that Meredith loves and is very attached to her career (although the yarn-spinners over at Shondaland could likely figure out a way to make even this story arc work!). At the same time, audiences would also find it unrealistic if Harry Potter and his friends decided to mow Voldemort and his minions down with machine guns instead of fighting them with magic. This isn't because machine guns don't exist in the real world and magic does, but because the use of magic is consistent with the story world of the *Harry Potter* series.

In research on how people judge the realism of stories, media psychologists Michael Shapiro and Hyekyung Kim (2012) found that when initial realism judgments of 30-second narrative TV commercials were high, final realism judgments tended to be lower. In contrast, when initial realism judgments were low, final realism judgments tended to be higher. So, initial judgments of realism seemed to anchor how people perceived the realism of the ads as a whole. This effect happened if viewers had cognitive resources available to adjust their initial assessments of realism. If participants were distracted or were processing information other than the reality of the ads, however, their initial realism judgments stayed the same. While Shapiro and Kim's study used short TV commercials, if their results hold for other kinds of narratives, perceptions of realism most likely depend on people's understanding of both stories and genres that are similar to the ones they are reading or watching. Just as our *Grey's Anatomy* and *Harry Potter* examples demonstrate, different realism criteria are applied to different kinds of stories. So, when we say a story is "real," our definition of real varies with the kind of story we're describing.

Suspension of Disbelief

Of course, you might be thinking, "Wait a minute, this is getting awfully complicated—doesn't suspension of disbelief explain why we get involved in stories in one concise phrase?" Samuel Taylor Coleridge introduced the idea of "willing suspension of disbelief" in 1817. Since Coleridge coined the phrase, it's become a common explanation for why we become interested and invested in fictional stories we know aren't real. While suspension of disbelief has certainly had staying power, the idea that we have a switch in our brains that we turn off to accept story worlds without judgment isn't consistent with the scientific evidence. Today, there's more or less a consensus among psychologists that suspending disbelief isn't really what we do when we take in a story (Shapiro & Kim, 2012). So, although we still hear about it all the time, we really aren't suspending disbelief when we're reading or watching a story any more than we might be in any other context.

Instead, many psychologists agree that when we take in information, we first comprehend it without judgment, regardless of whether its source is a news program, our best friend, or a fictional story. Then, after comprehension we evaluate the information to determine how much we believe it (Gerrig & Pillow, 1998). A series of studies by Daniel Gilbert and his colleagues indicate that when we comprehend information our automatic reaction is to believe it's true (Gilbert, Krull, & Malone, 1990). Rejecting information as false requires a lot more mental effort than believing it, and because of this, it's less likely to happen, especially if our mental resources are being used elsewhere (Gilbert, 1991). For example, in one experiment, research participants' mental processing was interrupted as information was presented to them, which prevented them from focusing on judging the information. As a result, they were more likely to say false propositions were true but not that true propositions were false (Gilbert et al., 1990). This suggests that more mental resources are needed to reject something as untrue than to accept it as true. So, accepting information as true is our default.

If we automatically accept information as true, we don't have to suspend disbelief to become involved in a story. We just have to watch or read. In fact, psychologist Richard Gerrig and his colleagues argue that to reject the information we encounter in a story, we have to engage in *"the willing construction of disbelief"* (Gerrig & Rapp, 2004, p. 267; also see Gerrig & Pillow, 1998). That is, we must make an effort to retrieve counterinformation that contrasts with the information provided by the story.

When we get transported into a story, it may be especially difficult for us to prevent ourselves from believing it. If you remember from Chapter 1, transportation is the process of getting immersed into a story. When we're transported, our mental efforts go toward involving ourselves in the story, leaving less energy for us to construct disbelief. In a series of studies, Melanie Green and Timothy Brock (2000) showed that readers who were more transported into a story were more likely to believe things that were consistent with ideas from the story and were more likely to feel the story rang true, regardless of whether they were told the story was fiction or nonfiction. So, when we are transported into a story, we are even less likely to disbelieve the story than we are in other circumstances.

This doesn't mean we literally think we are seeing or reading a factual account of a real-life situation. Instead, we believe the emotional content of the story. This enables us to laugh, cry, or scream in accordance with the plot and characters (Busselle & Bilandzic, 2008). If we're transported into a narrative, we don't need to expend extra effort to experience emotions. Furthermore, when we're transported, we are more inclined to accept the perspectives and worldviews in the narrative as true and relevant to our lives. This is why some of the ideas we encounter in fiction can change the way we understand, think about, and respond to the world.

Fictionality

Although we don't suspend disbelief when we take in a story, according to Busselle and Bilandzic's (2008) model of narrative comprehension, one thing we do utilize is our understanding that the story is fictional. Our knowledge of what it means for something to be fiction is incorporated into our mental models, becoming an additional part of our understanding of the story. While the idea of fictionality is included in the mental models we construct, typically the concept remains tucked away in the back of our heads, rarely acknowledged unless something in the story specifically activates our understanding that the story is fictional. However, the tacit knowledge of a story's fictionality enables viewers and readers to follow the story world's logic even if it doesn't conform to real-world logic. Logic that deviates from that of the real world is relatively typical in fiction. So, incorporating the concept of fictionality into our mental models of a story helps open us up to the narrative. Meanwhile, our understanding of the real world is kept separate so it doesn't conflict with the mental models we've created specifically for the story.

For example, Cynthia and Kristin Hopper-Losenicky (2016) researched how online fans discuss science fiction and fantasy genre TV shows and found that fans of these shows rarely mentioned the supernatural or magical parts of the show. Instead, they focused on the real-life elements of the show like the characters' relationships and their interpretations of the various storylines. While fans were aware what they were viewing was fictional, they were still interested in applying the lessons of the shows to their lives and were able to ignore the more overtly fictional elements of the shows to do so.

Similarly, in a study by media scholar Ranjana Das (2016) on British adolescents' perceptions of the *Harry Potter* series, Das found that the young participants often ignored or dismissed the magical and fantastical elements of the narrative in favor of the parts that were applicable to their lives. As a result, the participants focused on the parts of the story they could relate to their personal real-life experiences, including how the friendships between the characters mirrored their own friendships, the relevance of the story's lessons about growing up, and the meaning of the values championed by the narrative, such as the importance of family. So the story's meaning was rooted in the ways it could be connected to reality, not in the magic and fantasy elements. Although people know *Harry Potter* is fictional, their focus is on how the narrative reflects their understanding of life. It's in this way that the story becomes pertinent to people's everyday reality.

Metaphor and Allegory

Further, many stories or story elements function as allegories or metaphors, enabling fiction to examine real issues indirectly. Through metaphors something can stand both for itself and for something else. This is something we see frequently in popular culture narratives, especially in the genres of science fiction and fantasy. For example, superhero stories are ripe with metaphor. Many have pointed out the way stories featuring the X-Men—superheroes who discover they have powers during their adolescent years—could be seen as metaphors for coming out of the closet. Similarly, Superman's origin story can be seen as an allegory for the immigrant experience. This is also the case for Supergirl, something that has been explored extensively in the CW network's recent television depiction of the character. In the show, a significant number of aliens from space have taken up residence on Earth, many fleeing from hostile conditions on their own planets, and there is a conflict between the humans who want to grant the aliens citizenship and the rights that come with it and those who do not—a metaphorical reflection of the debates that take place in the United States and elsewhere about whether or not to welcome immigrants and refugees from other countries.

By using metaphor and allegory as a way to explore difficult topics, fiction allows us to examine our feelings in the safe space provided by the story. It may also help us relate to people in a way we couldn't before. While we may not personally experience what it's like to come out as LGBTQ or know someone who has, engaging with stories in which characters come to terms with their special abilities and the persecution that comes with them in X-Men movies, comics, and TV shows gives us direct insight into how emotionally challenging such an experience could be. Whether we recognize the metaphorical nature of these stories or not, meeting people that may not be like us through stories can help us become more accepting of people's differences.

As psychologist Keith Oatley (2011) points out, it is our mental models that enable us to experience both the world we live in and worlds we can only imagine. So, we can map our mental models of the immigration debate or the experience of coming out onto stories that, on their surface at least, don't deal with these issues. Oatley says our ability to discover metaphors in fiction is an extension of the pretend play we engaged in when we were children. By the age of 3, make-believe is frequent. Children's toys become both something they can hold and manipulate as well as the real-life object it represents. So, a stuffed animal is both a cuddly toy one can hug and a real animal. And a dollhouse is both a miniature space the child can decorate and a full-size home. As adults, we bring our ability to map our mental models of one domain onto another into our interactions with fiction.

This also lets us take personal meaning from stories. If a fictional story resonates with us, we may map the mental models we've created for the story onto components of our own life story. In this way, we notice how certain characters or plot points could be metaphors for our own real-life experiences. For example, anyone who has harbored a hidden part of themselves may apply the story of the X-Men to their personal experiences and struggles. This can alter both their comprehension of the story itself and their comprehension of their struggles with a hidden stigma, perhaps even leading them to change how they deal with this issue.

So, metaphors and the mental models that enable us to understand them can be a powerful force in our comprehension and emotional involvement with stories. Just like many of the other elements of story comprehension we've discussed in this chapter, the amount of attention different people pay to the metaphors and allegories contained in stories will vary. Some may simply ignore them, while others will be powerfully impacted by a story's use of one thing standing for another.

Clearly, although it comes to us naturally, comprehending fiction is a complex process. And when we find a story that really speaks to us, it's a process that can absorb us completely. This is one reason we love immersing ourselves in stories. In addition, becoming immersed in a story can evoke new thoughts and ideas that we wouldn't have arrived at any other way (Oatley, 2011). Our desire to become immersed in a story that exposes us to contrasting perspectives and ideas could be one reason interconnected stories with a plethora of settings and characters, like the Marvel Cinematic Universe, are so popular right now. When we spend enough time getting to know characters like Iron Man, Captain America, and Thor, it is fun for us to bring together our character models of these individuals into a single movie like *The Avengers* or *Captain America: Civil War*. We become emotionally invested in seeing how these characters interact and how their different perspectives drive their conflicts and reactions. But these stories also invite our cognitive engagement, expanding our mental models of the story world and how the story connections fit and work together. We construct an expansive, constantly growing model of an imaginary world and models of the people that occupy it in our minds. This experience not only absorbs and diverts us; it also gives us the opportunity to explore ideas about teamwork, good and evil, and friendship, if we want to.

While watching a movie or reading a book may look like a passive experience, the cognitive and emotional activities we take part in when we get lost in a story are anything but. In the next chapter, we turn to our ongoing love of stories. We'll explore the reasons some kinds of stories capture our imaginations over and over again and why they continue to have meaning to us.

REFERENCES

Bettencourt, B. A., Dill, K. E., Greathouse, S. A., Charlton, K., & Mulholland, A. (1997). Evaluations of ingroup and outgroup members: The role of category-based expectancy violations. *Journal of Experimental Social Psychology, 33*, 244–275.

Busselle, R., & Bilandzic, H. (2008). Fictionality and perceived realism in experiencing stories: A model of narrative comprehension and engagement. *Communication Theory, 18*, 255–280. https://doi.org/10.1111/j.1468-2885.2008.00322.x

Coleridge, S. T. (1817). *Biographia literaria*. Retrieved from http://www.english.upenn.edu/~mgamer/Etexts/biographia.html

Das, R. (2016). "I've walked this street": Readings of "reality" in British young people's reception of *Harry Potter*. *Journal of Children and Media, 10*(3), 341–354. https://doi.org/10.1080/17482798.2015.1094671

Gerrig, R. J., & Pillow, B. H. (1998). A developmental perspective on the construction of disbelief. In J. de Rivera & T. R. Sarbin (Eds.), *Believed-in imaginings: The narrative construction of reality* (pp. 101–119). Washington, DC: American Psychological Association.

Gerrig, R. J., & Rapp, D. N. (2004). Psychological processes underlying literary impact. *Poetics Today, 25*(2), 265–281.

Gilbert, D. T. (1991). How mental systems believe. *American Psychologist, 46*(2), 107–119.

Gilbert, D. T., Krull, D. S., & Malone, P. S. (1990). Unbelieving the unbelievable: Some problems in the rejection of false information. *Journal of Personality and Social Psychology, 59*(4), 601–613.

Graesser, A. C., Olde, B., & Klettke, B. (2002). How does the mind construct and represent stories? In M. C. Green, J. J. Strange, & T. C. Brock (Eds.), *Narrative impact: Social and cognitive foundations* (pp. 229–262). New York, NY: Psychology Press.

Green, M. C., & Brock, T. C. (2000). The role of transportation in the persuasiveness of public narratives. *Journal of Personality and Social Psychology, 79*(5), 701–721. https://doi.org/10.1037/0022-3514.79.5.701

Hall, A. (2003). Reading realism: Audiences' evaluations of the reality of media texts. *Journal of Communication, 53*, 624–641.

Kukkonen, K. (2013). Navigating infinite earths. In C. Hatfield, J. Heer, & K. Worcester (Eds.), *The superhero reader* (pp. 155–169). Jackson, MS: University Press of Mississippi.

Oatley, K. (2011). *Such stuff as dreams: The psychology of fiction*. Malden, MA: Wiley-Blackwell.

Potter, J. W. (1988). Perceived reality in television effects research. *Journal of Broadcasting & Electronic Media, 32*(1), 23–41.

Shapiro, M. A., Barriga, C. A., & Beren, J. (2010). Causal attribution and perceived realism of stories. *Media Psychology, 13*(3), 273–300. https://doi.org/10.1080/15213269.2010.502874

Shapiro, M. A., & Kim, H. (2012). Realism judgments and mental resources: A cue processing model of media narrative realism. *Media Psychology, 15*(1), 93–119. https://doi.org/10.1080/15213269.2011.6449666

Hawkins, J. (2007, May). How brain science will change computing [Video file]. *TED2003*. Retrieved from http://www.ted.com/talks/jeff_hawkins_on_how_brain_science_will_change_computing.html

Vinney, C., & Hopper-Losenicky, K. (2016, March). *Monsters and metaphor: How fans derive meaning from science fiction and fantasy television*. Paper presented at the Popular Culture Association/American Culture Association Annual Conference, Seattle, WA.

Wenzel, W. G., & Gerrig, R. J. (2015). Convergent and divergent thinking in the context of narrative mysteries. *Discourse Processes, 52*, 489–516. https://doi.org/10.1080/0163853X.2015.1023966

Zwaan, R. A., Magliano, J. P., & Graesser, A. C. (1995). Dimensions of situation model construction in narrative comprehension. *Journal of Experimental Psychology: Learning, Memory, and Cognition, 21*(2), 386–397.

5
The Timelessness of Stories

> What do you think stories are for? These stories? The classics. There's a reason we all know them. They're a way for us to deal with our world. A world that doesn't always make sense.
> —Mary Margaret (Ginnifer Goodwin),
> *Once Upon a Time* (Mylod, 2011)

Ask a writer, an actor, or a filmmaker what people can't live without, and they're likely to say stories. Ask an evolutionary biologist what the meaning of life is, and she might say to survive, to reproduce, and to help see that our children survive and reproduce. The artists and the scientists are both right. And, maybe more surprisingly, those seemingly lofty artistic yearnings and those almost brutally practical evolutionary imperatives are actually much more intertwined and interdependent in our own lives than we may realize. In fact, this whole book is precisely about how art and science both reveal fundamental truths about our existence.

People may say that human beings love stories, that stories have always been around, or that humans are drawn to stories. Those observations only skim the surface of the reality of the importance of story to our very existence. After all, there is a relationship between "existence" and survival and reproduction.

To see how this is true, we can explore the importance that Lee Roy Beach and Byron Bissell (2016) place on story in their book about the theory of narrative thought. The authors differentiate between story and narrative, explaining that narrative includes more than the story itself. Narratives "are a rich mixture of memories and of visual, auditory, and other cognitive images, all laced together by emotions to form a mixture that far surpasses mere words and visual images in their ability to capture context and meaning." (Beach & Bissell, 2016, p. 49). In other words, narrative includes not only the story contained in the movie, TV show, or book, but also things like the memories and emotions that it evokes in the viewer or reader. However, important this distinction maybe to scholars, we've used the terms "story" and "narrative" relatively interchangeably throughout this book. One of our reasons for this is that everyone knows what a story is, but the concept of narrative as defined by Beach and Bissell is less accessible. Also, we don't want to go all super-nerd on you! (We know what you're thinking: "Too late!")

In any case, stories include people and things, events and causes. For example, we all know the story of Jack and Jill who went up the hill. That story includes people (Jack and Jill), events (fetching, falling, breaking) and causes (falling causes breaking). According to the theory of narrative thought, our brains automatically assemble actors and events, causes and effects into the form of a storyline rather than seeing them as a jumble of people, things, and behaviors. The storyline evokes our personal memories and concerns; thus, we naturally contribute to any narrative we take in. That means that narratives encompass not only the storyline on the screen or page, but also what's in the mind of the viewer.

To say that people love stories sounds fanciful or even frivolous. It makes it sound like stories are just something we do to amuse ourselves. But narratives are far from simple entertainment devices and more than excellent teachers. Narrative is the fundamental structure of human thought. In other words, stories are, quite simply, the way we think.

We don't only experience narratives when we pick up a book or tune into a television show. We are forming narratives in our minds constantly.

They are the water we're swimming in. Whenever someone dismisses movies, television shows, or books as a waste of time or "not real," whenever they dismiss fans or lovers of stories as "out of touch with reality," that tells us that they don't understand the very serious and important role of story in our lives. It comes down to this: Our human experience doesn't exist without story. Period.

THIS IS YOUR BRAIN ON NARRATIVE

Why are narratives indispensable? What do they do for us that we can't live without? Our minds receive all kinds of input, from sensory experiences to conscious thoughts to unconscious content, and the brain puts it all this input together into a story. Narrative is a structure imposed on our ongoing conscious experience to make sense of and organize the world. We turn whatever's going on around us into a story. If we must think in story, then naturally we'd prefer to find input that is already crafted as a story. If you hand us the ingredients for a pie (flour, sugar, apples, etc.), we can make a pie. But we'd rather you just handed us the baked pie. It makes things much easier.

In other words, the whole is greater than the sum of the parts. This is a basic principle of Gestalt psychology. Gestalt psychology was a school of thought in Germany from the early years of the modern field of psychology. We associate it with the University of Leipzig and with scholars like Köhler, Koffka, and Wertheimer. To go back to our pie analogy, a pie is more than flour plus water plus sugar, etc. When all those ingredients are put together, the pie becomes a new thing. The great American psychologist William James used this pie analogy to describe his perspective, called functionalism. The philosophy of functionalism asks the question, "What is it good for?" A pie is good for feeding people and giving them pleasure. What is story good for? Story is good for understanding the world, especially the social world, and for readying us to be successful at the two imperatives highlighted by evolutionary biologists: survival and reproduction. As we know, stories can also give us pleasure. The savvy reader will recognize these two motives for consuming stories as the hedonic and eudaimonic motives for consuming stories that we spoke of in Chapter 2 of this volume.

If you took an introductory psychology course in high school or college, you likely covered human perception where you learned about the Gestalt principles of perceptual organization. These principles include the laws of similarity, proximity, continuity, and closure. The law of similarity, for example, means that similar objects are grouped together; the law of proximity that objects that are closer together are seen as groups. The law of continuity assures that a dashed line is seen as a single, continuous line and the law of closure means that a circle made from a dashed line is still seen as a circle; we fill in the gaps in our minds. These are examples of what Beach and Bissell (2016) mean in their theory of narrative thought when they say we automatically group people and events into stories, including ascribing causes, personalities, and motives. We group the various parts of a story into a complete entity and label it "book." We group events, people, causes, etc. into a whole that we call a story. Add our own memories, sights, sounds, etc. and the whole thing is a narrative.

Psychologists have shown people light displays that flash in a particular way, and viewers are able to impute a story onto the light's movements. In other words, rather than saying they saw lights that turned off and on, people say that certain lights hit other lights and knocked them off the screen. (People are so funny, aren't we? It makes being a psychologist so much fun!) Similarly, psychologists had people view a video where a circle moves onto another circle. Viewers said that one circle was angry and hit the other circle, who was the victim! We take simple perceptual events and turn them into stories complete with actors, motives, and causes. If this is what we do when we watch flashing lights and moving circles, imagine what we do with the actual people and events we see! And, to push it further, we tend to think the story we crafted in our minds about an event or experience is a faithful rendition of what happened, when really it is simply the story we made up when perceiving those events and people.

Imagination

Stories are imaginative. Our imaginations produce simulations or "what if" scenarios. Through story, we imagine what might happen in the future or reimagine what might have happened differently in the past. We judge those imaginings in terms of how good or bad they would be for us. We want to avoid doing things in the future that we would live to regret. Therefore, people mentally calculate the "regret potential of the future you expect to occur if you stay on your present course" (Beach & Bissell, 2016, p. 23). We're trying to go for a more desirable/less regrettable future. (Nerdy dating scene: "Sandra, please go to dinner with me. I think you would make my future less regrettable than if I continued on my current trajectory." "I concur, Tad. I calculate that accepting this date will make my future 25% more desirable than dating Mark.") Imagining the story of your potential future if you make various choices helps you figure out what to do with your life. Beach and Bissell (2016) suggest using "your imagination productively, as a tool, rather than merely as a diverting pastime" (p. 20). This is applicable to our favorite films, TV shows, and books, too, which we can use to inform and improve our own lives.

Human beings without imagination would be, well, unimaginable. What if we couldn't ask "What if?" How could we project even the simplest possibility into the future? For example, we can imagine what would happen if we fell asleep while driving home from the airport. Imagining this enables us to envision the negative consequences and motivates us to prevent it from happening. Thus, imagination is necessary for our very survival. There was an educational cartoon on *Sesame Street* in which a little girl wonders aloud what would happen if she popped her balloon. The cartoon speculates on the various possibilities. In the end, the girl decides not to pop her balloon because she wants to avoid the possible and perhaps likely consequences, which include waking up her baby brother and causing him to cry.

In life, we do our best to predict how likely various outcomes would be and to make the best choices for ourselves. (Clearly, we could write a whole book about how our thinking is often unclear or incorrect on this front, but, hey, we try our best!) Stories help us imagine these outcomes.

And because books have authors, and films and television shows have the added perspectives of actors, directors, etc., stories give us human input that help us analyze the possibilities. In other words, if *The Wonder Years, Sixteen Candles, Clueless,* or *The Perks of Being a Wallflower* communicate something to us about teenage romance, that lesson originates with the people who wrote the story, the actors who brought the story to life, and the rest of the crew who helped make it relevant for us.

Imagine All the People

Some of the primary questions we ponder with our imaginations are social in nature. We imagine whether certain actions, if we had done them in the past, might have helped us build better relationships. For example, if we worked less and paid more attention to our significant other in college, would we have forestalled a painful breakup? Because social support is so important for our ability to survive and reproduce, anything—including movies, TV shows, and books—that helps us strengthen relationships and secure mates gets us that much closer to our life goals.

In previous writing (e.g., *Mad Men Unzipped*; Dill-Shackleford, Vinney, Hogg, & Hopper-Losenicky, 2016), Karen mentioned that the relationship between Don Draper and his daughter Sally on *Mad Men* helped her reimagine her own relationship with her father. Through the interaction of these characters Karen could see, for example, that her dad was doing the best he could, given his circumstances, and that she was a pretty strong girl for taking on some of the "adulting" in that relationship. Now, Karen's dad wasn't an alcoholic ad exec who lived in Manhattan in the 1960s. But there are still things about Don Draper that remind her of her father. Stories that move us can evoke scenarios from our lives even if they aren't precisely the same. Part of what makes a story popular is the universality of its underlying themes, evoking real things in our own lives. That's one reason we go back to certain stories again and again—they apply to our own experience. Fiction is written by real people to explore real-life experiences. Fiction truly helps us understand our own lives better.

(Dill-Shackleford, Hopper-Losenicky, Vinney, Swain, & Hogg, 2015; Vinney & Dill-Shackleford, 2018).

You Complete Me

In 1927, graduate student Bluma Zeigarnik described a phenomenon that became known as the Zeigarnik effect. The Zeigarnik effect states that a lot more psychological energy goes into thinking about what is incomplete than what is complete. Successful writers often take advantage of our tendency for the unfinished to preoccupy us. This applies to any series that employs cliffhangers to keep us hooked.

For example, the TV show *Downton Abbey* is certainly a beloved and timeless story for many reasons. One of the reasons it draws us in is it places characters viewers care about in precarious situations, leaving us to wonder what will happen to them in the next episode. In one storyline from the show (spoiler alert!), long-suffering Lady Edith, poor dear, is left at the altar, then left pregnant and alone when the baby's father dies, then seems to have finally found love again. Will her supposedly superior sister, Lady Mary, scare away her rich and titled fiancée? The questions the story asks keep audiences guessing. It's the kind of thing that drives fans away from social media to avoid spoilers posted by friends who've seen an episode we haven't gotten to yet.

Downton Abbey plays on timeless themes: the desire for a mate, to have children, to have a job that will feed us, to have friends who will help us through the rough spots, and to leave a legacy. Since it's a period show (the story begins in the wake of the sinking of the *Titanic*) and produced with detailed and lavish costumes and sets, it should remain eminently watchable to our kids and grandkids.

Authentic Emotion

Karen had the privilege of working with the late great social psychologist Jack Brehm before he died. In the later years of his career, Jack was working on a theory of motivation. Jack spoke about how each emotion we feel is designed to motivate a behavior that is adaptive for us. For instance, if a bully shoves you and it makes you angry, the anger can fuel the motivation to fight back, thus potentially increasing your social status, your access to resources, your mate value, or even your very survival. Anger can be adaptive.

> We have a biological tendency to mirror the emotions we see, and the more invested in the person we are mirroring, the more we mirror it.
> —"10 Most Emotional Movies of All Time" (CineFix, 2016)

When a story triggers authentic emotions, that's a signal to the viewer or reader that "this is important." There's a concept called "psychological realism," which, for our purposes, basically means that it doesn't really matter how you get someone to feel something, as long as the feeling is authentic. You can make someone happy by offering them a cookie or by having them think about a vacation. (And by the way, yes, those are actual manipulations for happiness that psychologists have used in their research labs. We are such adorable nerds, aren't we?) Anyway, getting back to authentic emotions, if a story triggers a feeling, an idea, a belief that rings true for the person and connects to ideas from the person's life, then the story triggered something real. In that way, stories are a "way in."

Because that's the way our minds work, it's so much more effective to tell a story about, say, wrongful punishment followed by redemption, rather than to say all scientifically, "Okay, human, imagine a scenario with punishment followed by redemption. Got that? Okay, what did you learn?" That nerd stuff may work for people like us, but we've spent a lot of time training our brains to work that way. For most people, watching *The Shawshank Redemption* would be a much more effective way to learn about redemption. Plus, a great movie is much more fun and interesting than a cold scientific analysis—even for us.

Catharsis Through Stories

While the emotions we experience when we take in stories may motivate us and help us understand something fundamental about life, stories can also help us release our pent-up emotions. Aristotle originally proposed the idea of catharsis within the context of media, which, for the Greeks at the time, largely meant theater. For Aristotle, watching drama enabled theatergoers to vicariously release difficult or negative emotions—something Lee Shackleford will discuss in more detail at the end of this chapter. Hundreds of years later, Sigmund Freud claimed that if people did not vent their aggressive energy their mental health would suffer (Aronson, 2008), an observation that resulted in the catharsis hypothesis. The catharsis hypothesis states that consuming media violence enables viewers to vicariously "purge" their aggressive impulses, which leads to decreased aggression in real life (Giles, 2010; Wilson, 2011).

There's limited research on the catharsis hypothesis, but perhaps the most well-known study involved assigning boys at six boarding schools to either watch violent television programs or nonviolent television programs for six weeks (Feshbach & Singer, 1971, as cited in Giles, 2010). Although the study found that the boys in the nonviolent group were more aggressive than those in the violent group, the nonviolent group was also unhappy that they weren't allowed to watch violent television. The study's methodological problems have reduced it to something of a footnote in the study of violent media, and the catharsis hypothesis has been largely rejected by psychologists (Giles, 2010; Wilson, 2011).

Although media effects researchers haven't found support for the idea that watching violence leads to the catharsis of aggression, studies have shown that emotional catharsis does happen. In his book, *Human Aggression,* social psychologist Russell Geen (2001) explains that while there is a venting that happens emotionally or physically, there's not a decrease in our instigation to aggress. So, while we may feel emotionally satisfied after watching a violent film, it doesn't mean we're any less likely to do something aggressive or violent.

Love Stories

From the storybook story of *The Princess Bride* to the dancing teenagers of a certain *West Side Story*, we are riveted by what happens when two hearts find each other and want to be together. Most people have a serious romantic relationship at least once in their lives. Most of us long for it. And we generally never tire of watching or reading about it.

Whether you're one to shrug off romantic movies as "chick flicks" or they're your favorite genre, one way or another, stories are full of romance and people falling in (and out) love. It might be sweet and innocent like when Frankie Avalon and Annette Funicello dance on the beach in *Beach Blanket Bingo*, or it might be dark and difficult like when Rick Deckard attempts to protect replicant Rachel, in *Blade Runner*. Or it might be all those things at once—dark and difficult, sweet and innocent—like in what is perhaps the most famous love story of all, *Romeo and Juliet*. What matters is not so much the particulars, but the universals. We unravel the peculiarities and the appearances on the surface of the particular story to unearth the lasting truths that we can take away with us, such as what romance is like and what we can expect from it, and what we might hope for in a partner.

In stories like *Casablanca*, the truth we find may be that love does not override the needs of the many. When Han and Leia fight, we may learn that the one who drives you crazy is the one for you. *When Harry Met Sally* might teach us that sometimes friends make the best lovers. Or from *Pride and Prejudice* we might come to understand how first impressions can be deceptive or how our prejudices sometimes blind us. We take all of the things we learned from fiction into our personal love stories, for better or worse.

Survival Stories

We've said before that our two evolutionary imperatives are survival and reproduction. Let's assume that the love stories address the reproduction part. The survival part, well, that explains a great deal of the appeal of stories like *Independence Day, The Poseidon Adventure*, and *Jurassic Park*. There are also survival stories where part of what the protagonist is fighting through is to come of age, including in *Stand by Me, Stranger Things*, or the *Life of Pi*.

We argue, along with other narrative scholars that fiction offers us a rich array of opportunities to simulate possible futures and possible selves (Dill-Shackleford et al., 2016; also see Mar & Oatley, 2008; Mar, Oatley, Hirsh, dela Paz, & Peterson, 2006). Perhaps we've never been to India. Probably we've never been trapped on a lifeboat with a Bengal tiger named Richard Parker Figure 5.1. But if we have read or seen *Life of Pi*, perhaps we've empathized with that situation as it takes place in that story. And, being vicariously in that fantastic life-or-death situation is bound to help us think about what's important in life.

We are just skimming the surface of these narratives. But let's go a bit deeper into one of them, by way of example. We are both big fans of the Netflix series, *Stranger Things*. If you haven't watched it, you should. (Okay, put it on your Netflix queue; we'll wait.) There's a reason that over 361,000

Figure 5.1 Pi faces off against the tiger, Richard Parker, in the *Life of Pi*. Although it's unlikely we've faced this situation, we understand that the story is about the struggle to survive.

people binge-watched all nine episodes of the second season the day it dropped on Netflix and 15.8 million watched the first episode of Season 2 within three days of its Netflix release (Abrams, 2017). *Stranger Things* has so many timelessly appealing elements. It has the rawness of first love and the determination of an unshakeable mother's love. It has tragedy, betrayal, friendship, loyalty, and, of course, demogorgons. But let's zoom in on one of those for a bit: the intensity of a mother's love, connected with the need for survival and layered with so many stranger things.

Here's the scene: It's the 1980s in middle America, and Joyce Byers (Winona Ryder) is a single mom living on the wrong side of the tracks with very little to offer her sons Will and Jonathan, or so it would seem. When Will goes missing and is presumed dead, Joyce refuses to give up on him. In desperation, she hatches a plan to communicate with Will by painting the alphabet on the wall of her living room and nailing Christmas lights above the black letters so that Will can spell her a message.

The story itself is engrossing. What hit both of us hard was how willing Joyce was to throw aside everything she'd previously understood and focus all of her energy on doing whatever it took to save Will. She didn't care how it looked. She didn't put her energy into a Plan B. Her focus was relentlessly directed at saving her son. Even though Karen is the mother of a teenaged son and daughter, and Cynthia is not a parent, both of us took the story's message of unwavering commitment to the people you love to heart. While on the surface the story shows a woman in a 1980's living room nailing Christmas lights to the wall and chain smoking, the message underneath is much more universal. What's important is that feeling of the absolute commitment of a mother to her son, of one person to another. And that's what those letters on the wall ultimately symbolize.

So, when someone smiles at us and says, "Oh, I love *Stranger Things*," or when we see a fan wearing *Stranger Things* sweatshirt featuring the lights shown in Figure 5.2, we are automatically drawn to that person. Those declarations of love for the story are a kind of shorthand for our mutual attraction to what matters in that world. We might also love 1980s music and clothes and the other fascinations of that time and place. All of those intense emotions and attractions get mixed together. When Karen and her

Figure 5.2 Winona Ryder as Joyce Byers in *Stranger Things*. This mother is going to do whatever it takes to find her son.

son Jason randomly yell, "Nancy!" and "Jonathan!" at each other, they're really taking themselves back to that shared world and what it all meant.

Minimally Counterintuitive Narratives

Speaking of *Stranger Things*, this is a good time to pause and examine why we can become so engrossed in supernatural stories like this one. Yes, Joyce desperately wants to get Will back and will do anything to make that happen. But those letters and Christmas lights on the wall are there so she can communicate with her son in another dimension called the Upside Down. When we just talk about it, it may sound absurd. But often supernatural, science fiction, fantasy, and horror stories involving aliens, gods, ghosts, magic, and demons speak to us in ways that are just as powerful as stories that are firmly grounded in reality. Why do these stories "work" for us?

Stories like *Stranger Things* challenge our basic assumptions about how things are. For example, while we know there are animals in the world that could kill us and that trees and holes in the ground may house some pretty creepy critters, as far as we know there are no alternative dimensions that we can travel to through trees and holes in the ground, and monsters who are out to get us don't live there. These ideas are outside our experience of reality and, consequently, counterintuitive.

Norenzayan, Atran, Faulkner, and Schaller (2006) propose that the most culturally successful narratives contain a small number of counterintuitive concepts mixed with a larger number of concepts we understand intuitively. According to the researchers, these minimally counterintuitive narratives are easier for us to remember than narratives that only have intuitive concepts or have mostly counterintuitive concepts. The idea of minimally counterintuitive narratives helps explain the enduring popularity of fairy tales, folklore, myths, and even religious stories. From Moses parting the Red Sea to *Sleeping Beauty* being woken by true love's kiss, stories containing minimally counterintuitive elements tend to stick with us and are often passed from generation to generation. For example:

> In the Grimm Brothers folktales, the tale of "Little Red Riding Hood"—one of the most celebrated folktales in Western culture—is mostly a series of mundane occurrences, seasoned with only two counterintuitive ones (the talking wolf, and Grandmother and the little girl coming out of the wolf's belly alive). Similarly, the "Beauty and the Beast" has only three such violations (the Beast as an animal with human properties, the magic mirror, and the transformation from beast to human). (Norenzayan et al., 2006, p. 535)

Many of the popular culture stories that contain supernatural elements and endure today are also minimally counterintuitive narratives. These include often revisited stories like *Dracula* and *Frankenstein*, the concept of zombies originated in George Romero's *Night of the Living Dead*, and classics like *The Exorcist* and *Big*, in which Tom Hanks stars as a young boy who wishes on a carnival machine to be older. We remember these stories where the supernatural breaks into our mundane world better than stories that only capture the mundane or only capture the supernatural. Once we have something familiar to latch onto, it seems it's easier for us to accept a few fantastic elements in our stories. And those fantastic elements help those stories stay with us and even become cultural touchstones, as legends and fairy tales have been for centuries.

A Storied Relationship

Speaking recently at a Sherlock Holmes fan meeting, Karen asked fans what was their greatest attraction to that story world. They told her it was the relationship between Holmes and Watson. For individual fans, that might mean the relationship between the characters on the written page or between actors who have played the duo such as Basil Rathbone and Nigel Bruce, Benedict Cumberbatch and Martin Freeman, Robert Downey Jr. and Jude Law, Jeremy Brett and Edward Hardwicke, and Jonny Lee Miller and Lucy Liu. But whichever team captures one's imagination, Holmes and Watson are perpetually popular fictional characters, and it seems it is their relationship that leads to their story being revisited over and over again.

There are Tumblr feeds that show moments from the Holmes/Watson relationship, or "ship" as it's known in fan circles. Ships encompass the romantic relationship between any two characters, while the term "slash" more specifically refers to a same-sex relationship. On Tumblr, Holmes/Watson slash may be celebrated by a looping 7-second video from the BBC's *Sherlock* series where Benedict and Martin's hands almost touch that fans around the world excitedly view on their Tumblr screens. Fans may be fascinated by the idea of Holmes and Watson finally getting together, but more than anything, what may lead creators to revisit these characters time and again is the dynamics of a relationship between a difficult person and the individual who accepts and supports him. After all, isn't acceptance and love what all of us are looking for?

In addition, fans enjoy Holmes himself for his ability to see and figure things out that the rest of might miss. The Baker Street tube station in

London features Sherlock Holmes décor and a statue of Holmes outside the station. There is also a statue of Holmes in Japan, as well as Japanese manga and anime with Holmes characters.

As Tsukasa Kobayashi (2013) of the Japanese Sherlock Holmes Society puts it,

> The Holmes stories have had a profound influence on our culture. Sherlock Holmes in widely used in Japan as a symbol of the detective in literature and is one of the most frequently used motifs in advertising. For those of us in the "Japan Sherlock Holmes Club" and for many others he stands for more than the deerstalker and Inverness cape. He provides an outstanding example of justice and fair play. and teaches us the nature of detection and induction. His stories are even included as part of the "textbook of logic" which is used in the senior high schools in Japan.

The Stories That Fill Our Dreams

As Holmes and Watson make clear, there are stories that people love and want to revisit time and again. People may do this by either watching a single work over and over again and look for new incarnations of a specific kind of story. For example, when she was younger, Cynthia loved vampire stories and would read or watch anything she could get her hands on that featured this mythical monster. When she found a vampire story she especially loved, like *Buffy the Vampire Slayer* (movie and TV show!), *Interview with the Vampire*, or *Near Dark*, she'd revisit it over and over. But she was also always searching for new incarnations of the vampire story, or old vampire stories that she hadn't gotten to yet. Vampire stories helped her work through her teen angst and her transition into adulthood, by helping her envision what it would mean to take on grown-up responsibilities and obligations and commit to a set of ideals and values. Besides, it was a lot more fun imagining life through the lens of vampire stories.

Evidence for the way the characters and stories we love ignite our imaginations can be found in the content of our dreams and daydreams. Our fantasy lives reveal a lot about what matters to us.

Dreams, Daydreams, and Fantasies

Yale psychologist Jerome Singer did some of the seminal work on daydreaming. Singer (1961) found that people who daydream more are more self-aware, better creative storytellers, accept their inner experiences to a greater degree, and have a higher need for affiliation and achievement than those who daydream less frequently. We hope this reminds you of what we said earlier when referring to the theory of narrative thought—the part about how we use our imaginations to decide whether we should stay on our present course or try something else to reach the best outcomes for ourselves.

Jim Blascovich and Cade McCall (2013) classify dreams and daydreams as virtual reality experiences, noting that people's minds wander for about a third of every waking day! If we spend a third of our lives with our minds wandering in some way, and we think in story, then it only makes sense that our mental "free time," so to speak, is constantly telling us stories about what might happen. How would outcome X make us feel? How would outcome Y change our lives? So, like fiction produced by someone else, daydreams are fantasies that could become realities, they are simulations of possible futures. How amazing is that?

In his book, *Social: How our Brains are Wired to Connect*, Matthew Lieberman (2013) argues that every time we are not actively doing something else with our brains (you know, math problems, measuring a cup of sugar, dancing a ballet) our brains automatically return to a default network. This default network is social, and it's social because we need other people to survive. Being social is so important that Mother Nature made sure that when we don't need our brains for anything else, we mostly think of social stuff so as to make sure we become social experts. So, daydreaming (aka, mind-wandering, fantasizing, mental simulation playground) is a chance to try out a bunch of social stuff in our minds and see how it goes—how we feel, how we would thrive if we did that stuff, and so on.

In 2009, Singer wrote a large-scale review of daydreaming research. In it, he mentions that daydream content has been described as typically one of three styles: (a) positive/constructive—ranging from playful or wish fulfilment fantasies to more deliberately constructive or creative thought; (b) guilty/dysphoric—angsty daydreams; or (c) mind-wandering. A lot of our ongoing stream of consciousness moves back and forth between task engagement (doing whatever we are doing) and mind-wandering/daydreaming. When we're little kids, we say this stuff aloud. When we're older, we keep it to ourselves. But it serves a function—practice for our social worlds.

Patty Valkenburg and Tom van der Voort (1994) noticed that over the years many scholars proposed that watching television "hinders our imagination" (p. 316). But they also noticed that the waters were muddied because the scholars who said this weren't specific. Did they really mean "imagination," or did they actually mean "dream potential," or "creative play," or something else?

Valkenburg and van der Voort (1994) studied the relationship between television watching and daydreaming, defining daydreaming as "mental processes such as musing, mind-wandering, internal monologue, and being lost in thought" (p. 316). They did not distinguish in their work between creative imagination, which tends to be publicly disclosed, and daydreaming, which tends to be treated as very private. They also used the term "fantasies" to describe daydreams. They proposed that there are two arguments pertaining to TV and imagination, one pro and one con. On the con side, some say that TV blunts our imaginative abilities because it hands us ready-made stories so we don't have to make them up ourselves, promotes mental passivity and barrages our minds with various attention-grabbing strategies. On the pro side, some say that, to the degree that TV is fantastic, it promotes fantasies about that fascinating content. The authors reviewed a number of studies and came to the conclusion that, to the best of their knowledge, TV tends to increase daydreaming. Nonviolent TV tends to produce positive daydreams, and violent TV can produce violent daydreams. Our interpretation of this is that if stories bring us to different places to meet interesting people, then these stories supply fodder for our daydreams that tends to be more attractive and fantastic. Simply put, stories give us ideas.

If we put this together with Singer's idea that daydreamers are more self-aware and better creative storytellers, then daydreaming generally and daydreaming about scenarios and people we saw on TV specifically may actually help us reflect on our circumstances and dream up possible future for ourselves, increasing the possibility we'll be able to make informed choices with positive outcomes.

Recently, we conducted a study (Greenwood, Dill-Shackleford, Clifton, Vinney, Sadeghi-Azar & Couvillion, 2018, May) where we asked *Doctor Who* fans to share their thinking about the characters from the show. We asked them three questions about how the characters factor into their daily lives, including daydreaming about them. These items were worded as follows: (a) "I like to imagine my favorite *Doctor Who* characters as people I know personally"; (b) "I often feel like characters from *Doctor Who* are people I know and care about"; and (c) "I like to talk to others about what my favorite *Doctor Who* characters are like as people." Eighty percent of people said they imagine the *Doctor Who* characters as people they know. Ninety percent said they feel the *Doctor Who* characters are people they know personally. And almost 90% said they talk to others about what their favorite *Doctor Who* characters are like as people.

As we've said, when reporting statistics like this, this would be about the time that journalists would launch into a "crazy fans" discussion, and we would try to steer them through understanding that mental illness has nothing to do with it. We're social people. We are built to imagine and fantasize about social scenarios. We tell stories to expand the limits of our experiences and our imaginations. Thinking about TV and film characters isn't crazy. In fact, our data demonstrate that, in fact, it's normal and something that a majority of people who love a particular character or characters do.

What do fans think of when they daydream? We asked our survey respondents who their favorite Doctor on *Doctor Who* is. The Doctor also has traveling companions, so we asked who participants' favorite companion is too. We learned that the favorite Doctor was the 10th Doctor, played by David Tennant, and the favorite companion was his companion, Donna Noble, played by Catherine Tate. When we asked fans who they think of when they daydream about the characters, they often mentioned people like David Tennant's Doctor, Donna, and two of the Doctor's other companions, Amy and Rory.

Many of the *Doctor Who* fans we surveyed were comfortable saying not only who they think about when they muse about the show, but what it means to them. For example, one fan offered, "More than anything, *Doctor Who* reminds me to have hope and faith that even though humans can be terrible, we also have the capacity for great beauty." Another offered that they were "thinking of moments on the show that emotionally move me." Another said that the Doctor's travels and helping people made them want to do more of that in their real lives. One fan offered, "It's more than just a television show. To me, it's a hope delivery system."

We've mentioned Karen's husband, Lee Shackleford, before. Now we'll let him talk to you himself. Lee is a theater professor at the University of Alabama at Birmingham where he teaches playwriting and screenwriting. He's also an accomplished playwright as well as an actor. We talked him into sharing some of the ideas he teaches his playwriting and screenwriting students about what makes a story timeless.

A FICTION WRITER'S PERSPECTIVE

By Lee Eric Shackleford

This book explores end results, in a way—the effects movies and TV shows may have on us as audience members. The authors of this book have very kindly asked me to offer some insight into the other end of the process: where and how those scripts began.

When you're watching a play, film, or TV show, all the dramatic, hilarious, and heartbreaking things you see may appear to be happening spontaneously. They're supposed to! Extraordinary energy goes into helping you forget that what you're watching is fiction. The creators of these works of art want you to feel it's all *true*, it's happening *right now*, and it's happening to *you*.

That effort begins with a script written by a fiction writer like me, and I can tell you, we're always thinking about how to deliver to you the experience you're seeking. As we craft our stories (stage play, feature film, TV episode, or whatever) our end goal, the result we're after is that you feel the things you came to our show to feel.

But how can such a thing be calculated? How can a lone writer—or a dozen writers in a conference room—put words down on paper that will inspire and guide the collaborating actors, designers, and directors to create something that will leave you laughing, crying, cheering, or staggering?

I can't give away all the secrets (even if I knew them!), but I can tell you that we can always draw on the works of two extraordinary men: the Greek philosopher Aristotle and the mythologist Joseph Campbell.

Aristotle and the Three-Act Paradigm

Even though the term "psychology" wouldn't be coined for another 2,000 years, the Ancient Greek philosopher Aristotle (384–322 BCE) was nonetheless fascinated by the psychology of a new art form called θέατρον—*theater*. So much so, that he wrote what we call *Poetics*,[1] the first definitive book about creating works of tragedy and comedy for the stage, what I like to call "performed narrative." He was writing about live theater, of course, because film, radio, and television had not yet been invented. But when they were, and when we began creating performed narratives through those media, all of Aristotle's observations still applied. And they still do today.

---

1. "Why is it called *Poetics*?" you may reasonably wonder, since it has little to do with what we think of as poetry. It's about playwriting (and screenwriting, even though he didn't know it) so why not call it *On Playwriting*, or something like that? The answer is that terms like "playwright" and "screenwriter" are fairly recent inventions (like "psychology"). For most of history the writers of performed narrative have been called "poets."

Aristotle was driven by scientific curiosity. He was interested in how the audience reacted to various aspects of various productions and wanted to record his findings. In other words, he studied and reported on responses to stimuli. And in the process, he realized what made some plays "work" while others did not. He noted what made audience members laugh, cry, swoon, or gasp.

In short, he decided it's all in the script.

And since he set down his findings and feelings on paper (bless him!), playwrights and screenwriters like me have returned again and again to drink deeply at the well of Aristotle's *Poetics* because, as writers, we are in constant search of the best ways to stir our audience's emotion, and Aristotle scouted this path for us thousands of years ago.

Now, Aristotle wasn't trying to hand down arbitrary rules or to set eternal standards according to the fashion of the day. He was merely reporting his findings based on observations of his fellow audience members and the reputations of certain poets (playwrights) and their scripts.

Alas, we're pretty sure we only have half of *Poetics*. In the part we have, which is all about tragedy, Aristotle writes about what he'll say in the second part, which is about comedy. But if we had to lose one, it's a lucky thing it was the second part because it's in the first part that Aristotle related his observations about effective character creation and story structure. And for playwrights and screenwriters, that's where the gold is buried.

Aristotle's idea was that there are many aspects of drama that can vary and differ but that any writer who neglects the importance of character, which he called *ethos*, does so at the risk of creating a script that will not emotionally resonate (my words, not Aristotle's) with the audience.

Specifically, he wrote that the audience of a tragedy will feel more deeply for the characters if their problems are brought about by some mistake they have made rather than by a random chain of events. For example (warning: plot spoiler for *Oedipus Rex*), if there's a plague rampant in a country ruled by a particular king, we may feel sad for him, but we don't think his problem is unique or personal and therefore is easy to dismiss. But if that same king has a plague in his country and we learn it's his punishment from the gods for his long-ago road-rage crime in which he killed a man who is only now revealed to have been his own father, now we have an unforgettable tragedy. (The whole situation made famously worse because we already know our young king had dragged the grieving widow off and fathered two children with her.) It's extremely unlikely that anyone in the audience will ever have that exact experience (thank goodness), but we all know what it's like to make a stupid mistake and experience its repercussions later, even after many years. So, his tragedy matters to us.

I'll cite a more modern example. When Jack and Rose meet aboard the American-bound ocean liner in James Cameron's 1997 film *Titanic*, we all know what's going to happen to the ship and to hundreds of people aboard. It's not Jack's fault. It's not Rose's fault. Neither of them in any way causes the *Titanic* disaster to happen. So, without another factor added to the script, we may not be emotionally involved with them when the ship hits that iceberg. And screenwriter Cameron knows this. So, he has them separated by class: Rose is rich and Jack is poor; she has prospects on the other side of the Atlantic and Jack has none. But they fall in love anyway, and that's when we begin to worry about them. In other words, the masterstroke of this script is to make it *Romeo & Juliet* in addition to being about a doomed passenger ship. Because their love affair is their choice; the coming disaster is not. Surely very few of us will experience a tragedy like the sinking of the *Titanic*, but falling in love with the "wrong" person? Pfft. Who hasn't? So, we relate to that.

And that's what Aristotle was saying: If written with human empathy in mind, the tragedy has the potential to move every member of the audience for reasons known only to each person in that audience.

Perhaps the most profound (and artistically useful) observation Aristotle made was that a powerful drama will build with absolute inevitability toward a clear *climax*, at which point the audience will experience *catharsis*—emotional release. The audience knows what's going to happen, he observed, they can see it coming from a mile off. So, they're waiting for the moment, for the payoff, for the big reveal. And an audience will endure almost anything—in fact, embrace the tension of endurance—as long as they know that moment of revelation is coming, and their *catharsis* will follow.

It's worth noting here that *catharsis* doesn't necessarily mean the audience member is happy. It just means their pent-up emotions are released. And this is crucial because as humans we do seem to find this release gratifying even when the feelings would otherwise be considered unpleasant (as with "having a good cry" or "righteous indignation"). So, when you're watching a movie or TV show or play or whatever, at the climax your catharsis may be relief, or laughter, or tears, or that wonderful "I knew it!" feeling that makes you punch the air. It may be a combination of all them.

To return to the example of *Titanic*, everyone in the audience knows the ship will go down and that hundreds will die. We don't know the names of those hundreds of people. We care about this only in a remote, that-should-not-have-happened way. But Rose and Jack! We've gotten invested in them; we want them to escape their oppressive life circumstances and make a new life together. But when the ship starts to sink, it's likely that one or the other of them—or both—will die. We knew such a tragedy was possible, especially given how many people really did die on that terrible night, so it's been in the backs of our minds throughout the film. But now, suddenly, the climax is upon us, and we know we are about to experience catharsis: the question of who lives and who dies is going to be answered. We may not like the answer we get, but that's not the point: We will get an answer, and the result will be catharsis.

Aristotle further observed that effective scripts have distinct *phases* of complication and resolution. In other words, to evoke the desired emotions in the audience, the story must introduce us to a character we care about, establish what they desire and seek, and then a major portion of the script will be about why our principal character can't have what they want and how their efforts to achieve it will repeatedly fail. This is the "complication phase."

But the well-structured plot will then shift into a different gear, so to speak, creating the "resolution phase," because our main character will make a life-altering decision, usually an all-or-nothing approach to achieving their overall goal.

Later writers and scholars have built on (and endlessly debated) *Poetics*, to the extent that we now speak of "the Aristotelian paradigm" as if the ancient sage had described it in detail with accompanying flow charts. And he did not. But many, if not most, contemporary writers of performed drama (plays, TV, movies) like to think he would agree that the most powerful, more profoundly moving scripts, do indeed have this specific shape or timeline:

"Act I" Roughly the first 25% of script: Introduction

"Act II" Roughly the next 50% of script: Complication

"Act III" Roughly the final 25% of script: Resolution

With that final "act" or "phase" culminating in the *climax* and *catharsis*.

At that Act III point in *Oedipus Rex*, for example, Oedipus decides to send for the prophet, Tiresias, who knows everything and always speaks the truth. ("Don't do it," the chorus wails at Oedipus. "You won't like what he tells you.") The last quarter of that play is simply about Tiresias coming with the truth: *That woman you had the two children with is your own mother.* Boom! *Climax. Catharsis.*

At the equivalent juncture in *Star Wars* (*Episode IV: A New Hope*), the technical plans for the evil Empire's Death Star reveal a flaw: If a small spaceship could shoot a missile at one precise spot, the whole thing will explode. Some of the good-guy pilots say hitting that target is impossible. But the idealistic new recruit Luke Skywalker says, "It's not impossible!" And the last quarter of the film is simply about whether or not Luke will be able to hit that target. With the aid of the mystical Force, he does. And boom! *Climax. Catharsis.*

And, again, writers are *not* writing this way because Aristotle said they have to. They do it because they know he was right in the emotional effects he observed 2,400 years ago and that people really haven't changed that much in all that time.

I have students who tell me, half-jokingly, that knowing how this structure works has "ruined the movie-watching experience" for them. But I believe when we can recognize and appreciate that structure we may love our beloved stories even more for their elegant craftsmanship. (I know I do.) And it may help us understand why other narratives frustrate or annoy us: It's because their structure is somehow out of whack. Think of any film that you felt was boring or meandering; I can almost guarantee you experienced this because the film either (a) spent too much time in one part of its structure and not enough in another or (b) failed to demonstrate to the audience how the objective of the main character is related to his or her wants and needs.

A filmmaker may deliberately mess with the paradigm for the sake of giving the audience an experience they did not expect. The 2007 Coen Brothers' pursuit-of-a-killer film *No Country for Old Men*, for example, builds toward a powerful climax and then refuses to give it to us. The audience leaves frustrated and perhaps experiencing the feelings of the foiled police officers in a way that a conventional narrative could never provide (which I think was what the Coen Brothers were hoping for).

That approach is, of course, a calculated risk. I know people who swore, after seeing *No Country for Old Men*, to never pay to see another Coen Brothers film. I know one person who vowed to never pay to see *any* movie again. (I'm not sure he was serious.)

Now, here's an almost eerie way in which Aristotle's observations are as prescient today as they were back then. In one section of *Poetics*, he writes "Fear and pity may be aroused by spectacular means; but they may also result from the inner structure of the piece, which is the better way, and indicates a superior poet" (Aristotle, 1895, p. 45). In other words, if he was at the multiplex cinema with you today watching a film that is basically 90 minutes of exploding vehicles, he would probably lean over to you and whisper, "All the nerve-jangling special effects in the world can't make up for the fact that this script is crap."

And as a fan of radio drama—and a writer, producer, and performer of radio drama—I am fascinated by Aristotle's observation that an effective plot "ought to be so constructed that, *even without the aid of the eye,* he who hears the tale told will thrill with horror and melt to pity at what takes place (Aristotle, 1895, p. 45)." What a delight to find him writing, more than two millennia ago, about how a well-written drama can have profound emotional power even if you visualize the drama in your own mind. No multimillion-dollar CGI necessary.

It's all in the script!

The Hero With a Thousand Faces

The stories we all consume today also owe colossal debts to the works of the countless fiction writers of the past, and very often we don't even know their names. Their identities are lost to antiquity, forgotten because they first told their stories so very long ago. But modern playwrights and screenwriters deliberately use the same "template" those long-forgotten writers use. And we do it because it works. It's worked for millennia, and it keeps on working. As the old saying goes: *If it ain't broke, don't fix it.*

It's amazing to think that stories from, say, 3,000 years ago really have an impact on the TV shows and movies of today. But you know they do, especially if you're familiar with the life work of Joseph Campbell (1904–1987), author of (among many other things) *The Hero With a Thousand Faces*. This is where he explores most fully the idea that there are certain stories—one story in particular—that world cultures have been telling and retelling since the dawn of written language. It forms the basis of *Gilgamesh* and *Beowulf*. It forms the basis of *Jane Eyre* and *Moby-Dick*. And it forms the basis of *The Hobbit* and *Star Wars*.

That story that gets told and retold is what Campbell called "the monomyth." (Trivia: The word "monomyth" comes from a work of narrative drama—James Joyce coined the term in *Finnegan's Wake*.) Here's Campbell's (1968/2008) famous one-sentence summary of the monomyth:

> A hero ventures forth from the world of common day into a region of supernatural wonder: fabulous forces are there encountered and a decisive victory is won: the hero comes back from this mysterious adventure with the power to bestow boons on his fellow man. (p. 23)

If you think about it, that story sounds familiar, because (depending on your definition of "supernatural"), it's pretty much every "hero myth" story from the dawn of civilization to *Stranger Things*.

An Internet meme I've enjoyed for years makes this phenomenon plain using two familiar examples. The authorship of the precise wording is debated, so I'll simply give the gist here:

(Harry Potter/Luke Skywalker) is an orphan forced to live with his aunt and uncle. He is rescued by wise, bearded (Hagrid/Obi-Wan), who turns out to be a (wizard/Jedi). (Hagrid/Obi-Wan) reveals to (Harry/Luke) that (Harry's/Luke's) father was also a (wizard/Jedi) and was the best (Quidditch player/fighter pilot) he's ever known. The boy learns how to use a (wand/light saber) as he trains to become a (wizard/Jedi).

And so on—right down the line, every plot point of those stories matches up. And why not? They're drawn from the monomyth. Harry and Luke are among the thousand faces of the hero.

Campbell was a devout follower of the teachings of Carl Jung, particularly Jung's ideas about how the unconscious mind makes sense of the experiences of life. This led Campbell to the notion (or revelation, if you prefer) that all human cultures reveal their basic interconnectedness in the way we continually tell the same essential story. His idea, in other words, was that there is something innate in the human unconscious that reveals itself through a story that is retold throughout history, its details reworked and reinterpreted in various cultures. Campbell was saying, in essence, that we create myths (like books, plays, TV shows, and movies) because an unstoppable inner drive compels us to do so.

This would explain why the monomyth is so loaded with "emotional hooks," with story points that tug at our heartstrings. Campbell (1968/2008) notes that one sure-fire method is to make the central character one for whom we immediately feel empathy or pity, such as "the abused youngest son or daughter, the orphan, stepchild, ugly duckling, or the squire of low degree" (p. 280).

Certainly the "orphan alone in the world" story has been told time and again, and with good effect, possibly because we have all had parents and feel that in general a parent is something no one should be without. Harry Potter is an orphan; in fact, he will learn he's the most famous orphan in the wizarding world. Luke Skywalker at first believes himself to be an orphan, searching for the truth about how his father died. And Jerry Siegel and Joe Shuster may have been mere lads when they created Superman in 1938, but they knew to hook their audience with the most tragic backstory imaginable: an orphan whose selfless parents died in the explosion of their distant planet shortly after launching that child into space, desperately hoping he'll find a safe haven on the distance planet Earth.

The sheer preponderance of such tales shows how much we love to follow the adventure of fictional orphans. Cosette, Mowgli, Jane Eyre, Oliver Twist, Anne of Green Gables, Huckleberry Finn—the "orphan paradigm" is deathless, because the audience's sympathy is immediately extended to the character.

The stages or steps of the monomythic story, according to Campbell, are similar to the Aristotelian paradigm; similar enough, in fact, to make an argument for the underlying truth of both concepts. In Campbell, the three acts are thought of as departure, initiation, and return. An interesting similarity, for example, is in the way the final event in the introduction phase of screenplay structure mirrors the final event in Campbell's departure phase. Typically, a screenplay or TV script, reaching that "roughly 25% mark" that ends the introduction phase, will grab hold of the audience's heart by having the main character make a decision or discovery that sets them irreversibly on a dangerous journey. Campbell calls the corresponding part of the monomyth "the belly of the whale." In both cases, it is the final separation between the world our hero used to know and the world they will live in from now on.

I remember letting out an embarrassing "Ha!" in the movie theater when first watching James Cameron's 2009 film *Avatar*—not because the situation onscreen was humorous or absurd, or to mock the picture; my laugh was a happy one of recognition. Just when I was thinking the film had reached its one-quarter mark in terms of running time, the avatar form of our hero Jake Sully was chased over a cliff by a wild beast, losing his all-important walkie-talkie (last contact with the life that was) and plunging into the community of the natives (his life that will be)—end of the introduction and into the belly of the whale. I was delighted because screenwriter Cameron so clearly knew to use what he's learned from Aristotle *and* Campbell.

And remember the parallels I previously demonstrated between *Harry Potter* and *Star Wars*? You can do it with *Avatar* and the 1995 Disney animated feature *Pocahontas*. And for the same reasons: It's the same paradigm still at work:

In (2154/1607) a ship carrying (Jake Sully/John Smith) arrives in the new world: (Pandora/America). He's part of a crew mining for (unobtanium/gold). He soon meets (Neytiri/Pocahontas) who is at first distrustful of him. But guidance from (the Tree of Souls/Grandmother Willow) urges her to open her heart to him. Soon (Jake/John) begins to learn from (Neytiri/Pocahontas) that all life is valuable and all nature is connected.

And so on. Once again, the same structure appears in popular, successful stories because the paradigm is successful in creating emotional involvement with the characters and their situation.

And smart writers know: When you get lost, Aristotle and Campbell are always there to point the way.

REFERENCES

Abrams, A. (2017, November 2). 361,000 people binge-watched all of *Stranger Things* in a day. *Time Magazine*. Retrieved from http://time.com/5008471/stranger-things-2-neilsen-ratings-binge/

Aristotle. (1895). *Poetics* (S. H. Butcher, Trans.). London, England: Macmillan.

Aronson, E. (2008). *The social animal* (10th ed.). New York, NY: Worth.

Beach, L. R., & Bissell, B. L. (2016). *A new theory of mind: The theory of narrative thought*. Newcastle Upon Tyne, UK: Cambridge Scholars.

Blascovich, J., & McCall, C. (2013). Social influence in virtual environments. In K. E. Dill (Ed.), *Oxford handbook of media psychology* (pp. 305–315). New York, NY: Oxford University Press. https://doi.org/10.1093/oxfordhb/9780195398809.013.0017

Campbell, J. (2008). *The hero with a thousand faces*. Novato, CA: New World Library. (Original work published 1968)

CineFix. (2016). 10 most emotional films of all time. Retrieved from https://www.youtube.com/watch?v=6GMQ0F_YUCs

Dill-Shackleford, K. E., Hopper-Losenicky, K., Vinney, C., Swain, L. F., & Hogg, J. L. (2015). *Mad Men* fans speak via social media: What fan voices reveal about the social constructionofrealityviadramaticfiction. *Journal of Fandom Studies*, 3(2), 151-170. https://doi.org/10.1386/jfs.3.2.151_1

Dill-Shackleford, K. E., Vinney, C., Hogg, J. L., & Hopper-Losenicky, K. (2016). *Mad Men unzipped: Fans on sex, love, and the sixties on TV* (1st ed.). Iowa City, IA: University of Iowa Press.

Geen, R. G. (2001). *Human aggression*. Columbus, OH: Open University Press.

Giles, D. (2010). *Psychology of the media*. New York, NY: Palgrave Macmillan.

Greenwood, D. N., Dill-Shackleford, K. E., Clifton, A., Vinney, C., Sadeghi-Azar, L., & Couvillion, M. (2018, May). *When sexism trumps fandom: Hostile sexism and social dominance predict negative reactions to Doctor Who's first female Doctor*. Poster presented at the annual meeting of the Association for Psychological Science, San Francisco, CA.

Kobayashi, T. (2013). Sherlock Holmes in Japan. *Japan Sherlock Holmes Club*. Retrieved from http://www.holmesjapan.jp/english/history.html

Lieberman, M. D. (2013). *Social: why our brains are wired to connect*. New York: Crown.

Mar, R. A., & Oatley, K. (2008). The function of fiction is the abstraction and simulation of social experience. *Perspectives on Psychological Science*, 3(3), 173-192. https://doi.org/10.1111/j.1745-6924.2008.00073.x

Mar, R. A., Oatley, K., Hirsh, J., dela Paz, J., & Peterson, J. B. (2006). Bookworms versus nerds: Exposure to fiction versus non-fiction, divergent associations with social ability, and the simulation of fictional social worlds. *Journal of Research in Personality*, 40(5), 694-712. https://doi.org/10.1016/j.jrp.2005.08.002

Mylod, M. (Dir.). (2011). Pilot. In E. Kitsis & A. Horowitz (Executive Producers), *Once upon a time* (Season 1, Episode 1). Burbank, CA: ABC.

Norenzayan, A., Atran, S., Falkner, J., & Schaller, M. (2006). Memory and mystery: The cultural selection of minimally counterintuitive narratives. *Cognitive Science*, 30, 531-553.

Shackleford, L. E. (2007). *Holmes & Watson*. Charleston, SC: BookSurge.

Singer, J. L. (1961). Correlates of daydreaming: A dimension of self-awareness. *Journal of Consulting Psychology*, 25(1), 1-6.

Singer, J. L. (2009). Researching imaginative play and adult consciousness: Implications for daily and literary creativity. *Psychology of Aesthetics, Creativity, and the Arts*, 3(4), 190-199. https://doi.org/10.1037/a0016507

Valkenburg, P. M., & Van Der Voort, T. H. A. (1994). Influence of TV on Daydreaming and Creative Imagination: A Review of Research. *Psychological Bulletin*, 116(2), 316-339. https://doi.org/10.1037/0033-2909.116.2.316

Vinney, C., & Dill-Shackleford, K. E. (2018). Fan fiction as a vehicle for meaning making: Eudaimonic appreciation, hedonic enjoyment, and other perspectives on fan engagement with television. *Psychology of Popular Media Culture*, 7(1), 18-32. https://doi.org/10.1037/ppm0000106

Wilson, B. J. (2011). Media violence and aggression in youth. In S. L. Calvert & B. J. Wilson (Eds.), *The handbook of children, media, and development* (pp. 238-267). Malden, MA: Wiley-Blackwell.

6

Story and Identity

How Stories Influence Who We Are

> There are people. There are stories. The people think they shape the stories. But the reverse is often closer to the truth.
>
> —Alan Moore (1985) *Swamp Thing Annual, Volume 2*

Many beloved stories revolve around a protagonist "finding themselves" or "going on a journey of self-discovery." In stories like *Eat Pray Love, Life of Pi*, and even animated movies like *The Lion King, Kung Fu Panda*, and *Frozen*, we watch protagonists overcome challenges that help them figure out who they want to be and what they want from life and usually become stronger, more fulfilled, and more confident because of it. These stories resonate because in many ways they represent what we're striving for in our own lives—to wade through our personal struggles and become the best version of ourselves. Can watching and reading stories help us get there?

Throughout this book we've talked about how personal our love for our favorite stories can be. But does this personal connection have any impact on who we are? Does your favorite story contribute to what makes you, well, you? Our identity is deeply individual and specific to each of us, but we still develop it in the context of our families, our schools, our communities, and our society as a whole. Consequently, who we are is a social construction, as well as a mixture of personal traits and individual characteristics. If you were born in feudal Japan or Renaissance-era Rome, you might still be open and extroverted, but the world views and values imparted by your culture and the choices available to you would cause you to become a very different person. Even today, as social media, mobile phones, and instant news updates make the world seem smaller and more connected, the culture we grow up in helps shape us.

Cornell University professor Qi Wang and her colleagues have shown that culture profoundly influences how we see ourselves, and even how we remember our lives. For example, in one study, Wang (2001) discovered that Americans' earliest childhood memories occurred at around 3½ years old, and these memories consisted of specific events involving personal emotions and experiences. In contrast, Chinese participants' first memories occurred at around 4 years old and involved general or collective events that included their family or communities. Furthermore, when asked to complete descriptions of themselves, Americans were more positive and focused on private, individual aspects of the self, while Chinese were more negative and more likely to point to collective aspects of the self.

The culture in which we grow up plays a big role in how we see ourselves and, therefore, how our identities develop. Because we live our whole lives in it, the culture we're surrounded by seems natural. It becomes second nature to us. Despite how normal it seems, however, our culture also establishes often unspoken and even unconscious standards that citizens are expected to uphold. These standards drive us not only in terms of how we think, feel, and act, but also in terms of how we understand who we are (Wang & Brockmeier, 2002).

As part of culture, the stories we tell, including those told through media, help impart and set cultural standards. For example, *Star Trek* fans may recall how over the years of the original television series and the first *Star Trek* movies, Spock (Leonard Nimoy) changes his personal philosophy from the one he learned on his home planet of Vulcan to a new one: that sometimes the needs of the one outweigh the needs of the many. Spock's story communicated the value of one perspective over another. For fans, it was powerful to follow Spock over years and across mediums—including TV, movies, and books—as he changed his world view from the one he was raised with to one he came to understand. In his case, Spock adopts this new perspective after being resurrected! For viewers who were also considering their world view, the ideas championed by the story may have seemed monumental. Watching Spock think, feel, change, and grow over his lifetime, while fans were thinking, feeling, changing, and growing themselves may have influenced their points of view.

Today, more stories are available through media than ever before. From our earliest years, stories impact who we are and who we want to be. But how do stories shape us? And what role do stories play in who we become? Questions like these are challenging to answer, especially since it's difficult to track stories' influence on people in the complex world in which they grow up. While we spend our lives surrounded by stories, it may be a challenge for people to see the role story has played in who they are. At the same time, people might be reluctant to attribute any part of who they are to the stories they've read and seen throughout their lives.

We saw these issues first-hand when we conducted research on the ways fans construct a fan identity around their favorite TV show or movie (Vinney, Dill-Shackleford, Plante, & Bartsch, 2019). In the original version of the survey we created to assess how often fans took part in different fan experiences and behaviors, we asked several questions about how important fans' favorite show or movie was to their self-concepts—things like "I wouldn't be the person I am today without my favorite television show or movie" and "Being a fan of my favorite television show or movie is important to my identity." We were surprised to discover that fans rated these items very low. On a 1 to 9 rating scale, these items averaged around a 3. In comparison, scores for items about fans' passion and enthusiasm for their favorite show or movie averaged around a 7.5. We thought maybe our wording for the items had been too positive or too on the nose. So we changed the way some of them were stated. For example, the original item "I wouldn't be the person I am today without my favorite television show or movie" became "I would still be the person I am today without my favorite television show or movie." We retested these reworded items with a new group of fans, and the average ratings still stayed very low—around a 4 on a scale of 1 to 9. In contrast, the enthusiasm items averaged around a 7.7. (For more about this study, take a look at Chapter 2 of this volume.)

We realized that fans' largely negative reactions to these items probably had to do with the continuing negative stereotypes that still exist about popular media fans in Western cultures. Even though fans are becoming more accepted, there's still a perception that not only is popular culture frivolous and a waste of time, but popular culture fans are weird, hysterical nerds (Hills, 2005; Zubernis & Larsen, 2012). Because of this, fans might be comfortable admitting they love a popular movie or TV show, but they aren't that comfortable with the idea that their favorite story might have played a role in who they are. At least not when they're asked as directly about it as we did in our survey questions.

This doesn't mean that people can't recognize when a story plays a significant role in their lives. In a study Cynthia did with Kristin Hopper-Losenicky (Vinney & Hopper-Losenicky, 2017), almost 800 fans of *Buffy the Vampire Slayer* were asked if the show impacted their lives. Over 95% agreed that it had and explained how the show positively affected them in a number of ways, including helping them determine what they value, learning to accept themselves and others, and inspiring them to confront personal challenges and hardships. Many of these fans readily admitted that the show was an important part of who they were. One wrote, "[*Buffy*] has become a part of my identity, . . . a key way people 'know' me." And another explained, "I'm not usually one who ties my identity to pop culture, but *Buffy* is the sole exception to that. I feel like it has hugely informed who I am as a person." So, for some people, a profound experience with a particular story causes it to become a defining part of themselves.

CHANGES IN THE SELF

While the *Buffy* fans had moving, important experiences with the show, research indicates that the stories we encounter can impact who we are and how we see ourselves in more subtle ways. For example, we mentioned a study in Chapter 1 that found that people who read a short story by Chekhov, in contrast to a group who read a documentary-style report, experienced significant changes in their self-reported personality traits (Djikic, Oatley, Zoeterman, & Peterson, 2009). Other research has also shown that the way people perceive themselves is impacted by the stories they encounter. Another study showed that viewers who experienced more of a character's perspective while watching a movie clip and became more absorbed into the story were more likely to say personality traits that described the character also described themselves after, but not before, watching the clip (Sestir & Green, 2010). Similarly, in a third study participants read a chapter from *Harry Potter and the Sorcerer's Stone* (Rowling, 1999) that emphasized the story's focus on wizards or from *Twilight* (Meyer, 2005) that emphasized the story's focus on vampires. Afterwards, participants completed measures where they specified if they felt wizard- and vampire-related words were descriptive of themselves and answered questions about whether they attributed wizard or vampire traits to themselves, such as, "Do you think, if you tried really hard, you might be able to make an object move just using the power of your mind?" and "How sharp are your teeth?" Readers' responses showed that they psychologically adopted the traits of the fantasy character they read about, ascribing the characteristics of either wizards or vampires to themselves (Gabriel & Young, 2011).

Taken together, this research demonstrates that watching and reading stories can alter how we perceives ourselves. It's important to keep in mind, however, that the self is complex and different parts of who we are can be relevant at different times. It all depends on where we are, who we're with, and how we're feeling. So someone could be sullen and defensive when having dinner with his family, but jubilant and open when he goes to a party with his best friend, and serious and mature at his job. People contain all kinds of selves. And all these different selves make up one identity, one you. And when we take in different stories, as the previously described studies show, different parts of who we are may come out or become more apparent to us, leading to differences in how we might describe ourselves, depending on when we're asked.

THE WHAT, WHEN, AND HOW OF IDENTITY

Identity is a bit of a fuzzy concept. While everyone has an idea of what their identity is, it's hard to define it in words. Even psychologists don't always agree on what it means when we use the term "identity." Let's take a step back for a minute and discuss what identity is, and how it develops.

While the different identities we possess are often mentioned (social identity, sexual identity, gender identity, etc.), according to preeminent developmental psychologist and psychoanalyst Erik Erikson (1968), the general concept of identity is a psychosocial construct that refers to the continuity of what we know of our self and our world from our past memories, our current self, and our imagined future. Identity plays a synthesizing function binding a person's life together into a single unit, giving us a sense of how we got where we are in the present based on our past and where we're going in the future based on our present. And as we mentioned earlier, while identity is highly personal, it's also a product of our social environment, incorporating the people we know and the cultural objects we come in contact with, including the stories we encounter through the media.

Sometimes a story even reflects the very process of coming to terms with who we are. For example, on an episode of the series *The Crown*, a dramatization of the monarchy of Queen Elizabeth II, her first prime minister, Winston Churchill (John Lithgow), then age 80, confronts the artist Graham Sutherland (Stephen Dillane) who has painted what, in Churchill's mind, is a grossly unflattering portrait of him (see Figure 6.1). The following exchange showcases Churchill's struggle to deny how others see him, and reflects the difficulties we sometimes have with seeing ourselves as we really are.

> *Churchill:* It is not a reasonably truthful image of me!
> *Sutherland:* It is, sir!
> *Churchill:* It is not! It is cruel!
> *Sutherland:* Age is cruel! [pauses] If you see decay, it's because there's decay. If you see frailty, it's because there's frailty. I can't be blamed

Figure 6.1 John Lithgow as Winston Churchill with a portrait of himself he considered insulting in *The Crown*. Churchill's reaction to the painting reflects the difficulty we may all have at one time or another understanding how others see us or accepting ourselves for who we are.

>   for what is. And I refuse to hide and disguise what I see. If you're engaged in a fight with something, then it's not with me. It's with your own blindness.
>   *Churchill:* [Sits heavily down on the sofa] I think you should go.

Interestingly, psychologists have speculated that identity may be a modern problem specific to Western societies (McAdams, 1993). Before the late 18th century, people's choices were extremely limited. Because of this, their identity was assigned to them based on external factors, like social class, gender, and family ties. Today, in contrast, we're confronted with more and more choices in everything from what job to choose to who to marry to what values and beliefs to commit to. These choices all contribute to identity being the major, life-long project it has now become (Baumeister, 1987).

Of course, a sense of identity doesn't spring to life on its own. We aren't born knowing exactly who we are and who we're going to be. Identity is something that develops throughout our lives as we grow, learn, and change. The process begins in infancy as a child realizes she is an autonomous entity, separate from everyone else. This realization enables the child to start to develop a sense of self. But it isn't until adolescence that our cognitive abilities have matured and we have amassed enough life experience that we are fully prepared to engage in the process of developing an individual identity. Erikson (1968) specified that the task of adolescence, the fifth stage in his eight-stage theory of the human lifespan, was identity development. While we'll discuss other life stages in the next chapter, we'll talk about adolescence here because of its crucial role in the formation of our identities.

Adolescence begins with the onset of puberty but, according to Erikson (1968) its end is variable and based on both the individual person and the society in which they live. In his stage theory, Erikson said that prolonged adolescence was possible. Today, it has become normal for young people to continue to focus on their own identity development into their mid-20s (Côté, 2009; Elliott & Feldman, 1990), a change brought about by demographic, ideological, and technological shifts in Western societies over the last century or so that led to increased college attendance and delayed entry into marriage, parenthood, and career. This period in life is now often referred to by psychologists as "emerging adulthood" (Arnett, 2000, 2004).

Regardless of when adolescence ends, however, adolescence begins when a variety of physical, cognitive, and social changes take place. During puberty, adolescents begin to notice changes to their bodies and develop new sexual desires. Socially, there is an expectation that adolescents will start to focus on and prepare for what comes after childhood, especially in terms of school and career aspirations. And cognitively, adolescents enter what renowned psychologist Jean Piaget called "formal operations," enabling them to think abstractly for the first time, giving adolescents the cognitive skills needed to imagine who they could be in the future (McAdams, 1988, 1993).

This doesn't mean that children don't have a sense of self or an idea that they'll have a future before they reach adolescence. A child knows that she has blue eyes or that she's good at math. And a child can easily tell you what he wants to be when he grows up. But children's sense of self is fairly secure because it is wrapped up in their attachment to their parents and limited by the social expectations of childhood (Larson, 1995).

Adolescence is the first time that developmental changes and social expectations come together to trigger the desire to develop a sense of continuity between who one was, who one is, and who one eventually wants to become. At first, this can be very destabilizing. Early adolescents question the self they've been throughout their childhood and search for who they could become, exploring and trying out multiple self conceptions in the process (Larson, 1995). By late adolescence and emerging adulthood, people start to choose the roles and attachments they want to commit to and work towards as they become adults, as well as the values and worldviews that matter most to them. It's in this way that we eventually develop a coherent sense of identity, someone who is both different from everyone else—unique in our own special ways—and who is a unified, continuous individual over time, even as we change and grow (Baumeister, 2011).

WHERE FICTION FITS IN

So where do fiction and the media we consume it through fit in? While children are exposed to stories of all kinds from an early age, during adolescence, identification with parents decreases and identification with peers and media increases (Cramer, 2001; Arnett, 1995). As adolescents work on forming their identities, the fictional stories they can access through the mass media give them opportunities to discover new things and vicariously try on different possible selves. After all, most adolescents are students, but they won't stay that way forever.

Media help adolescents discover things above and beyond what's available to them in their daily lives alone, including new and unfamiliar careers they might enjoy, different kinds of relationships they might find fulfilling, and various perspectives on values, attitudes, and beliefs (Giles & Maltby, 2004). Through stories, adolescents can get insight into what it might be like to be a private investigator, a dog trainer, or a doctor; what it would feel like to be married with three kids, to get divorced, or to party every night; and how being admired, lonely, or strongly committed to a religious or political philosophy would suit them. One can experience almost anything through a story and all of these options represent possible selves that adolescents might wish to strive for, or possible selves they may want to avoid. What they find out provides a roadmap, giving adolescents a template for the choices they should make to become who they hope to be in the future (Markus & Nurius, 1986).

Media can also provide adolescents with information they can't get anywhere else. For example, coming of age is a common trope in many movies including *The Breakfast Club, Lady Bird, Ferris Bueller's Day Off,* and *Almost Famous*. These stories may help adolescents grapple and negotiate with the freedoms and constraints of this time in their lives. Similarly, adolescents struggling with their gender or sexual identity might turn to media representations, like those in the TV shows *Supergirl* or *13 Reasons Why*, or the movies *Call Me by Your Name* or *Blue Is the Warmest Color* to help them better understand and accept this aspect of themselves (Arnett, 1995). Similarly, media can provide examples of what to expect from and how to negotiate new situations, especially those that may be difficult to discuss with parents or peers, such as the newly accessible world of romance, dating, and sex, including depictions in *Sixteen Candles, Bring It On,* and *Say Anything*... (Brown, Dykers, Steele, & White, 1994). In addition, media helps adolescents learn about the kinds of roles, relationships, and behaviors that are considered culturally valued and, therefore, worth working toward, while also demonstrating what might be less culturally valued and, therefore, worth passing up (Lloyd, 2002).

Research suggests that the stories experienced through media work in conjunction with the things adolescents discover in their "real lives" to help them learn and grow, enhancing their ability to work toward becoming the people they hope to be as adults. In a series of case studies exploring the lives of three middle school students, New York University professor JoEllen Fisherkeller (1997) showed that while each student's family and community set the parameters for their social goals and future aspirations, the TV shows they watched helped the students develop "imaginative strategies" for reaching these goals. Thus, television gave them tools to work on and cope with their personal issues, serving as a complement to what they learned locally.

Similarly, young people who star in movies and TV shows may find their identities influenced by the characters they play. For example, the acclaimed coming-of-age story *Boyhood* was filmed over 12 years as Ellar Coltrane, the boy playing the central character, Mason, grew from childhood to adulthood. Speaking with the Los Angeles Times (Zeitchik, 2015), Coltrane, then age 20, was asked how starring in *Boyhood* influenced the formation of his own identity. Coltrane explained:

> When you're at an age that your ego and identity are being forged, I think it would be hard to do this. I'm still figuring out who I am, but I'm a lot more stable in my ego and personality than when I was 10 or 15. Just having done all this and seeing how much strain it's put on my mind, people telling you crazy things about yourself. It does [mess] with your head.

Not only does this conversation suggest Coltrane learned things through his experience on the film that likely impacted who he became as an adult, it also shines a light on our earlier discussion in Chapter 3 of this volume about the difficulty of separating the actor from the role.

There is also the question of who chooses the stories adolescents (and everyone else) consume. Parents and other adults often select the stories presented to young children, but as we grow we're more and more capable of selecting among the available options. In adolescence, as less time is spent with parents and more is spent alone and with friends, people are increasingly able to select stories and media that best reflect their interests and preferences—a skill people carry into adulthood. So although media consumers are often characterized as mindless, passive slaves to the messages they take in, really they are active in selecting the media with which they interact. As we mentioned earlier, this idea is reflected by the uses and gratifications approach, which says that we choose what we watch or read based in part on our needs and desires (Rubin, 1993).

Furthermore, people's responses to media differ. So while people may watch or read the same story, what they pay attention to and how they interpret it is specific to the individual because each person's capabilities, characteristics, experiences, and social ties constrain what they take from the experience (Arnett, Larson, & Offer, 1995).

As fiction researchers Mar, Peskin, and Fong (2010) point out, there are three perspectives at work when it comes to stories: the story's perspective, the audience member's perspective, and where those two perspectives meet. It's at the intersection of the story's perspective and the audience member's perspective that a person's identity interacts with the story to arrive at an interpretation of the narrative. Thus, the act of "interpretation itself becomes a part of the ongoing development of the reader's [or viewer's] self-identity" (p. 76), as one's life experience and individual points of view provide a means for making a story personally relevant and meaningful. In other words, when we read or watch a story, we make sense of it by referencing our own knowledge and perspectives, and in the process we determine what our take on the story means for who we are and who we could be (Jones, 2010).

THE MEDIA PRACTICE MODEL

Building on the uses and gratifications approach to explain how media choices influence identity, especially in adolescence, media researchers Jeanne Steele and Jane Brown (1995) developed the media practice model. To better understand young people's relationship with media and how it impacted them, Steele and Brown spent hours interviewing male and female adolescents and emerging adults from a variety of races in their bedrooms or college dorm rooms. Their model was based on their analysis of the data they collected. It specifies that the media one consumes and the identity one constructs influence each other in a cyclical process.

The first step in this model is selection. That is, we choose which media options we wish to consume. As the uses and gratifications approach explains, media selection is dictated by personal motivations, and people can be quite clear and directed about their reasons for consuming specific media. For example, someone might watch *The Walking Dead* because she wants to use the show as a vehicle to vicariously experience what it would be like if the world as we know it came to an end and to consider how she would react in that situation. Other times, however, media selection is habitual, such as when we check the news on our smartphone or flip on a morning show as soon as we wake up.

We usually have higher-quality media interactions when our choices are strongly motivated, but habitual interactions can also influence us over time. Moreover, a motivated choice might not actually be as good a fit with our desires and needs as we originally believed it would be, leading us to pay less attention to it. So if someone selected a movie like *Twilight* hoping for a gory horror film, he likely would have a less intense interaction with it once he learned the story was, in fact, a teen romance that happens to feature vampires.

The second step of the model is interaction. In this step, we engage with media in different ways, interpreting and evaluating the messages media communicate. People who interact intellectually may analyze the story, evaluate its messages, or become psychologically involved. When interacting emotionally, we might cry, laugh, or feel our hearts pound in response to the story. And behavioral interaction can include talking to the characters in the story, flipping back and forth between different web videos, or paging through a book in search of a particular passage.

In the third step, we apply what we've taken from our experiences with media in our daily lives. Steele and Brown (1995) specify two ways this can happen: appropriation and incorporation. When we appropriate our favorite media, we actively incorporate it into the decoration of our home or office, and we can explain how the media impacted us. In this case, we use media in a conscious way to enhance our mood, express ourselves, or spark our imaginations. Incorporation, on the other hand, is usually less conscious. In this case, we incorporate media into our lives in an associative way, taking meaning from it and making that meaning part of what we know, how we feel, and what we value. Some media messages will be applied because we accept and agree with them, but we may also resist specific media messages, applying them in our daily lives as examples of how not to be or what not to do.

Finally, both our sense of identity and our lived experience, including factors like race, gender, and social circumstances, impact the media we consume and what we get out of it. On the flip side, the media we consume impacts our identities, influencing how we think of ourselves right now and who we might become in the future. So our media choices are constantly influencing our identity, and our identity is constantly influencing our media choices.

The media practice model was developed from research with adolescents and emerging adults and created specifically to explain how adolescents apply media to their developing identities (Steele & Brown, 1995). However, we believe the cycle it specifies, where media and identity are constantly impacting and changing each other, might apply at any point in life, especially at times when we're considering who we are and who we want to be.

SELF-SOCIALIZATION AND REPEATED EXPOSURE TO STORIES

Today, with countless and diverse media options available to us, we can choose the stories that best speak to our specific preferences, interests, and moods on any given day. For adolescents and emerging adults, this means they can effectively select some of the agents of their own socialization, using the media they watch and read to glean information pertinent to their specific identity-related concerns (Arnett, 1995).

A recent study by psychological researchers Garmon, Glover, and Vozzola (2018) showed that emerging adults chose to repeatedly watch or read the books or movies of the *Harry Potter* series, *The Hunger Games* trilogy, or the *Twilight Saga* due to their desire to foster their own identity development. In the study, identity development was described as a desire "to cultivate [a] conception of [one's] own values, abilities and hopes for the future" (p. 8). Identity development was associated with repeated exposure to the books and films of all three franchises, meaning there was a relationship between higher levels of exposure and the goal of identity development, although it wasn't clear if the goal of identity development led individuals to read or watch the books and movies more or if the repeated exposure led individuals to believe the books and movies helped with identity development. Through some statistical magic, the authors showed that the goal of identity development predicted that participants had read the *Harry Potter* books and watched the *Twilight Saga* films a greater number of times, meaning individuals were motivated by the goal of identity development to reread the *Harry Potter* books and rewatch the *Twilight Saga* films.

This study demonstrates that not only do adolescents and emerging adults decide to watch and read stories based on their unique wants and needs, but that when they discover a story they find especially useful for meeting a goal, they will revisit it repeatedly in an effort to get the most they can out of the experience. Like the media practice model, since identity development is a process that continues throughout our lives, we likely continue to look to media to develop our identities in adulthood too. In adolescence and emerging adulthood, however, identity development may be an especially important reason people have for consuming specific stories (Arnett, 1995).

EXTENDING THE SELF THROUGH STORIES

Today, the rise of technology and fast, affordable transportation has freed people to follow their dreams more than ever before, but it also means people's lives are that much more uncertain at whatever age they happen to be. One person may be born in one place, but move to many others over a lifetime, learning about the ins and outs of many different cities, towns, states, and countries along the way. Another could switch careers every few years, trying out one possibility, but then growing curious about and pursuing new professional opportunities. Another may be downsized out of a long career and forced to figure out other options that will keep the mortgage paid and food on the table. Yet another may marry and divorce multiple times, constantly looking for a better fit romantically. With so many choices tempting us, stability is often temporary, and for some, may not even be desirable. But careers, relationships, even where we live are all factors people use to define themselves. Since these things are no longer stable anchors we can stake our identities on, we engage in identity work regularly, especially when we experience a life event that makes us reconsider who we are and how we think about ourselves. Everything from graduating from high school or college to a career change to having a child to a divorce to the death of a loved one to retirement can cause upheaval and lead us to reformulate parts of our identities.

As we grow older, however, some possibilities are no longer available to us. For example, when he was a child, Cynthia's husband, Michael, dreamed of becoming an astronaut. By adolescence, however, he realized his less-than-perfect vision and NASA's strict standards for astronauts would prevent him from ever reaching his goal. Although we must let go of certain options, other opportunities can present themselves. For example, because of his involvement in martial arts, Michael discovered a talent for teaching new martial arts students, and now he teaches multiple forms of martial arts in locations throughout Los Angeles—something he wouldn't have considered doing when he was a kid, but something he truly enjoys and excels at now. So our identity is always being created in conversation with our personal history, our abilities, our interests, our social environment, and our culture. These things open up avenues for us to pursue, while limiting us in other ways.

Of course, our identities are multifaceted and complex, and what one thinks of as "me" can be highly personal and specific to the individual. The father of American psychology, William James (1890/1918) suggested that the self includes extensions. James explains:

> In its widest possible sense, however, a man's Self is the sum total of all that he CAN call his, not only his body and his psychic powers, but his clothes, and his house, his wife and children, his ancestors and friends, his reputation and works, his lands and horses, and yacht and bank-account. All these things give him the same emotions. If they wax and prosper, he feels triumphant; if they dwindle and die away, he feels cast down,—not necessarily in the same degree for each thing, but in much the same way for all. (pp. 291–292).

While James doesn't mention media or stories (after all, he was writing in 1890 when movies had just been invented, TV was decades from becoming a reality, and computers, the Internet, smartphones, and tablets were probably beyond imagination), today the ubiquity of books, movies, TV, and the Internet provide us with myriad opportunities to find fiction that can act as extensions of our identities.

James (1890/1918) indicates that the key to seeing something as an extension of oneself is emotional investment. So, popular culture fans who become emotionally attached to a specific fictional story may be especially prone to seeing that story as an extension of self. Although this could be true of anything one feels an emotional tie to, including any story whether one is a fan or not. For example, if someone spent her formative years reading the *Wizard of Oz* books or watching Bugs Bunny cartoons, she may see those stories as important extensions of her identity due to her emotional attachment to them, even if she hasn't read or watched them in a long time. Richard Belk (1988), a business scholar, argues that one way we incorporate objects into the self is by knowing them passionately. Acquiring knowledge of a given story with passionate interest, then, may cause it to evolve from being something one simply reads or watches to something that is part of the self.

Research on the way we integrate people, objects, and things into our conception of self is minimal. However, one study by Monika Lisjak, Angela Lee, and Wendi Gardner (2012) showed that when participants read a negative editorial about Starbucks or Facebook and the participant identified with the brand, their response was the same as it would be if they had read a negative editorial about themselves. More specifically, participants who identified with these brands and were prone to responding defensively when their identity was threatened found a threat to the brands personally threatening and reacted as they would if the threat was to themselves. The researchers took this to mean that participants who defended the brands saw them as part of their extended self.

More research is necessary to find out if fans and audiences of fictional stories would react in similarly defensive ways, but social psychologist Henri Tajfel's social identity theory suggests this might be the case. Social identity theory says that people become deeply cognitively and emotionally invested in the groups of which they are a part and that identification makes up part of who they are and how they see themselves (Tajfel, 1982). So if we consider ourselves part of any kind of group—a religious group, an ethnic group, a nationality, or even a story fandom—we will see ourselves as part of an in-group that contributes to our sense of self.

Studies suggest that fans of many interests view themselves as part of a distinct social group (Reysen & Branscombe, 2010; Tsay-Vogel & Sanders, 2017). In one study on *Harry Potter* fans, communication scholars Mina Tsay-Vogel and Meghan Sanders (2017) found that fans felt they were members of the fandom even when they didn't directly communicate with other fans. In another study, Samantha Groene and Vanessa Hettinger (2016) showed that when *Harry Potter* fans had their fan identities affirmed via a computer test, they put in more effort and were more successful at writing a *Harry Potter*–themed essay than when their fan identity wasn't affirmed. This was not the case for *Twilight* fans, however, who put in equal effort when writing a *Twilight*–themed essay regardless of whether their fan identity was affirmed or not. These researchers interpreted the results to mean that the *Harry Potter* fans were more highly identified with *Harry Potter* than *Twilight* fans were with *Twilight* and that high identification meant *Harry Potter* fans had incorporated their fan identity into their self-concept. This made them more sensitive to both affirmations and threats to that part of their identity. This research suggests that when someone identifies with and is emotionally invested in a specific story, it can be a source of great pride and self-esteem when the story is valued and appreciated. But if the story is disparaged or dismissed, it can be bruising. This could cause a fan to become defensive, as if the criticism of the story is a threat to the self.

We've seen this happen in fandoms before. For example, within the *Twilight* fandom, passionate debates took place about the merits of Bella Swan's two suitors: Edward, the vampire, and Jacob, the werewolf. Team Edward and Team Jacob became so well-known in popular culture that some fans literally wore their affiliation by donning T-shirts of their chosen love interest—something Taylor Lautner, the actor who embodied Jacob in the movies, satirized on a *Saturday Night Live* sketch (see Figure 6.2). For some fans, these debates seemed just as important as they might be if they were part of a love triangle in their real lives. As a result of these fans' emotional investment, their fan identity as not only a *Twilight* fan but a Team Edward or Team Jacob fan may have become an important extension of self. It follows that if we're emotionally invested in specific stories and what they mean to us, we will utilize those stories to inform our identities and include them in our extended self.

We can see this played out in the way people communicate their affiliation with a particular story through the clothes they wear or the decorations they use in their personal spaces, such as bedrooms, offices, or cars. As fan studies scholar Lawrence Grossberg (1992) observes, such symbols of affiliation with a story give it the authority to "speak for and as him or her, not only as a spokesperson but as surrogate voices" (p. 59). For example, this happens when we use a movie quote to make a point or wear a T-shirt of a specific TV character as a representation of

Figure 6.2 Taylor Lautner and Jenny Slate in the sketch "Lab Partners: Team Edward vs. Team Jacob" from *Saturday Night Live*, parodied the *Twilight* phenomenon and the way its fans took sides on whether the best suitor for main character Bella was Edward or Jacob.
Screen capture from http://www.nbc.com/saturday-night-live/video/lab-partners/n12640?snl=1

who we are and what we care about. In this way the stories we love can speak for us and as us, and these affiliations contribute to the construction of our identity.

In the studies that contributed to the creation of the media practice model, Steele and Brown (1995) showed that adolescents decorated their bedrooms with posters and other objects representing their favorite popular culture stories and figures to express themselves, integrate themselves into the cultural and social world, remind themselves of people they admire, and help them fantasize about what they might experience and who they might become. So material possessions that represent a story can help us present who we are to the outside world, while at the same time inviting feedback that would not be offered to us independently (Belk, 1988). Thus, our identities evolve in conjunction with the stories we emotionally invest in and use to symbolize and explore who we are.

NARRATIVE IDENTITY

> We tell ourselves that we're in a movie
> WhoaWhoaWhoa
> Each one of us thinks we've got the starring role
> RoleRoleRole
>
> —from the song "The End of the Movie"
> *Crazy Ex-Girlfriend*

As media psychologists who study stories, we believe one of the most interesting ways to think about identity is as a story. Psychologists call the internalized, ever-evolving story people are always creating and recreating about their lives "narrative identity." While objectively, as the song from *Crazy Ex-Girlfriend* quoted at the beginning of this section states, "Life doesn't make narrative sense," we tell ourselves stories about what happens to us for this exact reason—it gives our lives coherence and meaning that it wouldn't have otherwise (McAdams & McLean, 2013). Essentially, we're all starring in our own personal life story and that story helps us understand and make sense of who we are (Josselson, 2006). In personality psychologist Dan McAdams' (1988, 1993) life story model of identity, not only does identity take the form of a story, but it also features all the traditional story features we're familiar with, including genre, plot, settings, themes, characters, and scenes.

Of course, as preeminent psychologist Jerome Bruner (1990, 2001) reminds us, our life stories are not a perfect reconstruction of what happened to us from the time we were born to the current moment. Our memories are selective and imperfect and bound by our personal perspectives and histories, both in terms of what we paid attention to when the memory was made and what we remember when we recall the memory later. Instead of an unbiased documentary of our personal history, our life stories include only the memories that support our specific interpretation of what our lives have been like and what they mean. When we tell ourselves our life story, we are reconstructing our past in order to tell ourselves a story in the present. As a result, who we are today influences the story we tell and may alter our memories of the past. Often the things we remember the best are emotionally loaded, so we construct our story as a means for explaining those emotional experiences. The important thing is that these autobiographical stories feel real and true. So, the life stories we tell, both to ourselves and others, don't need to pass a test of verifiable proof, but they must pass a test of verisimilitude. In other words, they must feel true.

For example, at the beginning of the chapter we mentioned Cynthia and Kristin's (Vinney & Hopper-Losenicky, 2017) study about *Buffy the Vampire Slayer* fans' impressions of how the show impacted their lives. While the fans had many stories to tell about how the show's effect on them and the role it played in shaping who they are, these stories can't be verified. We have no way of confirming that the fans' experiences with *Buffy* actually led to the real-life impacts they attribute to it. What the fans' stories do indicate, however, is that they've incorporated their interpretations of the show's role in their lives into their life stories and, therefore, the show occupies a significant place in these individuals' narrative identities. So, ultimately, the factual basis of the fans' stories isn't the point. What's important is what fans remember and how it informs their understanding of themselves. The stories fans told about *Buffy* demonstrated that it had a meaningful place in their memories and that those memories were a source of ongoing strength. So when fans revisited those memories, the stories they told about their association with the show were positive, and often triumphant, tales of learning to face problems, confront demons, and take what they've learned into a bright, optimistic future.

Buffy fans and other pop culture watchers might be interested to know that the data for this study was collected before the scandal involving *Buffy*'s creator, Joss Whedon, that happened in late summer 2017. Whedon's ex-wife accused him of being a hypocrite for preaching feminist ideals publicly while privately cheating on her repeatedly throughout their 15-year marriage (Cole, 2017). We address how we cope when a celebrity we adore does something we despise in Chapter 8 of this volume. The relevant thing to keep in mind here is that this scandal could alter the way fans view how *Buffy* impacted their lives, and this could affect its place in their life stories as a result. (Although the Whedon scandal didn't set off the media frenzy that surrounded subsequent Hollywood players accused of repeated sexual harassment and abuse in fall 2017, for fans of *Buffy* and other Whedon properties, it was a significant revelation.) Our life stories are always shifting and changing in response to newly acquired information as well as our personal perceptions. Given the perception of Whedon as a champion of feminist values, the revelations by his ex-wife might cause fans who originally felt *Buffy* had taught them how strong women can be to question how much it really did so. The show's place in fans' life stories may change depending on their responses to this new information about its creator. The stories some fans tell about the show's impact on their lives might stay the same if the information doesn't influence their perceptions of the show. On the other hand, for some fans, the scandal might cloud how they view the show to the point where they no longer view it as a significant part of their lives or, by extension. include seeing it in their life stories.

Narrative identity is malleable. At the same time, however, it gives our lives continuity. The story we tell about ourselves connects our past to our current self and our current self to our imagined future self. As our current self learns new things and moves towards the future, our stories must constantly adjust to accommodate new circumstances, relationships, experiences, values, and thought processes.

Psychologists who study narrative identity often emphasize the importance of culture in the construction of life stories. The culture we grow up in often dictates how we tell a story, including the stories of our lives. As Wang (2001) found in her studies on how Americans and Chinese remember their lives, early parent–child interactions introduce children to the style of personal storytelling that is culturally expected. American and Chinese children as young as 3 exhibit different approaches to storytelling and emphasize different values when they talk about their personal experiences because they grow up in such different narrative environments. In parent–child interactions, American children are often encouraged to tell elaborate stories that focus on the child's unique opinions, feelings, and reactions. In contrast, such interactions in Chinese culture are less elaborate and individual, instead focusing on the facts of an event with great attention paid to social standards and rules. These differences impact the way people remember their own lives, resulting in different kinds of life stories. As we've discussed, people in Western cultures create elaborate, coherent life stories where the individual telling the story is the star. In many East Asian cultures, however, collective experiences are emphasized over one's unique life story, resulting in memories that have a social orientation.

Interactions with parents and other family members are typically our first introduction to the kinds of stories that are valued in our culture. But the stories we interact with through media can introduce, reinforce, and critique culturally endorsed narratives as well. Psychologists call the stories that communicate such cultural standards "master narratives." Whether a person conforms to them, ignores them, or resists them, master narratives help members of a given culture understand and make sense of their experiences (Thorne & McLean, 2003). So narrative identity becomes a fusion of a culture's master narratives and one's personal history (Hammack, 2008).

For instance, McAdams (2006) specifies a uniquely American master narrative in his book *The Redemptive Self*. As we mentioned in Chapter 2 of this volume when we discussed the appeal of the story of *It's a Wonderful Life*, stories of human redemption tell of "a deliverance from suffering to a better world" (McAdams, 2006, p. 7). The life stories of generative American adults, those who are highly committed to leaving a positive legacy for future generations, often emphasize this theme of redemption. This is a story Americans know well and is reflected all around them. It is the story of the person who suffers many trials and tribulations throughout their life, but never gives up, and eventually triumphs and decides they will use their good fortune to help others. McAdams

(2006) contends this story is wrapped up with American cultural identity. It is reflective of Americans' early understanding of their country as a "city on a hill," a special place where anything is possible. This story reproduces ideas about American exceptionalism, manifest destiny, individualism, and independence that have become intrinsic, often unconscious, ideas underlying American society. We see this reflected in the stories in American popular media. From Spider-Man's origin story to *The Shawshank Redemption* to countless slave narratives, such as *12 Years a Slave*, to recent television character arcs like that of Damon Salvatore on *The Vampire Diaries* to Regina, the (formerly) Evil Queen, on *Once Upon a Time* to Luke Cage on several Netflix-Marvel shows, American popular culture continues to champion this kind of story. And for highly generative American adults, this story arc becomes the framework for the story of their lives, shaping their narrative identity and how they understand themselves.

While stories of redemption work on a macro level, master narratives also convey standards to members of a society based on characteristics including gender, race, sexuality, religion, and age. For example, in one study, Avril Thorne and Kate McLean (2003) found that when European American college students told a story of their experience of a life-threatening event, women were significantly more likely than men to take an emotional position that emphasized care and concern for others, a master narrative the researchers referred to as the "Florence Nightingale position." The authors posited that their finding is a product of the different ways European American girls and boys are socialized—girls are socialized to express their feelings, while boys are socialized to consider their emotions in a pragmatic way. The master narratives told by parents, peers, and the media as kids grow up repeatedly emphasize and reinforce these cultural expectations. By late adolescence, people's experiences within their culture shapes their perception, often unconsciously, of what's expected of them. This, in turn, influences how they understand and remember their experiences and, consequently, how they tell their personal stories.

Given the power of master narratives and how popular culture amplifies and augments them, the popular media stories people point to as important in their lives could provide insights into their narrative identities. Fan researchers C. Lee Harrington and Denise Bielby (2010), for example, suggest that becoming-a-fan narratives (i.e., the stories fans tell about first encountering the media that they develop a highly personal attachment to) represent important milestones in people's narrative identities. These stories represent turning points in people's lives that are remembered and discussed with other people. Becoming a fan often fundamentally changes people, both personally and socially, altering who they are and the course of their lives (Duffett, 2013; Harrington & Bielby, 2010).

As fan scholar Mark Duffett (2013) explains, "individuals who become fans do not exactly *transform* their identities, because they never actually *leave* any aspect of their previous identity *behind*. Instead, they find that a new vista opens up of self-identified possibilities. The individual changes *how they see* their identity" (p. 155). As a result, fans see themselves in ways they never did before and the story that marks this change in their life, their story of becoming a fan, becomes a vital part of their narrative identity.

While the many ways popular culture stories might impact narrative identity hasn't yielded a lot of scholarly attention, recent research suggests that the books, movies, and television shows people read and watch could play an important role in their life stories. In two studies, Breen, McLean, Cairney, and McAdams (2017) interviewed several white emerging adult college students and a group of African and European American mid-life adults. Almost all the participants could name at least one media story that was important to their lives. Participants described these stories as sources of information and influence regarding their personal traits, skills, and values, and served as inspiration for who they might become in the future. Media stories also served a relational function, helping people understand others and their personal connections to them. Women and men were more likely to identify with characters of the same gender. And as might be gleaned by our previous discussion of master narratives, the stories some interviewees told fell in line with the expectations about gender showcased in many master narratives. Some of the mid-life adult participants also noted that media stories had helped raise their social consciousness, enabling them to develop a critical lens through which they could understand the world and an appreciation of collective identity. It's noteworthy that the interviewees who brought this up also identified themselves as minorities.

In addition, the researchers pointed to a parallel in their findings between the themes that dominated participants' life stories and those in the media stories they said were important to them. For example, one interviewee, Anthony, a successful businessman with a wife and two children, named the books *The Adventures of Huckleberry Finn* and *The Adventures of Tom Sawyer* as his favorites. These stories of adventure reflected the themes of the life story Anthony told. In particular, they seemed to reflect the life he hoped to have as he transitioned to a new phase of semiretirement. These stories may have served as inspiration for who he could become in this new chapter in his life. Similarly, Anne, a recently divorced lawyer with two kids, said her favorite stories were television shows like *The Mary Tyler Moore Show* and *Rhoda* and books like the autobiographies of Anne Frank and Helen Keller. These stories were reflective of her new perspective on life after her divorce. Each of these stories centers on strong female characters who follow their own path without relying on others, mirroring the life story she was currently creating for herself as a single, independent woman.

Although much more work remains to be done to truly understand how popular culture stories impact who we are, and who we might become, these studies suggest that popular media stories can play an important role in our understanding of ourselves. Of course, throughout our lives, the stories we interact with, and the way they affect us, changes and evolves. We'll delve into the role stories can play at each stage of our lives in the next chapter.

REFERENCES

Arnett, J. J. (1995). Adolescents' use of media for self-socialization. *Journal of Youth and Adolescence, 24*(5), 519–533.

Arnett, J. J. (2000). Emerging adulthood: A theory of development from the late teens through the twenties. *American Psychologist, 55*(5), 469–480. https://doi.org/10.1037//0003-006X.55.5.469

Arnett, J. J. (2004). *Emerging adulthood: The winding road from the late teens through the twenties.* New York, NY: Oxford University Press.

Arnett, J. J., Larson, R., & Offer, D. (1995). Beyond effects: Adolescents as active media users. *Journal of Youth and Adolescence, 24*(5), 511–518.

Baumeister, R. F. (1987). How the self became a problem: A psychological review of historical research. *Journal of Personality and Social Psychology, 52*(1), 163–176.

Baumeister, R. F. (2011). Self and identity: A brief overview of what they are, what they do, and how they work. *Annals of the New York Academy of Sciences, 1234,* 48–55. https://doi.org/10.1111/j.1749-6632.2011.06224.x

Belk, R. W. (1988). Possessions and the extended self. *Journal of Consumer Research, 15*(2), 138–168.

Breen, A. V., McLean, K. C., Cairney, K., & McAdams, D. P. (2017). Movies, books, and identity: Exploring the narrative ecology of the self. *Qualitative Psychology, 4*(3), 243–259. https://doi.org/10.1037/qup0000059

Brown, J. D., Dykers, C. R., Steele, J. R., & White, A. B. (1994). Teenage room culture: Where media and identities intersect. *Communication Research, 21*(6), 813–827. https://doi.org/10.1177/009365094021006008

Bruner, J. (1990). *Acts of meaning.* Cambridge, MA: Harvard University Press.

Bruner, J. (2001). Self-making and world-making. In J. Brockmeier & D. Carbaugh (Eds.), *Narrative and identity: Studies in autobiography, self, and culture* (pp. 25–37). Philadelphia, PA: John Benjamins.

Cole, K. (2017, August 20). Joss Whedon is a "hypocrite preaching feminist ideals," ex-wife Kai Cole says. *The Wrap.* Retrieved from http://www.thewrap.com/joss-whedon-feminist-hypocrite-infidelity-affairs-ex-wife-kai-cole-says/

Côté, J. E. (2009). Identity formation and self-development in adolescence. In R. M. Lerner & L. Steinberg (Eds.), *Handbook of adolescent psychology* (pp. 266–304). Hoboken, NJ: Wiley.

Cramer, P. (2001). Identification and its relation to identity development. *Journal of Personality, 69*(5), 667–688.

Djikic, M., Oatley, K., Zoeterman, S., & Peterson, J. B. (2009). On being moved by art: How reading fiction transforms the self. *Creativity Research Journal, 21,* 24–29. http://doi.org/10.1080/10400410802633392

Duffett, M. (2013). *Understanding fandom.* New York, NY: Bloomsbury.

Elliott, G. R., & Feldman, S. S. (1990). Capturing the adolescent experience. In S. S. Feldman & G. R. Elliott (Eds.), *At the threshold: The developing adolescent* (pp. 1–13). Cambridge, MA: Harvard University Press.

Erikson, E. H. (1968). *Identity: Youth and crisis.* New York: W. W. Norton.

Fisherkeller, J. (1997). Everyday learning about identities among young adolescents in television culture. *Anthropology & Education Quarterly, 28*(4), 467–492.

Gabriel, S., & Young, A. F. (2011). Becoming a vampire without being bitten: The narrative collective-assimilation hypothesis. *Psychological Science, 22*(8), 990–994. https://doi.org/10.1177/0956797611415541

Garmon, L. C., Glover, R. J., & Vozzola, E. C. (2018). Self-perceived use of popular culture media franchises: Does gratification impact multiple exposures? *Psychology of Popular Media Culture, 7*(4), 572–588. https://doi.org/10.1037/ppm0000153

Giles, D. C., & Maltby, J. (2004). The role of media figures in adolescent development: Relations between autonomy, attachment, and interest in celebrities. *Personality and Individual Differences, 36,* 813–822. https://doi.org/10.1016/S0191-8869(03)00154-5

Groene, S. L., & Hettinger, V.E. (2016). Are you "fan" enough? The role of identity in media fandoms. *Psychology of Popular Media Culture, 5*(4), 324–339. https://doi.org/10.1037/ppm0000080

Grossberg, L. (1992). Is there a fan in the house? The affective sensibility of fandom. In L. A. Lewis (Ed.), *The adoring audience: Fan culture and popular media* (pp. 50–65). New York, NY: Routledge.

Hammack, P. L. (2008). Narrative and the cultural psychology of identity. *Personality and Social Psychology Review, 12*(3), 222–247. https://doi.org/10.1177/1088868308316892

Harrington, C. L., & Bielby, D. D. (2010). A life course perspective on fandom. *International Journal of Cultural Studies, 13*(5), 429–450. https://doi.org/10.1177/1367877910372702

Hills, M. (2005). Negative fan stereotypes ("Get a life!") and positive fan injunctions ("Everyone's got to be a fan of something!"): Returning to hegemony theory in fan studies. *Spectator, 25*(1), 35–47.

James, W. (1890/1918). *The principles of psychology* (Vol. 1). New York, NY: Dover.

Jones, R. A. (2010). "Talking brought me here:" Affordances of fiction for the narrative self. *Theory & Psychology, 20*(4), 549–567. https://doi.org/10.1177/0959354310361406

Josselson, R. (2006). Narrative research and the challenge of accumulating knowledge. *Narrative Inquiry, 16*(1), 3–10.

Larson, R. (1995). Secrets in the bedroom: Adolescents' private use of media. *Journal of Youth and Adolescence, 24*(5), 535–550.

Lisjak, M., Lee, A. Y., & Gardner, W. L. (2012). When a threat to brand is a threat to self: The importance of brand identification and implicit self-esteem in predicting defensiveness. *Personality and Social Psychology Bulletin, 38*(9), 1120–1132. https://doi.org/10.1177/0146167212445300

Lloyd, B. T. (2002). A conceptual framework for examining adolescent identity, media influence, and social development. *Review of General Psychology, 6*(1), 73–91. https://doi.org/10.1037//1089-2680.6.1.73

Mar, R. A., Peskin, J., & Fong, K. (2010). Literary arts and the development of the life story. In T. Habermas (Ed.), *The development of autobiographical reasoning in adolescence and beyond* (pp. 73–85). Hoboken, NJ: Wiley. https://doi.org/10.1002/cd.290

Markus, H., & Nurius, P. (1986). Possible selves. *American Psychologist, 41*(9), 954–969.

McAdams, D. P. (1988). *Power, intimacy, and the life story: Personological inquiries into identity.* New York, NY: Guilford.
McAdams, D. P. (1993). *The stories we live by: Personal myths and the making of the self.* New York, NY: Guilford.
McAdams, D. P. (2006). *The redemptive self: Stories Americans live by.* New York, NY: Oxford University Press.
McAdams, D. P., & McLean, K. C. (2013). Narrative identity. *Current Directions in Psychological Science, 22*(3), 233–238. https://doi.org/10.1177/0963721413475622
Meyer, S. (2005). *Twilight.* New York, NY: Little, Brown and Co.
Moore, A. (1985). *Swamp thing annual* (Vol. 2). New York, NY: DC Comics.
Reysen, S., & Branscombe, N. R. (2010). Fanship and fandom: Comparisons between sport and non-sport fans. *Journal of Sport Behavior, 33*(2), 176–193.
Rowling, J. K. (1999). *Harry Potter and the sorcerer's stone.* New York, NY: Scholastic.
Rubin, A. M. (1993). Audience activity and media use. *Communication Monographs, 60*, 98–105.
Sestir, M., & Green, M. C. (2010). You are who you watch: Identification and transportation effects on temporary self-concept. *Social Influence, 5*(4), 272–288. https://doi.org/10.1080/15534510.2010.490672
Steele, J. R., & Brown, J. D. (1995). Adolescent room culture: Studying media in the context of everyday life. *Journal of Youth and Adolescence, 24*(5), 551–576.
Tajfel, H. (1982). Social psychology of intergroup relations. *Annual Review of Psychology, 33*, 1–39.
Thorne, A., & McLean, K. C. (2003). Telling traumatic events in adolescence: A study of master narrative positioning. In R. Fivush & C. A. Haden (Eds.), *Autobiographical memory and the construction of a narrative self: Developmental and cultural perspectives* (pp. 169–185). New York, NY: Psychology Press.
Tsay-Vogel, M., & Sanders, M. S. (2017). Fandom and the search for meaning: Examining communal involvement with popular media beyond pleasure. *Psychology of Popular Media Culture, 6*(1), 32–47. https://doi.org/10.1037/ppm0000085
Vinney, C., Dill-Shackleford, K., Plante, C. N., & Bartsch, A. (2019). Development and validation of a measure of popular media fan identity and its relationship to well-being. Psychology of Popular Media Culture, 8(3), 296–307. https://doi.org/10.1037/ppm0000188
Vinney, C., & Hopper-Losenicky, K. (2017, April). *More than escapism: How popular media helps fans learn, cope, and live.* Paper presented at the Popular Culture Association/American Culture Association annual conference, San Diego, CA.
Wang, Q. (2001). Culture effects on adults' earliest childhood recollection and self-description: Implications for the relation between memory and self. *Journal of Personality and Social Psychology, 81*(2), 220–233. https://doi.org/10.1037/0022-3514.81.2.220
Wang, Q., & Brockmeier, J. (2002). Autobiographical remembering as cultural practice: Understanding the interplay between memory, self and culture. *Culture & Psychology, 8*(1), 45–64. https://doi.org/10.1177/1354067X02008001618

Zeitchik, S. (2015, February 21). Oscars 2015: "Boyhood's" Ellar Coltrane balances fame and the future. *Los Angeles Times*. Retrieved from http://beta.latimes.com/entertainment/movies/la-et-mn-conversation-boyhood-ellar-coltrane-interview-20150222-story.html

Zubernis, L., & Larsen, K. (Eds.). (2012). *Fandom at the crossroads: Celebration, shame and fan/producer relationships*. Newcastle upon Tyne, England: Cambridge Scholars.

7

Story and Life Stage

Turning to Stories Throughout Our Lives

> Some day you will be old enough to start reading fairy tales again.
> —C. S. Lewis (1950)
> Dedication of *The Lion, the Witch and the Wardrobe*

As kids, it's understood and accepted that stories are a big part of our lives. Our parents read to us, we watch cartoons with our friends, and we anticipate the next children's movie coming soon to theaters near us. As we grow older, our relationship with stories sometimes becomes less obvious, but that doesn't make it any less important. While different stories are marketed to different age groups—animation is often for kids, action extravaganzas for adults—we typically don't think about how our relationship with stories changes as we age, or how it stays the same. After all, we may discover a love for horror films with a hard-R rating as we grow up, but we also may continue to adore Disney cartoons.

Cynthia will admit that her undying love of almost all the shows on the teen-oriented CW network confounds even her sometimes. She can't get enough of *Supernatural*, *Riverdale*, and *The Originals* (why, oh, why did it have to end after only five seasons?!). Even though her perspective on these stories is probably different than it would have been when she was younger, Cynthia still has a deep love of these shows. And Cynthia's not alone. As the moms who loved *Twilight* or the adults who stood in line for the next *Harry Potter* novel can attest, sometimes the stories we love aren't "age-appropriate"—whatever that means.

Regardless of the age group that is expected to watch or read a particular story, different stories can speak to different people in different ways throughout their lives. Someone who loves *Annie* or *Charlie and the Chocolate Factory* as a child may continue to love them as an adult. While taste in stories may stay the same, our take on those stories undoubtedly changes as we grow older. This alters what we pay attention to and how we interpret the same stories over time and, by extension, which parts of the stories we find relevant and meaningful.

At the same time, sometimes new stories speak to us in ways we never could have imagined when we were younger. Or stories that seemed essential when we were younger no longer resonate with us. All of this represents the development and change that happens as we grow, experiencing and learning new things along the way. In the following pages, we'll discuss how our preferences and motivations for engaging with stories evolves throughout our lives and what this means for the ways stories can facilitate our goals at different ages. To start, we'll go back to when everyone's relationship with stories begins: childhood.

CHILDHOOD RELATIONSHIPS WITH STORIES

Childhood is a time of incredible growth and change. From the time they're babies until they're 12 years old, children grow rapidly. That growth isn't just physical; its cognitive and social too. In fact, children's interest in and comprehension of stories at a given age are highly dependent on their cognitive abilities. Also, many scholars note that stories serve important social functions throughout childhood. So stories can facilitate children's development, and children's reactions to and understanding of different stories change as they develop.

Today, children are exposed to an incredible amount of content through media. According to a 2017 survey by Common Sense Media, on average, American children 8 years old and under spend more than 2 hours a day with media. A majority of that time—almost an hour—goes to watching TV on a TV set. Watching TV or videos on a mobile phone or tablet takes up a little over 20 minutes. Meanwhile about half an hour is spent reading or being read to (Rideout, 2017).

Clearly television still dominates children's media time, but the activity parents and caretakers are encouraged to do with their children most is read stories to them, starting when they're first born. Reading to babies exposes them to simple stories, while encouraging parent–child interactions and increasing the bond between them. In contrast, in a 2016 policy statement, the American Academy of Pediatrics recommended that parents avoid letting children younger than 1½ to 2 years interact with screen media of any kind. Why would babies benefit from having stories read to them but not benefit from watching stories on screen? Reading to children is a way to introduce them to the literacy practices of our culture. An understanding of the importance of reading prepares children for their membership in a society that expects and values literacy. Babies as young as 6 months are able to pay attention to books and to understand that the stories parents read to them are a form of entertainment (Tamis-LeMonda & Song, 2012).

Reading to children promotes language development and the parent–child interactions that center around reading help socialize children by teaching them the cultural norms around speaking with and responding to another person. While they're reading to their children, parents ask kids questions related to what they're hearing. When language starts to develop around 2 years old, children not only learn to answer these simple questions, they also learn the cues that signal it is their turn to speak. This helps kids learn how to engage in conversation with another person, a skill that can facilitate their success when they start school (Tamis-LeMonda & Song, 2012). In addition, children whose parents read to them have better language and cognitive skills. The stories children hear introduce them to new words, as well as a greater variety of words, than they might hear otherwise, helping them develop their language skills and improving their chances of success when they start reading themselves. Reading to children also introduces them to new concepts, expanding their minds and improving their ability to label items (Ninio & Bruner, 1978; Tamis-LeMonda & Song, 2012).

Starting around 2 years old, children are able to begin to comprehend stories told on screens. However, the American Academy of Pediatrics (2016) cautions that between the ages of 2 and 5 screen time should be limited to 1 hour a day of quality, age-appropriate programs, like *Sesame Street*. Most important, parents should watch with their children so they can interact with them during the show in a lot of the same ways they do when they read to their babies. Parents can help children understand what's happening on screen and how the material is pertinent to their lives, whether they're learning about the letter C or the value of being neighborly. By watching with their kids, parents can also help children learn about the screens that seem to be so ubiquitous in our lives nowadays. Parents who model good habits like turning the television off when it isn't being used or setting the smartphone aside during dinnertime show their kids how to balance screen time with other activities. Something children certainly need to learn in this day and age.

Furthermore, parents who watch with their children can introduce their kids to the magic of screen stories by gradually immersing them in what these stories have to offer. Young children are limited in their understanding of screen stories by their cognitive abilities. When they're preschool age, children really can't keep up with fast-paced programs because their capacity to process information and their knowledge of the world is still fairly limited. At this age, children prefer slower shows with more repetition that are easy to understand like *Mister Rogers' Neighborhood* and *Blue's Clues*. However, around 5 or 6, kids start to get bored with these shows and can handle more rapidly paced stories (Valkenburg & Cantor, 2000).

Research shows that kids between 2 and 5 years old tend to pay attention to the most obvious features they see in a television show or movie, while missing subtler cues. This phenomenon, which is called perceptual boundedness, leads preschool age children to pay attention to characters' physical appearance, while far less of their attention is captured by characters' behavior and dialogue. Young children also tend to focus on only the most salient feature of a visual to the exclusion of all other elements. Referred to as centration, this makes it difficult for preschoolers to examine a picture in its entirety. Due to perceptual boundedness and centration, children base their emotional responses and understanding of screen stories on the story's most prominent visual features instead of other information (Sparks & Cantor, 1986; Valkenburg & Cantor, 2000).

Of course, this changes as children grow older and develop cognitively. To see how children in age groups from 3 to 5, 6 to 7, and 9 to 10 reacted to a combination of a story protagonist's behavior and appearance, media scholars Cynthia Hoffner and Joanne Cantor (1985) changed the appearance and behavior of the protagonist in several videos. The videos presented either an attractive or ugly woman interacting with a cat, which the woman was kind or cruel toward. When study participants were shown the videos where the attractive woman was kind and the ugly woman was cruel to the cat, children in all the age groups reacted similarly, finding the attractive woman nice and the ugly woman mean. But when participants were shown the videos where the attractive woman was cruel and the ugly woman was nice to the cat, the kids in the youngest age group still said the ugly woman was meaner than the attractive woman, relying on appearances over behavior in their assessments. Meanwhile, children in the older age groups paid more attention to the woman's behavior than her appearance to make their assessments, judging the kind, ugly woman as much nicer than the cruel, attractive woman. So, for the 3- to 5-year-olds, appearance influenced their assessments of the character far more than behavior, while the 6- to 7- and 9- to 10-year-olds were more influenced by behavior than appearance.

As children grow older, then, they are better able to understand that what people do says more about them than how they look—this includes characters in on-screen stories. Yet, up to the age of 5, young children take their cues about people from their most obvious features—their looks. These children are still early in their cognitive development and cannot process information as quickly as older children, so their understanding of screen characters is limited by the appearance cues to which they pay the most attention. It's this tendency that causes younger kids to believe that ugly characters are bad and pretty characters are good regardless of the characters' behavior. Of course, we still prize beautiful people even as adults, as our ongoing interest in and expectation that the protagonists of our favorite entertainment meet at least a minimum threshold of attractiveness demonstrates. Starting at around 6 years old, however, when an attractive protagonist behaves in a way that we find questionable, the behavioral information will override our previously positive assessment of the character. This is a switch that younger children are not yet able to make, so they remain reliant on appearances to understand characters.

Young children's focus on the visual over other cues leads them to miss other key information too, like causal relationships and changes from one state to another (Valkenburg & Cantor, 2000). Because of this, they find transformations like that of Dr. Banner into the Hulk surprising. For some preschoolers such surprising transformations might be accompanied by delight, but others could be frightened and unnerved. In fact, when the show *The Incredible Hulk* was being broadcast on television, Joanne Cantor and Glenn Sparks (1984) found that 40% of parents mentioned the show had scared their preschool-aged children. Following up on this information, Sparks and Cantor (1986) showed a group of 3- to 5-year-olds and a group of 9- to 11-year-olds a transformation scene from the show of Banner turning into the Hulk. In the sequence, Banner attempts to help a worker injured in an explosion but is unable to clear away the debris surrounding the worker. A subsequent explosion sets off Banner's transformation into the Hulk, after which the Hulk easily rescues the worker. The younger group of children's fear increased throughout the scene, and they were more scared after the transformation. But the older group of children was more scared before the transformation, and their fear decreased as the sequence played and they realized the injured worker would be saved.

The researchers explained the difference between the younger and older groups as a matter of development. The younger children were still in what the distinguished psychologist Jean Piaget referred to as the "preoperational" stage of cognitive development. In this stage, kids are unable to understand conservation from one state to another. So, for example, if they see water poured from a short, wide glass into a tall, narrow one, they will often believe that there's more water in the tall glass than the short one, because they're only paying attention to the most salient feature of the glasses—in this case, their height. The preoperational stage lasts from about age 2 to age 7. Around 7, kids enter the concrete operations stage at which point they can understand that the two glasses in our example hold the same amount of liquid. At this point they are able to recognize, first, that if water is poured directly from one glass to another it has to be the same amount because nothing has been taken away. And second, that the glasses don't just differ in height, but also in width, so the width of the glass compensates for the change in its height and preserves the amount of liquid from one to the other (Crain, 2005). Although not all developmental psychologists use Piaget's stage theory to explain these differences, they do tend to agree that specific cognitive differences, such as an understanding of liquid conservation, can be observed between preschool and elementary school children (Valkenburg & Cantor, 2000).

It is this growth in cognitive abilities that also enables concrete operational kids to understand that Banner can transform into the Hulk, a story point that eludes younger kids. Instead, younger kids fixate on the most salient visual information—that the Hulk looks scary—leading them to become frightened when the Hulk appears. In contrast, the older children are able to follow the logic of the character's transformation and therefore recognize that because they are the same individual, Banner and the Hulk share the same motivations. Thus, if Banner's motivations are worthwhile but difficult to achieve, his transformation into the Hulk is welcomed by older children, because they know the transformation enables Banner to reach his goals (Sparks & Cantor, 1986).

Distinguishing Fantasy From Reality

Children's frightened reactions to TV and movie characters that transform from one state to another speak to an issue of primary interest to anyone who deals with young children: When do kids begin to understand the difference between fantasy and reality? A great deal of the concern about the harm media can have on children comes from the belief that their inability to distinguish fantasy from reality makes them more vulnerable to media effects (Giles, 2010). Parents, educators, and even media researchers work off the belief that kids' lack of understanding that the fiction they see on their screens isn't real makes them more susceptible to suggestions from advertisers or may make them more aggressive or more worried about their looks if they're exposed to certain kinds of content.

It seems to us, however, that it's a great cultural irony that we willingly read our young children fairy tales and fantastic stories with talking animals, magical objects, and fantasy creatures, while at the same time worrying that the television stories they watch may "trick" them into believing things that aren't true. This also lends itself to the assumption that at a certain age kids will finally snap out of it and understand when something is fiction and therefore should be discounted as fantasy. Of course, if you spend time with children, you can't help but notice how immersed in fantasy they can be. Around 2 years old, children start playing pretend, something they spend a great deal of time doing, especially as preschoolers. Young kids also believe in fantasy characters like Santa Claus, the Easter bunny, and the ever-fearsome monster in the bedroom closet. They often have imaginary friends as well. While pretend play and belief in fantastical figures usually starts to decrease between the ages of 5 and 8, and imaginary friends are no longer important to kids by age 10, children's fantasy worlds are clearly much richer and more present in their daily lives than those of adults (Woolley, 1997).

But as we explained in Chapter 4, sometimes fiction can convey truth and feel real, even to adults who are well aware that something is a fantasy. For example, despite her ever-advancing years, Cynthia finds clowns terrifying. So, when she was exposed to the trailer for the film *IT*, whose central antagonist takes the shape of a diabolical clown, every time she went to the movies leading up to the release of this latest adaptation of the Stephen King novel it felt like torture to her. Cynthia would cower in her chair, cover her eyes, and cringe throughout the experience. She often had a hard time controlling her breathing and slowing down her heart rate after 2½ minutes with the creepy clown (who you can catch a partial glimpse on in Figure 7.1). Of course, on an intellectual level, Cynthia knew the screen clown wasn't really in the theater threatening her personally. But on an emotional level, Cynthia found the experience terrifying. And her emotional and physical responses of fear were still very real, despite the fact that she knew that she was seeing a fictional character played by an actor.

On the other hand, Cynthia has not believed in the tooth fairy or feared a monster is lurking in her closet for a very long time. The difference between her fear of on-screen clowns and her lack of fear of bedroom monsters can be understood as a matter of knowledge acquisition. Over

Figure 7.1 The clown in the teaser trailer for the 2017 adaptation of *IT*. Yes, there is a giant red balloon in front of his face. This was the only way Cynthia would agree to include his image. While we are often concerned about children learning to distinguish fantasy from reality, clearly, adults can still respond viscerally to fiction too.

time, we accumulate knowledge that tells us what is or is not real. When children don't see the monster in their closets over weeks and months, eventually they conclude he's unlikely to be real. But they must first acquire a wealth of evidence to the contrary. On the other hand, while Cynthia has no direct evidence that clowns are out to get her, clowns do exist in real life, and it's not completely implausible that one of them might not have the best intentions. In Cynthia's mind, this faint possibility of clown-based horror and mayhem leaves the door open for her fears. Because children lack as much knowledge of the world as adults, they are more willing than adults are to entertain the possibility that other fantastical creatures and phenomena are real. Moreover, through the stories we tell them, we often expose children to talking pigs, frogs that turn into princes, and people who can perform magic spells to get what they want. So it may take some time for children to acquire enough knowledge to realize these things aren't real (Woolley, 1997). Before then, in their minds it's possible that the pig they met at the farm might talk or the frog they saw hopping along could be a prince in disguise.

As they develop and gather more knowledge of the physical world, children have an easier time labeling monsters and magic as fantasy. Although, as can be seen by Cynthia's fear of the on-screen clown from *IT*, and as we discussed in Chapter 4 of this volume, adults can still respond emotionally and even physically to things they know are not real, especially when they see it presented as a story on TV or in the movies. So children don't suddenly learn the difference between fantasy and reality and no longer respond in any way to anything they know is fiction for the rest of their lives. They mature in their understanding of the world and become more adept at using their advancing knowledge to better assess the plausibility of the various fictional entities they encounter. By the time they enter early adolescence, then, children's responses become more like those of adults and are therefore more understandable and familiar to us. As a result, we worry about them less. At the same time, however, adults may not completely lose their faith in forces that cannot be proven by the observation of physical reality, but these beliefs may morph and shift as they grow older, manifesting themselves in areas that are more acceptable for adults.

For example, the child who believes that wishing will cause their dreams to come true may become an adult who believes in the power of prayer (Woolley, 1997).

Until children mature, however, sometimes their beliefs about fictional characters and situations can be unexpected. It's important to remember that this doesn't mean their reactions are wrong or dangerous. Kids' reactions are based on their developmental stage, and watching stories with an understanding parent can help them learn the best way to comprehend and respond to the fiction they encounter. Young children are more likely to become scared by things that look frightening, like a firebreathing dragon, a big bad wolf, or an ogre lurking under a bridge. As they age, older children recognize that dragons, talking wolves, and ogres aren't real and can't actually hurt them. Instead, older children's fears are more likely to center on real-world dangers that could present a true threat to them, like nuclear war, wild animal attacks, natural disasters, or even—you guessed it!—evil clowns (Cantor,1994). In their survey of parents, Cantor and Sparks (1984) found that although parents of preschoolers were most likely to mention fantasy stories like *The Incredible Hulk* as frightening to their children, parents whose children were in fourth grade were more likely to point to movies like *Jaws* as the source of their children's fear. While the man-eating shark in *Jaws* is certainly fictional, sharks can be dangerous, so it is possible events (somewhat) like those depicted in the movie could happen. Thus, as children get older, their ability to distinguish between impossible and real dangers improves. In other words, older children are better able to discern fantasy from reality, and the fantasy scenarios they see in stories become less scary than frightening scenarios that could plausibly happen in real life.

Learning From Screen Stories

Today, there are all sorts of stories that are designed to teach kids everything from words and numbers to moral lessons. But is this educational content really effective? Can children really learn from stories they watch on a screen? The answer is a qualified yes.

LEARNING FROM SCREEN STORIES FOR CHILDREN AGED 2 AND UNDER

While the American Academy of Pediatrics discourages the use of screen media for children under 2, 71% of children in this age group have watched TV and around one third watch TV daily (Rideout, 2017), so it's helpful to know if very young children can benefit at all from screen stories. Studies show that children may be able to learn from screen media, but that learning is very limited. One reason for this is that very young children experience a "video deficit" that causes them to learn more easily from a live model than from a videotaped model (Heintz & Wartella, 2012; Richert, Robb, & Smith, 2011). Researchers have speculated that this deficit may be due to very young children's inability to understand the relationship between the information conveyed on a screen and the real world (Richert et al., 2011).

Before children can understand screen media, they have to learn that screen media are a source of symbolic communication first. For example, a study by researchers Sophia Pierroutsakos and Georgene Troseth (2003) showed that 9-month-old infants hit at, rubbed, or grasped for toys that were shown on a video screen, indicating the children didn't understand the toys they saw on screen were symbolic representations of real toys. By 15 months, however, this behavior diminished, and by 19 months, it was very rare. Meanwhile, pointing and vocalizing at the video increased across the age groups with the 19-month-olds most likely to point instead of grasp at the toys shown on the video, suggesting the children had learned to see the on-screen objects as representative rather than real. Research has shown that this inability to grasp the relationship between screen images and reality can last until around 2½ years old. For example, Troseth (2003) found that while 2-year-old children were successful at finding a toy in a room a majority of the time when they could observe the toy being hidden by an adult in the room in real life, when they could only observe the toy being hidden on a television screen, they were able to find the toy less than half the time.

However, when very young children's attention is directed to a screen by either a parent or a researcher and the content is simple and appropriate to their stage of development, children are able to learn from the on-screen content (Heintz & Wartella, 2012; Richert et al., 2011). For instance, during one study, 14-month-old and 2-year-old children's attention was directed to a television screen that showed an adult manipulating a toy in a specific way. Afterwards, the children were presented with the same toy to see if they would reproduce the manipulation. A majority of the children imitated the action they had seen on screen, and many could also perform the manipulation 24 hours later (Meltzoff, 1988).

On the other hand, there is very limited evidence that children learn words from educational media like *Baby Einstein* DVDs. In a study, children from 4 to 23 months old watched as either an adult in real life or in a video presented unfamiliar objects while naming them. When the children were shown those objects along with a second, novel object and instructed to look at the objects using the words they were taught, the children who had learned the objects' names from the real-life adult looked at those objects longer. If they were taught the objects' name from the video, however, the children didn't look at the objects as long and actually looked at the incorrect distractor object longer (Krcmar, 2011). So this study didn't provide any evidence that children could learn from an educational video.

Similarly, researchers found that children between 1 and 2 years old didn't learn more words after multiple exposures to educational DVDs in their homes, and watching the DVDs also didn't have an effect on general language development. However, when parents watched the DVDs with the children and the parents either repeated the words highlighted on the DVD or drew their children's attention to the DVD, some children did appear to learn (Richert, Robb, Fender, & Wartella, 2010). So it seems that the context of viewing and the content of screen stories are key factors in whether children learn from what they watch (Christakis & Zimmerman, 2009). In particular, watching with an engaged adult who is willing to facilitate their interaction with the screen may help some very young children learn from educational screen stories (Heintz & Wartella, 2012).

One way or another, very young children learn the most when an adult is available to augment their engagement with the world. Synchronous social interactions between very young children and adults are vital for teaching children how to, among other things, interact with communication partners and convert negative emotions to positive or neutral emotions. In addition, successful interactions between adults and children can help children develop a sense of self-efficacy and a belief that their caregivers are trustworthy (Tronick, 1989). Thus, when parents can draw children's attention to the screen and repeat the information shown on a video, children are more likely to learn the educational content. In contrast, letting audible television or video play in the background at home decreases how much adults speak and how much children vocalize. This use of screen media can lead to delays in young children's language acquisition (Christakis et al., 2009). So, if TV and other screens become a barrier to interactions between children and their parents, it can negatively impact their development (Bronfenbrenner, 1986) Given the vital learning opportunities such interactions provide and the minimal learning opportunities offered by screen stories, substituting screen time for adult–child interactions results in diminishing educational returns for children.

Learning From Screen Stories After Age 2

After about 2 years old, the educational benefits of TV increase (Heintz & Wartella, 2012; Richert et al., 2011). As children develop cognitively, their ability to process information from television evolves as well. Further, at this point in their lives children have developed enough socially that their ideas about social interactions often transfer to their interactions with television as well.

It's this ability to interact with television socially that enables children to learn from it in the preschool and middle childhood years (Richert et al., 2011). For example, Sandra Calvert, the director of Georgetown University's Children's Digital Media Center, and her colleagues (Calvert, Strong, Jacobs, & Conger, 2007) found that when preschool-aged children interacted with the television show *Dora the Explorer* by responding physically and verbally to prompts by the characters, the children comprehended the story's content better than those who simply observed the content. Similarly, in another study, 3- to 5-year-old children who regularly viewed the program *Blue's Clues* talked to a character that the show encouraged them to help solve problems. Children reported that they believed they could help the character somewhere between a lot and a little, indicating that they became involved in solving the problems presented on the show (Anderson et al., 2000).

Children's programs whose characters mimic real-life social interactions by looking at the camera, asking direct questions, and pausing for responses create pseudosocial contexts that guide children, encourage their participation, and enhance their learning (Calvert et al., 2007; Richert et al., 2011). If you remember our discussion of parasocial interactions from earlier chapters, you'll notice that these shows use children's newly developed social skills to engage them in parasocial interactions with their characters and, as a result, give the children the opportunity to learn as they might from a real-life social partner. Not only do these parasocial interactions between the child and the TV characters enhance children's learning, they also increase children's comfort with and trust in the characters and the information they present on the show. This effectively leads children to form ongoing parasocial bonds with the characters that further enhance their desire to pay attention to, and learn from, the characters.

Children demonstrate greater mastery of the material presented in educational shows when they view them regularly and repeatedly. Repetitive viewing improves children's information acquisition as well as their cognitive skills, such as flexible thinking (Anderson et al., 2000; Calvert et al., 2007). For instance, in the *Blue's Clues* study, the researchers found that when preschool children viewed a single episode of the show five times over five days, their understanding of the show's content was greater, and in some cases, the children even applied the problem-solving strategies they learned on the show to real-world problems (Anderson et al., 2000). Repetitive viewing may increase the likelihood that children will form parasocial relationships with screen characters, enabling them to see the characters as socially relevant sources of trustworthy information and enhancing their ability to learn from these characters and apply what they've learned in their real lives (Richert et al., 2011).

From infancy people are hardwired to form social relationships. Once preschool-aged children acquire the cognitive skills needed to pay attention to and understand TV characters, shows that approximate real-life social contexts, including opportunities for children to respond and interact, and that provide socially relevant information, can have real educational benefits. By utilizing children's fundamental desire and ability to form social relationships, these screen stories can promote learning and cognitive development.

INCIDENTAL LEARNING

Another thing to keep in mind when it comes to learning from media is that children along with everyone else can experience incidental learning through these stories. Incidental learning happens when learning occurs that wasn't necessarily planned. There are entire books written about how parents make media decisions for children and sometimes children just happen to be in the room when adults are watching a television show or movie that wasn't necessarily intended for kids. In these cases, children may pick up on something parents or caregivers weren't intending because adults may underestimate the fact that children are always learning. Adults must constantly ask themselves what might my child learn about life from watching the Shopping Channel? The news? Or a film that presents ideas that are not yet appropriate?

Children may have trouble understanding content that is not meant for them. Exposure to these stories can lead to nightmares or waking worries because children are grappling with information that was too much for them developmentally. Even if children forget the source, such experiences can create associations or concerns that stay with them as they age.

On the positive side, sometimes we learn valuable lessons from unexpected sources. Even a comedic or seemingly silly story can give us an insight we remember for a long time. For example, on an episode of the sitcom *Superstore*, about employees of a big box store, it is revealed that

Jeff, a regional manager, is gay. Store manager Glenn expresses outrage because Jeff doesn't "look gay," explaining, "You're so blah!" Finally, Glenn decides that if Jeff is gay, "Anyone could be gay." A child watching this show, even amidst the laughs, might learn a valuable lesson about not judging books by their covers.

TWEENS, TEENS, AND STORIES

By the time children reach their tween (roughly the ages of 8 through 12) and teen years, their interest in the stories they can consume through media is even greater. As children grow older, they can make more and more choices about the stories they spend time with, tailoring their media diet to their personal preferences. As a result, the fictional stories they choose to read and watch are often even more powerful and meaningful to them, taking on greater importance during this time in their lives.

Media use increases throughout the tween and teen years. A 2015 Common Sense Media report found that tweens spend an average of almost 6 hours a day with media, and teens spend a whopping 9 hours a day, on average. Despite all the new media they use, both age groups still spend the largest amount of their media time watching TV, DVDs, and videos, with both groups spending around 2½ hours. Furthermore, as children become teenagers, their parents become less aware of their media usage. While 78% of tweens say their parents know a lot about the TV shows they watch, only 58% of teens say the same. And the difference in those percentages is even higher for online and social media activities. Over half of tweens saying their parents know a lot about what they do online and the social media they use, but less than a third of teenagers say the same.

As children grow up, they start to assert their autonomy. They spend more time alone in their rooms and with friends, and they become less attached to their parents and more attached to their peers, especially during the teen years. The characters tweens and teens encounter in stories can offer an additional outlet for their shifting attachments. For example, in one study, media psychologists David Giles and John Maltby (2004) showed that interest in celebrities and emotional autonomy increased with age in a group of participants ranging in age from 11 to 16 years old, while parental attachment decreased with age. In addition, high levels of attachment to peers predicted a positive attitude toward celebrities, but high levels of attachment to parents predicted a more negative attitude toward celebrities. Giles and Maltby (2004) concluded that celebrity attachments develop at the same time as peer attachments and that as parental attachments decrease throughout adolescence, media figures may replace some of the functions that parents fulfilled during their children's younger years. While this study is limited because the researchers didn't ask the participants to specifically name their favorite celebrity about whom they completed the study, it's reasonable to think that at least some of these celebrities might be actors who play fictional characters.

For those adolescents who consume fictional stories, then, the importance of the characters they enjoy and respect increases throughout these years. Due to this increasing importance and tweens' and teens' growing ability to make their own decisions about what they read and watch, psychologist Jeffrey Jenson Arnett (1995) points to several important functions stories and the media they're consumed through can play during adolescence. First, and most obviously, just as they can be for adults, media are a source of entertainment during leisure time.

Second, some stories, like action or horror movies, offer the kind of intense stimulation many crave during adolescence. Referred to by psychologists as "sensation seeking," people can be anywhere from low to high on this motivation, even as adults. But, in general, adults are less prone to sensation seeking than adolescents. The daily grind of school, afterschool activities, chores, and homework is often devoid of the extreme or fresh sensation many adolescents want. Stories can help fill that gap. For example, in a study by Garmon, Glover, and Vozzola (2018) of late adolescent and emerging adults found the desire to engage in intense stimulation influenced people to repeatedly read the books of the Twilight Saga.

Third, stories can be used to cope with the negative emotions brought on by the increased struggles and stresses many experience at home and school during the adolescent years. Something like watching TV can help tweens and teens distance themselves from their personal difficulties, a coping strategy that likely becomes more deliberate during the adolescent years (Larson, 1995). This can be seen in Garmon et al.' (2018) finding that the need to cope with and relieve negative emotions led participants to view the *Harry Potter* movies repeatedly.

Fourth, adolescents may consume stories to connect with their peer network. Stories often provide a common ground for people, and when tweens and teens watch and read the same stories it provides them with an automatic connection. In particular, some adolescent-targeted stories may be foreign to many adults. As a result, they offer a basis for adolescent-specific identification and connection. Further, stories can define and unite members of a given peer group. In Cynthia's (Vinney, 2011) research on *Buffy the Vampire Slayer* and *Twilight Saga* fans, many participants said that their fandom of these properties helped them meet and develop new friendships with other fans, or that they deepened their existing relationships by bonding with their peers over their fandom.

Finally, stories can be used to develop adolescents' identities. We discussed identity development, adolescence, and how stories help adolescents develop their identities in Chapter 6 of this volume, so if you skipped that chapter or need a refresher, take a look there.

These five uses of stories and media are not exclusive to adolescents, of course, but they may be especially important during this time in life. Because adolescents are independent enough, they are able to decide which stories best resonate with them and meet their individual needs from the many, many options available today. In making choices based on these five goals, different stories may give tweens and teens different ideas about the opportunities and options within their culture, and the various ways they might deal with new experiences or challenges they may encounter.

For parents who remain aware of their adolescents' media consumption, the stories their kids watch can provide a worthwhile platform for discussing issues tweens and teens must deal with as they grow up. For example, after Karen and her teenaged son, Jason, watched the film *Boyhood* together, Jason brought up a scene in which the teenaged main character smokes marijuana. This provided Karen with a good opportunity to talk about drugs with Jason. Because Jason brought up the topic, the conversation unfolded naturally, and Jason was able to take the lead by asking questions and expressing opinions. However parents can do it, talking to their kids in an authentic way about the stories tweens and teens take in can be valuable. Couching discussions this way can take some of the pressure off by centering the conversation on the story while still giving parents the ability to ask kids for their thoughts and to provide input.

The characters in the stories adolescents watch and read can also provide them with very different ideas about what their roles in the world should or could be. On the one hand, as adolescents spend less time with their parents, characters in fictional stories provide opportunities for pseudofriendships that can keep them company and provide a sense of belonging even when they're away from their peers. On the other hand, tweens and teens often look to these characters as role models. Characters can give them examples of how to handle their daily lives, what they should value and appreciate, and who they might want to become in the future. So, an adolescent who regularly watches *Riverdale* and looks to Archie and his pals as exemplars of how to be and what to value may develop a very different sense of what is meaningful in life and what roles he'd like to occupy than someone who enjoys bingeing on the small-town charms of the show *Everwood*. Media psychologists call the desire to be like and emulate the behavior of a fictional character "wishful identification." When a viewer or reader experiences wishful identification with a character, he looks to that character as a model of the qualities or characteristics he'd like to have. Often in identifying with a character as a role model, an individual will learn from that character by observing her actions and responses within her story. In his social cognitive theory, respected psychologist Albert Bandura (2001) characterizes people as active agents who, through observational learning, are able to adopt the behaviors, attitudes, and characteristics of those they admire, including media characters.

Observational learning relies on a sequence of four processes. First, attentional processes select the information that is observed. Next, through retention processes the observed information is committed to memory. Third, behavioral production processes recall and reconstruct the remembered observation so what was learned can be applied when an appropriate situation arises or can be modified to better fit the context. Finally, motivational processes determine whether or not an observed behavior is reproduced based on whether that behavior led to a good or bad outcome for the person who originally performed it (Bandura, 2001). So, if an adolescent experiences wishful identification with Elena on *The Vampire Diaries* and sees her confidently pursuing her desires in both her career and her love life, the individual can employ observational learning to emulate Elena's behavior. The adolescent would do this by observing how Elena asserts her needs, remembering what she did, noticing situations in his own life in which similar behavior can be performed and believing that he can effectively carry it out, and deciding he wants to deploy that behavior with the expectation of similar success.

The characters tweens and teens choose as role models hinge on their individual interests and preferences, as well as on their age and where they are developmentally. For example, research has repeatedly shown that people are more likely to experience wishful identification with same-sex screen role models with boys more likely to choose male role models, and girls being a bit more flexible in the gender of the role models they choose (Calvert, Strouse, & Murray, 2006; Hoffner, 1996; Zehnder & Calvert, 2004). This actually isn't too surprising if you think about it. Studies have shown that male characters are seen on-screen far more often than female characters. In a study of the top-grossing films of 2015, it was found that men were on screen twice as much as women and that even when a film had a female lead (which was only 17% of the time), men had about the same amount of screen time as women (Geena Davis Institute on Gender in Media, 2016). Girls don't grow up in a culture where they see themselves represented as often in screen stories, so they become more flexible in the characters they learn to identify with because they have to. Boys don't have a similar shortage of male characters, so they become much more used to having a same-sex character to identify with when they are watching screen stories. This becomes normal to them, and as a result, looking to male characters as role models becomes their default.

Yet, when selecting characters as role models, boys and girls often choose male and female characters who also have specific character traits. In a study of 7- to 12-year-old children by Cynthia Hoffner (1996), boys and girls experienced wishful identification with male TV characters they viewed as intelligent. On the other hand, the only trait that influenced wishful identification with female characters by girls was their physical attractiveness. Wishful identification was higher with characters that were considered caring, helpful, and less mean and selfish. Furthermore, two studies by Calvert and colleagues (Calvert et al., 2006; Zehnder & Calvert, 2004) showed that teens in mid- and late adolescence chose characters as role models that they felt had prosocial traits, including being compassionate, heroic, moral, honest, proud, thinking before they acted, and using their conscience as a guide. Interestingly, the mid-adolescents in one of the studies—who were around 15½ years old on average—were more likely to say the villain in the movie they were shown, Two Face in *Batman Forever*, was a role model, than the study's older participants—who were around 20 years old on average (Zehnder & Calvert. 2004). So, while people of all ages generally are drawn to characters with positive traits, age and developmental stage can also influence which characters some people gravitate toward. As people grow, what they value and appreciate changes, causing them to experience wishful identification with different characters at different points in their lives. However, media role models may be particularly salient during adolescence when people are figuring out who they are and what they can do to live the best version of their lives.

ADULTHOOD

While adulthood seems more static than the first 18 to 25 years of life (depending on who you ask), people grow and change during the adult years just like they do during childhood and adolescence. People go through a lot during adulthood. They develop their careers, get married and sometimes divorced, raise children, change careers, see their children leave the nest, retire, become grandparents, and many, many other things. As all this happens, people's relationships with stories, what they look for in them, and how they fit into their lives also evolves.

In his stage theory of lifespan development, Erik Erikson (1968) specified three stages during the adult years. They are aptly named young adulthood, adulthood, and old age. Erikson proposed that each of his stages revolves around a specific crisis that the individual must navigate to successfully move on to the next stage. In young adulthood, there is a crisis of intimacy in which one must develop true, mutual intimacy with another person. If this doesn't happen, it can result in isolation. The development of intimacy hinges on one's success at developing a sense of identity in adolescence, the previous stage of life. According to Erikson, if we can develop a genuine sense of who we are, this enables us to truly open ourselves up to someone else as young adults.

In adulthood, the crisis revolves around generativity, which means we contribute to and nurture the next generation. While Erikson primarily focused on generativity in the form of having and raising children, it also applies to the production of ideas, creative works, or anything else that can help guide others and contribute to future progress, even after one is gone. An individual who doesn't become a generative adult risks becoming stagnant, bored, and self-absorbed during mid-life.

Finally, in old age the goal is to attain integrity, which results from accepting one's life and finding a sense of meaning and order in all that one has experienced and attained, and all the significant relationships that were part of the journey. When one doesn't achieve integrity, it can lead to despair that comes from the knowledge that time is short, preventing the individual from fixing regrets and trying alternative life paths. Elderly people with integrity exhibit what we call wisdom, an understanding and acceptance of life that gives them a detached but mature perspective.

Pop culture fan researcher Gayle Stever (2011) has shown how story characters and celebrities can help people navigate through Erikson's stages. For example, in young adulthood, she found fans who had not yet found a real romantic relationship could turn to the fictional characters or celebrities they enjoyed via media to engage in vicarious romantic relationships. While this may sound odd, all the fans in Stever's research who did this were fully aware of it and had made a conscious choice to deal with their need for intimacy this way. Given the transient nature of modern life, where divorce and moving to new places where you don't know anyone are regular occurrences, these young adults' reliance on media and celebrities for intimacy they couldn't find otherwise actually makes a lot of sense. After all, these young adults are taking the tools available to them and using them to achieve intimacy they couldn't get in other ways. Stever discovered that her participants often felt intimacy with a celebrity they would never know in reality was preferable to the isolation they endured otherwise. And for some who had endured dysfunctional real-life relationships or suffered through the death of a spouse, this distanced intimacy was a plus, enabling them to feel safe, and ensuring their imagined partner couldn't leave or hurt them. So, given the isolation that can be a by-product of modern life, turning to stories and media for intimate parasocial relationships could be considered an adaptive way of coping.

During the stage of adulthood, middle-aged adult fans became involved in charity work inspired or sponsored by their favorite celebrities. This enabled these fans to participate in a generative activity that would make a positive difference in the world and contribute to the greater good. Although these fans became interested in a cause because a celebrity had championed it, they continued to participate in it because they liked helping others. For example, *Supernatural* fans may be aware that star Misha Collins, who plays the angel Castiel (check out Figure 7.2 to see him in action), started a nonprofit organization called Random Acts. Random Acts hosts events whose goal is to do social good each year. While fans may initially decide to participate because they hope to feel a connection with or even catch a glimpse of Collins, the positive experience of spreading kindness and warmth to others through these events could lead them to participate in future events, creating positive change and enabling middle-aged fans to achieve generativity through their love of Collins and

Figure 7.2 Misha Collins as the angel Castiel on *Supernatural*. In real life, Collins has parlayed his fame into charitable works by co-founding the organization Random Acts.

Castiel. So, stories, their characters, and the actors who play them can help people navigate through the ins and outs of adulthood.

Just like people at earlier life stages, adults may use media to answer some of their pressing life questions. For example, in the movie *Boyhood*, a mother played by Patricia Arquette confesses as her son leaves for college:

> You know what I'm realizing? My life is just going to go. Like that. This series of milestones. Getting married. Having kids. Getting divorced. The time that we thought you were dyslexic. When I taught you how to ride a bike. Getting divorced . . . again. Getting my master's degree. Finally getting the job I wanted. Sending Samantha off to college. Sending you off to college. You know what's next? Huh? It's my fucking funeral! . . . I just thought there would be more.

Similarly, in the TV show *Girls*, Loreen (Becky Ann Baker), mother of main character Hannah upon learning Hannah is pregnant with her first grandchild, gets high on marijuana gummies and laments, "Every time I look at your baby. I will see my own death."

Even though the *Boyhood* scene was poignant and sad and the *Girls* scene was played for laughs, both touch on real-life feelings many adults have when big life events happen, leading them to grapple with their own mortality and what their lives have added up to. For adults going through similar challenges, seeing their experiences reflected in a story can make them feel more understood and less lonely.

Adults' Changing Relationship With Stories

Although stories remain important throughout adulthood, the stories people choose to watch and read often evolve as people get older. Despite old age's reputation as a time of deprivation and loss, research has shown that emotional well-being actually improves with age. On the whole, older adults feel more positively about their lives than younger adults do. One explanation for this is social-emotional selectivity theory, which states that people have different emotional goals based on the amount of time they believe is left in their lives (Carstensen et al., 2011). Younger adults perceive themselves as having a great deal of time left and are therefore more willing to spend some of it on frivolous relationships and emotional experiences. Older adults, however, see their time as more limited and, consequently, are more deliberate about how they invest it. This means older adults spend their time engaged in things that have more emotional importance for them, including meaningful relationships and activities. Mares, Oliver, and Cantor (2008) used social-emotional selectivity theory to account for different story preferences at different points during adulthood. Their research has repeatedly shown that older adults prefer uplifting, positive, meaningful entertainment, while younger adults are more interested in experiencing negative emotions or consuming entertainment purely for enjoyment or to pass the time. For example, in a study that asked younger (aged 18–25), middle-aged (aged 26-49), and older (aged 50 and up) adults about their movie preferences, older adults were more interested than younger adults in watching heartwarming films. On the other hand, younger adults were more interested in watching films for fun or to alleviate boredom. In addition, all adults were interested in watching funny films, but younger adults were more interested in watching slapstick films than older adults. Furthermore, middle-aged and older adults said they had more interest in watching movies for fun or to alleviate boredom when they were teenagers than they did at their current ages.

In another study, Mares, Bartsch, and Bonus (2016) showed research participants movie trailers for stories with a great deal of gory violence. The movies were also either high in meaningfulness, like *Saving Private Ryan* or *Hotel Rwanda*, or low in meaningfulness, like *The Texas Chainsaw Massacre* and *The Hills Have Eyes*. While all the adults in the study were interested in the films that were high in meaning, older adults were less interested in films with low meaning. And like the previous study, great meaningfulness made older adults want to view a gory film more than it did middle-aged or younger adults. In other research Anne Bartsch (2012) found that a group of younger (aged 18–25) and a group of older (aged 50 and up) adults both said they wanted to have fun and share their emotional responses with others when they watched movies. However, the younger adults were more interested than the older adults in experiencing negative emotions like fear and sadness. Older adults were more interested in having socially and emotionally meaningful movie experiences.

When it came to preferences for television content, a set of studies by Mares and Sun (2010) found that older adults had a greater preference for TV news, but younger adults preferred sitcoms. Additional research showed that older adults (aged 55 and up) were more interested in watching sad and warm TV shows that they anticipated would be meaningful, while younger adults (aged 18–25) were more interested in watching sitcoms and scary TV shows. For all show genres, however, as age increased, anticipating that the story would be meaningful made a greater difference in viewing interest (Mares et al., 2016).

Older adults' preference for meaningful experiences with stories could be the result of older adults actually experiencing greater meaning than younger adults when they watch and view stories. When Hofer, Allemand,

and Martin (2014) showed study groups of younger (aged 18–28) and older (aged 62–87) adults a meaningful film, they found that older adults had more meaningful cinematic experiences than younger adults. More specifically, older adults, more than younger adults, connected with and related to the movies' characters, saw their values reflected in the events depicted in the story, were able to meet and master cognitive and emotional challenges presented by the story, felt good about their own lives in comparison to the trials and tribulations experienced by the story characters, and believed the story helped them feel that their lives had value and purpose. Older adults were also more likely to feel more poignant, mixed emotions in response to the film and to feel that their meaningful experiences with the film were quite positive.

Thus, older adults may be more likely to find meaning in their everyday lives, including when they're engaging with stories. They may even regulate their emotions so such meaningful experiences are even more likely. This helps older adults maintain a stable positive outlook and find more meaning in life as their time grows shorter. Although these studies show that younger adults are interested in a wide array of emotional experiences when they watch stories, this does not mean they aren't interested in meaningful entertainment experiences. These studies show that they are. Their interest is just not as exclusive as that of older adults. This falls in line with social-emotional selectivity theory. While younger adults have the time to take in and enjoy more frivolous entertainment experiences, as they become more aware of their pending mortality, older adults invest their time more deliberately to ensure that this limited resource is spent on things they truly value and find meaningful.

Stories as Anchors Throughout Adulthood

Older adults may seek more positive and meaningful story experiences as a general rule; however, adults who are long-term fans of a specific story like *Star Wars* or *Doctor Who* may find that the evolution of their relationship with their favorite story serves as a touchpoint throughout adulthood.

Harrington and Bielby (2010b) and Harrington, Bielby, and Bardo (2011) have argued that because traditional timetables for adopting adult roles no longer apply in Western societies, adults have turned to the stories of which they're fans as a way to find a source of stability in their lives. For example, in many cases, people no longer go through the stages of adulthood as Erikson (1968) outlined them. Instead people may take longer to commit to long-term romantic relationships, to have children, and to establish careers. They may change careers in middle age, have children at vastly different times in life, and marry and divorce numerous times. While the plethora of choices people have today leads to a great deal of flexibility during adulthood, it also increases uncertainty because there is no "normal" trajectory for adult life anymore. This means people can no longer refer to conventional expectations to guide their choices, give their lives value, or determine who they should be at various life stages. To fill the void left by this uncertainty, people use stories and other cultural objects, which have become increasingly available, as reference points throughout adulthood.

For long-term fans, favorite stories serve as emotional anchors throughout their lives. These stories create meaning and enable fans to evolve in conversation with their favorite story as the story's meaning for them changes as they grow and age. For example, Harrington and Bielby (2010a) surveyed long-term fans of soap operas, like *The Young and the Restless* and *General Hospital*, and found that being a fan of soap operas was frequently tied to family narratives because participants' mothers often introduced them to their favorites soaps when they were children. As a result, the stories told in the soap operas became the basis of shared family memories. Long-term soap fans looked to their favorite soap operas and the family memories they evoked to give their lives unity and continuity. This helped fans construct a coherent life story.

Long-term fans might also be able to track the shifts in their own lives based on their changing perceptions of stories. Cynthia (Vinney, 2011) found evidence of this in her study of long-term *Buffy the Vampire Slayer* fans. When she asked young adults about the characters they most identified with, participants said that they currently identified with the show's main character Buffy, but they said they previously had identified with Buffy's best friend and sidekick, Willow. Participants explained that they previously identified with Willow's struggles as a nerdy, shy high school student, qualities they felt were similar to their own challenges at that age. However, once these individuals graduated from high school and the show's characters left high school too, participants grew out of the qualities that led them to identify with Willow and no longer found her as relatable. Instead, as young adults, the participants identified with the heroic Buffy, particularly her challenges in meeting her responsibilities and fulfilling her obligations as the one chosen to defend the world against supernatural creatures. Metaphorically, the participants saw their own life struggles reflected in Buffy and could relate to the weight of the character's obligations and the loneliness they sometimes caused her. So, while these participants remained fans of the show, the characters they most identified with shifted as they entered a new stage of life with new challenges and difficulties.

Based on Cynthia's research, we would also suspect that for people who are fans of many stories throughout their lifetimes, their understanding of who they are in the present and who they were in the past could also be tied to these short-term fan involvements. Stories could mark a given point in one's life when the story was important to one's development at the time but is no longer pertinent to who one is now. In Cynthia's study (Vinney, 2011), she also talked to young adult fans of the *Twilight Saga*. Some said that although they had been fans of *Twilight* at one time, they no longer felt the same enthusiasm for the series they once did. One of the major reasons these fans cited for their dwindling fandom was that they felt they were getting older and, therefore, growing out of their interest in the story. For these fans, *Twilight* might serve as a reminder of a time in their life when they found meaning in a story about being the special high school girl that drew the romantic attentions of a sexy vampire. As young adults, however, the story no longer held the same allure for them, and these fans may have moved on to an appreciation of other stories that better reflected where they were in life.

Throughout our lives when we turn to stories we tend to see something of ourselves in them. Whether it's who we are now, who we used to be, who we aspire to be, the way we've evolved throughout our lives, or reminders of important relationships or events, stories can represent so much to us as individuals. As we choose the stories that matter to us throughout our lives, those stories can take on meaning beyond themselves. They can help us understand something fundamental about ourselves in the past, in the present, and even into the future. While all stories won't occupy this special place in our lives, those that do will remain meaningful and significant. In some cases, our association with these special stories can even help us overcome social ills, bigotry, and bias, something we'll discuss in the next chapter.

REFERENCES

American Academy of Pediatrics, Council on Communication and Media. (2016). Media and young minds. *Pediatrics, 138*(5), 1–6. https://doi.org/10.1542/peds.2016-2591

Anderson, D. R., Bryant, J., Wilder, A., Santomero, A., Williams, M., & Crawley, A. M. (2000). Researching *Blue's Clues*: Viewing behavior and impact. *Media Psychology, 2*(2), 179–194. https://doi.org/10.1207/S1532785XMEP0202_4

Arnett, J. J. (1995). Adolescents' use of media for self-socialization. *Journal of Youth and Adolescence, 24*(5), 519–533.

Bandura, A. (2001). Social cognitive theory of mass communication. *Media Psychology, 3*, 265–299.

Bartsch, A. (2012). As time goes by: What changes and what remains the same in entertainment experience over the life span? *Journal of Communication, 62*, 588–608. https://doi.org/10.1111/j.1460-2466.2012.01657.x

Bronfenbrenner, U. (1986). Ecology of the family as a context for human development: Research perspectives. *Developmental Psychology, 22*(6), 723–742. https://doi.org/10.1037/0012-1649.22.6.723

Calvert, S. L., Strong, B. L., Jacobs, E. L., & Conger, E. E. (2007). Interaction and participation for young Hispanic and Caucasian girls' and boys' learning of media content. *Media Psychology, 9*(2), 431–445. https://doi.org/10.1080/15213260701291379

Calvert, S. L., Strouse, G. A., & Murray, K. J. (2006). Empathy for adolescents' role model selection and learning of DVD content. *Journal of Applied Developmental Psychology, 27*, 444–455. https://doi.org/10.1016/j.appdev.2006.06.005

Cantor, J. (1994). Children's fright reactions to television and films. *Poetics, 23*, 75–89.

Cantor, J., & Sparks, G. G. (1984). Children's fear responses to mass media: Testing some Piagetian predictions. *Journal of Communication, 34*(2), 90–103.

Carstensen, L. L., Turan, B., Scheibe, S., Ram, N., Ersner-Hershfield, H., Samanez-Larkin, G. R., . . . Nesselroade, J. R. (2011). Emotional experience improves with age: Evidence based on over 10years of experience sampling. *Psychology and Aging, 26*(1), 21–33. https://doi.org/10.1037/a0021285

Christakis, D. A., Gilkerson, J., Richards, J. A., Zimmerman, F. J., Garrison, M. M., Xu, D., ... Yapanel, U. (2009). Audible television and decreased adult words, infant vocalizations, and conversational turns: A population-based study. *Archives of Pediatric & Adolescent Medicine, 163*(6), 554–558. https://doi.org/10.1001/archpediatrics.2009.61

Christakis, D. A., & Zimmerman, F. J. (2009). Young children and media: Limitations of current knowledge and future directions for research. *American Behavioral Scientist, 52*(8), 1177–1185. https://doi.org/10.1177/0002764209331540

Common Sense Media. (2015). The common sense census: Media use by tweens and teens. Retrieved from https://www.commonsensemedia.org/sites/default/files/uploads/research/census_researchreport.pdf

Crain, W. (2005). *Theories of development: Concepts and applications* (5th ed.). Upper Saddle River, NJ: Pearson Prentice Hall.

Erikson, E. H. (1968). *Identity: Youth and crisis.* New York, NY: W. W. Norton.

Garmon, L. C., Glover, R. J., & Vozzola, E. C. (2018). Self-perceived use of popular culture media franchises: Does gratification impact multiple exposures? *Psychology of Popular Media Culture, 7*(4), 572–588. http://dx.doi.org/10.1037/ppm0000153

Geena Davis Institute on Gender in Media. (2016). The reel truth: Women aren't seen or heard—An automated analysis of gender representation in popular films. Retrieved from https://seejane.org/wp-content/uploads/gdiq-reel-truth-women-arent-seen-or-heard-automated-analysis.pdf

Giles, D. (2010). *Psychology of the media.* New York, NY: Palgrave Macmillan.

Giles, D. C., & Maltby, J. (2004). The role of media figures in adolescent development: Relations between autonomy, attachment, and interest in celebrities. *Personality and Individual Differences, 36,* 813–822. https://doi.org/10.1016/S0191-8869(03)00154-5

Harrington, C. L., & Bielby, D. D. (2010a). Autobiographical reasoning in long-term fandom. *Transformative Works and Cultures, 5.* https://doi.org/10.3983/twc.2010.0209

Harrington, C. L., & Bielby, D. D. (2010b). A life course perspective on fandom. *International Journal of Cultural Studies, 13*(5), 429–450. https://doi.org/10.1177/1367877910372702

Harrington, C. L., Bielby, D. D., & Bardo, A. R. (2011). Life course transitions and the future of fandom. *International Journal of Cultural Studies, 14*(6), 567–590. https://doi.org/10.1177/1367877911419158

Heintz, K. E., & Wartella, E. A. (2012). Young children's learning from screen media. *Communication Research Trends, 31*(3), 22–29.

Hofer, M., Allemand, A., & Martin, M. (2014). Age differences in nonhedonic entertainment experiences. *Journal of Communication, 64,* 61–81. https://doi.org/10.1111/jcom.12074

Hoffner, C. (1996). Children's wishful identification and parasocial interaction with favorite television characters. *Journal of Broadcasting and Electronic Media, 40*(3), 389–402.

Hoffner, C., & Cantor, J. (1985). Developmental differences in responses to a television character's appearance and behavior. *Developmental Psychology, 21*(6), 1065–1074.

Krcmar, M. (2011). Word learning in very young children from infant-directed DVDs. *Journal of Communication, 61*, 780–794. https://doi.org/10.1111/j.1460-2466.2011.01561.x

Larson, R. (1995). Secrets in the bedroom: Adolescents' private use of media. *Journal of Youth and Adolescence, 24*(5), 535–550.

Lewis, C. S. (2009). *The lion, the witch, and the wardrobe.* New York, NY: Harper. (Original work published 1950)

Mares, M.-L., Bartsch, A., & Bonus, J. A. (2016). When meaning matters more: Media preferences across the adult life span. *Psychology and Aging, 31*(5), 513–531. https://doi.org/10.1037/pag0000098

Mares, M.-L., Oliver, M. B., & Cantor, J. (2008). Age differences in adults' emotional motivations for exposure to films. *Media Psychology, 11*, 488–511. https://doi.org/10.1080/15213260802492026

Mares, M.-L., & Sun, Y. (2010). The multiple meanings of age for television content preferences. *Human Communication Research, 36*, 372–396. https://doi.org/10.1111/j.1468-2958.2010.01380.x

Meltzoff, A. N. (1988). Imitation of televised models by infants. *Child Development, 59*(5), 1221–1229.

Ninio, A., & Bruner, J. (1978). The achievement and antecedents of labeling. *Journal of Child Language, 5*(1), 1–15.

Pierroutsakos, S. L., & Troseth, G. I. (2003). Video verité: Infants' manual investigation of objects on video. *Infant Behavior and Development, 26*, 183–199. https://doi.org/10.1016/S0163-6383(03)00016-X

Richert, R. A., Robb, M. B, Fender, J. G., & Wartella, E. (2010). Word learning from baby videos. *Archives of Pediatric & Adolescent Medicine, 164*(5), 432–437.

Richert, R. A., Robb, M. B., & Smith, E. I. (2011). Media as social partners: The social nature of young children's learning from screen media. *Child Development, 82*(1), 82–95. https://doi.org/10.1111/j.1467-8624.2010.01542.x

Rideout, V. (2017). The Common Sense census: Media use by kids age zero to eight. *Common Sense Media.* Retrieved from https://www.commonsensemedia.org/sites/default/files/uploads/research/csm_zerotoeight_fullreport_release_2.pdf

Sparks, G. G., & Cantor, J. (1986). Developmental differences in fright responses to a television program depicting a character transformation. *Journal of Broadcasting & Electronic Media, 30*(3), 309–323.

Stever, G. S. (2011). Fan behavior and lifespan development theory: Explaining parasocial and social attachment to celebrities. *Journal of Adult Development, 18*, 1–7. https://doi.org/10.1007/s10804-010-9100-0

Tamis-LeMonda, C. S., & Song, L. (2012). Parent-infant communicative interactions in cultural context. In E. M. Lerner, M. A. Easterbrooks, & J. Mistry (Eds.), *Handbook of psychology.* Vol. 6, *Developmental psychology* (2nd ed., pp. 288–342). Hoboken, NJ: John Wiley.

Tronick, E. Z. (1989). Emotions and emotional communication in infants. *American Psychologist, 44*(2), 112–119. https://doi.org/10.1037/0003-066X.44.2.112

Troseth, G. L. (2003). Getting a clear picture: Young children's understanding of a televised image. *Developmental Science, 6*(3), 247–253

Valkenburg, P. M., & Cantor, J. (2000). Children's likes and dislikes in entertainment programs. In D. Zillmann & P. Vorderer (Eds.), *Media entertainment: The psychology of its appeal* (pp. 135–152). New York, NY: Routledge.

Vinney, C. (2011). *High stakes:* The Twilight Saga, Buffy the Vampire Slayer, *and the development of identity in adolescence and beyond.* (Unpublished master's capstone paper). Fielding Graduate University, Santa Barbara, CA.

Woolley, J. D. (1997). Thinking about fantasy: Are children fundamentally different thinkers and believers from adults? *Child Development, 68*(6), 991–1011.

Zehnder, S. M., & Calvert, S. L. (2004). Between the hero and the shadow: Developmental differences in adolescents' perceptions and understanding of mythic themes in film. *Journal of Communication Inquiry, 28*(2), 122–137. http://doi.org/10.1177/0196859903261797

8

On Prejudice and Values

> Dear white people, our skin color is not a weapon. You don't have to be afraid of it.
> —Samantha White (Logan Browning)
> *Dear White People* (Season 1, Episode 6)

We have been telling stories about race, gender, religion, sexual orientation, and a myriad of other social categories for as long as stories have existed. Research has documented that we've told a lot of stereotypical stories over the years. The late, noteworthy communication scholar George Gerbner documented how people in prime-time TV were disproportionately white males in the prime of life, while women, especially women of color, were overrepresented as victims of violence. Gerbner published most of his work between the 1960s and early 2000s and is perhaps best known as the originator of cultivation theory, which describes how exposure to television over time can influence viewers to adopt the values embedded in the shows they watch (e.g., Gerbner, 1999). While the theory has typically been used to explain how people learn negative things from TV, it can also encompass how TV can pass on positive ideas, including tolerance and altruism, if there are shows available to convey those values.

Stacy Smith, who currently leads the Inclusion Initiative for the University of Southern California Annenberg School of Communication, and her team release yearly reports about the representation of marginalized social groups in popular films. The last report (Smith, Choueiti, & Pieper, 2017) revealed that in the top 100 films of 2016, only about 31% of speaking characters were female, only 14 of the films had lead characters from underrepresented racial groups, and only 1.1% of film characters were lesbian, gay, or bisexual. In short, there continues to be a lot of disappointing news about who we include in our fictional stories. This is problematic because when we don't see a diverse array of people represented in movies and TV, or we don't see them represented in anything other than stereotypical ways, our impression of people "like that" becomes woefully narrow.

Fortunately, there is some good news—especially when it comes to diversity on television. In recent years popular and acclaimed TV shows like *Dear White People*, *Black-ish*, and *Fresh Off the Boat* have included discussions of race from various nonmajority perspectives. There has also been progress with the representation of other social categories. For instance, shows like *Orange is the New Black* and *Pose* have included strong roles for female leads, including women of color, as well as depictions of transgender characters. There are many additional examples of increasing diversity in TV we could mention, but here are a few: *Grace and Frankie, Empire, Speechless,* and *How to Get Away With Murder*.

There are even some positive signs that film is becoming more inclusive. Recent movies that have seen critical, awards, and popular success include *Get Out, The Big Sick, Call Me by Your Name, Black Panther, Coco, Moonlight,* and *Crazy Rich Asians*. As of this writing, *Black Panther* surpassed $700 million at the U.S. box office ("2018 Domestic Grosses," 2018). And *Forbes* (Mendelson, 2018) reported that, adjusting for inflation, as of the summer of 2018 *Black Panther* was the 12th highest-grossing film of all time worldwide. The film also had the fifth-largest opening weekend of all time and the largest opening weekend ever for a Black director (Ryan Coogler; Khal, 2018).

In addition, after numerous protests of whitewashing, including over the casting of Scarlett Johansson in *Ghost in the Shell* and Tilda Swinton in *Doctor Strange* in roles that were originally conceived as Asian, actor Ed Skrein exited the movie *Hellboy* after learning the role in which he was cast is depicted as half-Japanese in the comic books (Stack, 2017). Furthermore, *Star Wars: The Last Jedi, Beauty and the Beast*, and *Wonder Woman* were the top three movies at the North American box office in 2017 and were all driven by female characters (Barnes, 2017).

Whether you're a fan of these particular movies and shows or not, it's important for people who've been on the receiving end of discrimination and prejudice to see their stories told on screen. For example, given is status as a major motion picture with a predominantly Black cast, *Black Panther* was a watershed moment for African Americans audiences and moviegoers of all kinds. We were inspired to seize the opportunity to study the reactions of young people of color to the film, especially Black youth (González-Velázquez, Dill-Shackleford, Keller, Vinney, & Drake, 2020). Working with a racially diverse sample of high achieving high school students, we measured several relevant factors before and after these participants watched the film. First, we wanted to see if a finding from the past still existed—that, for African Americans, a stronger racial identity predicted greater well-being. We found that same relationship existed in our sample. Furthermore, a stronger racial identity before watching the film predicted greater well-being after watching it for Black students. Furthermore, there was high identification with the character T'Challa/Black Panther for the participants in general, regardless of the race of the student. Interestingly, on average, identification with T'Challa was higher for Whites than for Blacks, although it should be noted that Blacks were the largest racial group in this sample, outnumbering Whites by 4 to 1. In general, having a greater number of participants means that the numbers are more likely to match the numbers in the larger population.

While it's invaluable for people who have been underrepresented on screen to finally see their stories told, it's also important for those who aren't in these groups to see people who aren't like themselves represented. After all, if watching stereotypical depictions of people from various groups leaves us with a narrow impression of them, watching stories in which underrepresented people share who they are in all their nuanced, human glory gives viewers the opportunity to get to know, appreciate, and sympathize with them. For those who may not have much interaction with people unlike themselves, this can be a powerful force for increasing understanding and reducing prejudice.

For example, the Netflix series *Grace and Frankie*, starring Jane Fonda and Lily Tomlin in the titular roles, explores issues of sexuality and aging, among other things. One of the most enjoyable storylines on the show happens when Grace and Frankie decide to start a company that sells vibrators designed for older women. Aging has often been portrayed in very stereotypical and negative ways by the media, but *Grace and Frankie* uses humor to bust some myths. More broadly, it explores liking and loving in a multigenerational, multiethnic, multireligious, nontraditional extended family. This is something you don't see every day, but hopefully we'll be seeing more of as entertainment like this is successful. Figure 8.1 shows a billboard featuring Grace and Frankie.

We begin this chapter by focusing on how we can reduce prejudice using stories. If stories can be persuasive, telling better stories can help us change minds. And there is research to back up this assertion. In the second half of this chapter, we'll revisit the subject of actors and roles in terms of what happens when the real-life actions of an actor don't match the roles for which they're known. We'll examine what happens when a celebrity you love does something you hate.

USING STORY TO REDUCE PREJUDICE

Given the plethora of issues it can pack into a single story, fiction is a very efficient purveyor of critical conversations. Writers create relationships, situations, and dialogue to draw people in. And when the story is meaningful and relevant enough, viewers and readers think about the ideas brought up in the story in ways that don't happen often enough in our everyday lives. Good writers, directors, and actors work together to show

Figure 8.1 Jane Fonda and Lily Tomlin as Grace and Frankie (Netflix Original Series). Grace and Frankie, both in their 70s, start a business selling vibrators designed for older women. Shown here is a billboard in LA bringing the show to the attention of Emmy voters.

us what's important and why. When we engage with a great story we may adopt the feelings and ideas it champions as our own, rather than feeling like these messages were forced on us like some kind of medicine. Call it a manipulation if you will, but the ideas of a story still must be filtered through our personal beliefs and values. Engaging with stories can introduce us to new ideas and perspectives that we may never have encountered on our own, making us more informed and more open in the process.

If a friend invited you to have a critical conversation about race at the local public library on a Friday night, would you want to go? Some would, but it might feel a bit like meeting an obligation or perhaps entering a battlefield. But if a friend invited you to watch a great movie, which ended up saying something deeply meaningful about race, would you be glad you watched it? After the movie, you'd probably feel a sense of fulfillment and satisfaction. We think in story, and we search for meaning in stories. Some things, many things, feel like eating our vegetables if delivered in the form of a lecture but feel pertinent and important when delivered via story.

In Chapter 1 of this volume, we mentioned a study that found that people who watch more complex dramas help people improve their theory of mind abilities, which enables them to more easily but themselves in the shoes of others and, consequently, helps them develop greater empathy (Black & Barnes, 2015). Also, as we mentioned in Chapter 4, fiction can be more persuasive than nonfiction because when we're transported into a story, we're less likely to question or argue against it, leaving us more likely to believe ideas that are consistent with those in the story (Green & Brock, 2000). These findings can help people use fiction to break down prejudice. There are other methods as well.

Consider a set of studies conducted in Europe by Vezzali, Stathi, Giovannini, Capozza, and Trifiletti (2014) in a research paper called "The Greatest Magic of *Harry Potter*," which we touched on in Chapter 2 of this volume. These scientists noted that the Harry Potter books are the best-selling book series of all time, giving rise to the films, the lands in amusement parks, and many other highly popular outlets. Prejudice and discrimination are recurring themes throughout the franchise. Integral to the story is the central conflict between the "pure blood" wizards and the "mudbloods," those with mixed "muggle" (nonwizarding people) and wizard ancestry. Those on the dark side favor the pure bloods, those on the light side favor equality.

> We've talked a lot about parasocial relationships with characters and our love of stories can help us in our everyday lives. And we're no exception to this rule. For example, on a regular basis, when Karen's faced with a situation where she's feeling pressured by someone to do something that doesn't feel right to her, she flashes to the scene from *Harry Potter and the Sorcerer's Stone* (or *Philosopher's Stone* for you Brits) where Harry has just arrived at Hogwarts to find out what house he's going to belong to. Quickly, if you haven't read the books, "house" basically means the kids will be sorted into four groups based on their personalities and values. Gryffindors are brave. Ravenclaws are bright. Hufflepuffs are sweet. Slytherins are snakelike. (Side note: You can take a quiz to see what house you are in on J. K. Rowling's website, Pottermore, which is dedicated to all things Harry Potter. Cynthia and her husband discovered they are both Ravenclaws. Clearly, their relationship is meant to be.)

At the top of the stairs, Harry, known to be a famous wizard, is greeted by Draco Malfoy, veins full of Slytherin blood:

"You'll soon find out some wizarding families are much better than others, Potter. You don't want to go making friends with the wrong sort. I can help you there."

He held out his hand to shake Harry's, but Harry didn't take it.

"I think I can tell who the wrong sort are for myself, thanks," he said coolly."

Throughout the books, there are these pivotal moments where a person must decide to embrace her own values despite the consequences, which range from social awkwardness to death. These scenes are beloved by many. If you want to see how many, do a Google search on Harry's line ("I think I can tell who the wrong sort are for myself, thanks"). Fans have lovingly turned the quote into art and used it in memes. It means a lot to a lot of people. One of the hardest parts about sticking to your guns is facing each scary moment. But it's always worth it. This scene reminds Karen of that. She brings it to mind over and over again. Figure 8.2 shows the warm relationship between Harry Potter and his friends Ron, and Hermione.

Figure 8.2 The enormous popularity of the Harry Potter books and movies relates to the timeless insights the stories offer about things we value, from the importance of authentic relationships, to the value of treating people with kindness and equality.

Before we tell you more about the research, here is a bit more Harry Potter magic you should know to understand the research. If you're a fan, then this is a chance to think about one of your favorite things (brilliant!).

Background: Harry Potter is raised by an aunt and uncle who loathe him following the murder of his parents by an arch-villain, the wizard Voldemort (aka "He who must not be named"). Harry learns that he is a wizard when Hagrid, the groundskeeper from Hogwarts School of Witchcraft and Wizardry, comes to recruit him for the school on his 11th birthday. Harry goes to Hogwarts to train as a wizard, meeting his two best friends, Hermione Granger and Ron Weasley, in the process. He is also antagonized by a pint-sized bully, Draco Malfoy. Harry is our hero. Voldemort is our villain. They are fated to fight an epic battle that only one can survive. (For you *Star Wars* fans, remember from Chapter 5 of this volume that Harry is Luke Skywalker; Voldemort is Darth Vader. Harry is the hero with a thousand faces.) Okay, that's enough to set the story in context. Now, back to our scientific discoveries, already in progress.

Vezzali et al. (2014) believed they could use the Harry Potter books to teach children and youth to value of equality and less prejudicial viewpoints. They began in an elementary school in Italy where, over six sessions, an adult read passages from *Harry Potter* and discussed them with the children. The children either read and discussed passages related to prejudice or passages unrelated to prejudice. For example, one of the prejudice-related passages is a scene from *Harry Potter and the Chamber of Secrets* where Draco Malfoy calls Hermione Granger "a filthy little mudblood." Hermione is ashamed and humiliated, while Harry and Ron are irate. One of the nonprejudice-related passages is where Harry buys his first magic wand (ah, good times!). The researchers factored the amount of *Harry Potter* exposure each child had prior to the study into their analysis. They also gave the kids a brief plot summary to make sure everyone understood the passages they read.

What the researchers found was that reading and discussing the prejudice-related content with an adult improved the children's attitudes toward immigrants, but only for the children who highly identified with

Harry Potter. What does this tell us? The scholars believe that the reason they got these results can be explained social cognitive theory. You may have run into this theory and the studies it's based on, such as Albert Bandura's Bobo doll experiments, if you've taken a psychology course. In these studies, children watched adults beat up an inflatable doll (the Bobo doll). These doll-abusing adults were then either rewarded and encouraged for their aggressive behavior or were discouraged from acting aggressively. Results showed that kids who watched this whole thing on closed-circuit TV were more likely to imitate the adults' aggressive behavior if the adult they watched was rewarded for attacking the doll.

Well, Albert Bandura is one of the most famous psychologists in the history of modern psychology, and Bandura's social cognitive theory is an interesting bridge between the behaviorists who said everything was a response to a stimulus and the cognitive psychologists who said thinking is where it's at. (Nerd fact: Bandura is a social cognitive behaviorist. Nerds, go out and impress your dates!) According to social cognitive theory, if we see another person try a behavior (aggression) and get a response (social reward), we'll make the simple calculation that "If I do that, I'll get rewarded too." Or, "I'm gonna punch that doll, and people will think it's cool" (thought bubble over the head of a little boy in a daycare somewhere as we speak). In other words, Bandura demonstrated that kids may imitate violence if they see it on TV. Using the same basic principle, our colleagues in Italy (Vezzali et al., 2014) demonstrated that kids can learn that being prejudiced is uncool from reading about it in a book.

In a second study, our intrepid researchers headed to a high school classroom in northern Italy where they asked teens how many Harry Potter books they'd read and films they'd watched. They also measured the participants' identification with Voldemort and with Harry Potter. Here "identification" was measured by rating the truth of the following statements: "I wish I could be more similar to Harry/Voldemort"; "Harry/Voldemort represents the type of person I'd like to be"; and "I often think of how it would be to be like Harry/Voldemort." (We're thinking that a person should give their daughter's potential dates the "I wish I could be like Voldemort" questions before they're allowed to take their daughter out, with the understanding that the potential date gets blackballed if they endorse any of those Voldemort items.) The results of the study showed that teens who wanted to be like Harry Potter and who had read more Harry Potter books were less prejudiced against LGBTQ persons than teens who'd read fewer Harry Potter books and/or who identified more with Voldemort. Naturally, we don't know, if reading *Harry Potter* or identifying with Harry Potter caused the positive attitudes toward LGBTQ persons. But we do know that it caused the changes in the elementary school kids, thanks to the research design of that study. Either way, we can come away from this second study knowing this: If kids read *Harry Potter*, they are less likely to harbor prejudice based on sexual orientation.

In a third and final study, the research team went to England to study university students. This time they investigated attitudes toward refugees, a timely topic if there ever was one. The college kids thought they were taking part in two studies, one on their media habits and another on their views on refugees. The researchers asked the students if they felt they could take the perspective of refugees and what their general attitudes were about them. They discovered that the students who were less identified with Voldemort and had read more Harry Potter books found it easier to take the refugees' perspective. This perspective-taking ability was associated with more positive attitudes toward refugees.

This set of studies is important. In people from elementary school to college, from Italy or England, reading and watching *Harry Potter* is associated with a reduction in prejudice toward immigrants, LGBTQ persons, and refugees. Further, the studies used different research designs, some showing cause and effect and some showing naturally occurring relationships. In science, we can generalize our findings to similar others, so these studies give us a lot of power to generalize—in others words, to say that this seems to be a robust set of findings that should also apply to people more generally.

Something that's quite significant here are the groups who benefited from reduced prejudice among *Harry Potter* readers and viewers: immigrants, LGBTQ persons, and refugees. Reduced prejudice toward LGBTQ persons in *Harry Potter* readers indicates that even if the story itself is about race or ethnicity, the lessons it teaches about tolerance can transfer to other groups—in this case, sexual orientation. Immigrants and refugees are usually distinguished by race and ethnicity, so increased tolerance of these groups represents a more direct transfer of values. If characters model the value that a mixed or different ancestry does not make a person inferior, it doesn't matter that the story was fiction. As fiction authors know, thinking about "mudbloods" and "purebloods" in the context of a fictional story makes the message of the value of tolerance easier to digest. It helps us think about the underlying value—discriminating based on race or ethnicity—without thinking about the particular players in real-world politics. It takes away some of our resistance, like the shame we might feel for the mistakes of our own ancestors, which can result in cognitive dissonance and lead to victim blaming. Nobody has a dog in the fictional fight (well, there's Fluffy) when it comes to muggles, mudbloods, and dark wizards, which leaves readers and viewers more open to the messages championed by the story.

What does this mean? Most of us, if we're honest, don't feel especially enthusiastic about the prospect of, say, reading a book or watching a documentary on racial prejudice, even if we feel passionately about the subject. This is because of the many negative feelings this kind of experience can bring up. For those who feel empathy, the topic of racial prejudice can lead to guilt, shame, a desire for avoidance and, for those who want to retain the status quo, the desire to remain in power and to feel "better than" someone else. But fictional stories can set aside these threats to our self-concept and put us in a more receptive state.

Here's another study that demonstrates the power of story to break down prejudice. Cameron, Rutland, Brown, and Douch (2006) went into elementary schools in England. This time, they brought with them storybooks to read to the children. For half of the children, the stories showed English children being friends with refugee children; the other half didn't read stories containing this theme. The study's results showed that the children who read about people like themselves having friendships with refugee children had more positive attitudes about real-life refugees than the other children. One important caveat: the stories of English children with refugee friends only improved children's attitudes if the children had a specific attitude about how people are related to each other. Researchers call this important attitude "inclusion of self in others." Cameron et al. defined inclusion of self in others this way: "within the context of close relationships individuals spontaneously perceive and overlap in concepts of the self and the other" (p. 1209).

Here is the same idea described in different ways. First, let's take it from the scientific to the poetic:

> In a real sense all life is inter-related. All men are caught in an inescapable network of mutuality, tied in a single garment of destiny. Whatever affects one directly, affects all indirectly. I can never be what I ought to be until you are what you ought to be, and you can never be what you ought to be until I am what I ought to be. . . . This is the inter-related structure of reality.
> —Martin Luther King Jr., Letters from a Birmingham Jail

And now let's hear from the world of pop music:

> There's a little bit of something me
> In everything in you
> "If You're Gone," Matchbox Twenty

Harry Potter and kids' books are far from the only sources in the world of fiction that promote this self-in-other framework that scientists have found to be so beneficial in reducing prejudice. We can think of several stories that fit this mold. These stories take the tactic of recategorization theory (Dovidio et al., 1997) to redraw the boundary between "us" and "them" and instead put everyone in the same group: "us" (Brewer, 1979; Tajfel & Turner, 1979). Because people are invested in the groups that they're a part of, recategorizing people into the same group with us is valuable because we are biased in favor of ourselves and the people in our groups. The latter are usually people we perceive to be like us: people who go to our church, who look like us (i.e., race), dress like us (i.e., socioeconomic status), talk like us (i.e., education), etc. As we mentioned in Chapter 5 of this volume, we want to survive and reproduce, to preserve our genes. We implicitly believe that people who look like us share some of our genes (Tajfel & Turner, 1979).

Heck, this attitude of giving to our own and depriving others is so ingrained that scientists have found we act this way even if the groups we find ourselves in aren't based on anything meaningful. In a classic study, Brewer (1979) constructed what she called "minimal groups," groups basically formed at random. Let's say we tell you we're going to form two groups, Group A and Group B, simply by drawing numbers out of a hat. We tell you that your group is Group A, and then we ask you to say who you like and who you'll give resources to. Do you know what happens? If you guessed we say we like people in "our group" more, and we allocate more resources to "our group," you're correct. This goes back to our discussion in Chapter 6 of this volume of William James's idea that our sense of self extends to other things, including brands, objects, TV shows, and even random groups of people who are unrelated to us, but who are labeled as "mine."

We bet you can think of any number of storylines that use this approach to remind us we're on the same team. Take, for example, movies where aliens attempt to take over planet Earth. At the beginning of these films, people have their differences. Then, when the aliens attack, the characters realize they have to work together to survive and, hopefully, to save the planet and/or take out the aliens. One classic in this genre is H.G. Wells's *War of the Worlds*, which was adapted by Orson Welles's Mercury Theater into a radio show that blurred the lines between fantasy and reality. When it was originally broadcast, the people of planet Earth weren't used to "fake news" or the tropes of mockumentaries. If a newscaster said it, they believed it. When the radio announcer on *War of the Worlds* revealed that Martians were attacking the planet, many thought it was a real newscast. Mass hysteria ensued.

The story has also been adapted several times subsequently. There was a 1953 film version of *War of the Worlds* featuring "Gene Barry . . . as Dr. Clayton Forrester, an improbably hunky scientist who is enjoying a fishing trip outside the fictional town of Linda Rosa when a meteorite falls from the sky" ("10 Great Films About Aliens," 2016, ¶5). And the most recent version of the story was directed by Steven Spielberg and starred Tom Cruise. In addition, *Independence Day* is a retelling of *War of the Worlds*, and *Mars Attacks!* is a parody of the storyline. Clearly, we enjoy "us" against "them" stories where the us is all of humanity.

We also enjoy twists on this theme. For example, in the 2004 Syfy (originally Sci Fi) channel series *Battlestar Galactica* there are people and there are Cylons. In the 1970s series of the same name, the Cylons were depicted as robot servants. In the 2004 series, the Cylons, colloquially called skinjobs, have evolved into complex cybernetic organisms who look just like humans and can therefore hide among them. After the Cylons kill off a large hunk of humanity, the remaining humans take to space in search of Earth, which they refer to as the 13th colony. Part of the show's central mystery is discovering which human characters are actually Cylons.

As we know, a person's belief that there is part of them in the "other" and part of the "other" in them can be a crucial factor in reducing prejudice. One of the underlying questions on *Battlestar Galactica* is whether people can accept Cylons as part of human society. Since the skinjobs look and act like we do, it begs the question: What makes the skinjobs so different from "real humans"? If the us-in-them philosophy can reduce prejudice so that humans can accept Cylons as part of their group (or as players for the same team, to use the language of recategorization theory), then perhaps they can stop killing each other and live together in peace.

Again, this science fiction story enables us to grapple with our own prejudices, but from a safer distance. If the show had been a documentary set in modern times and the two groups who struggled against each other were Whites and non-Whites, there would be more psychological baggage standing in the way of changing minds. A show like that could be useful, don't get us wrong. But the fact that *Battlestar Galactica* is fiction, set in a different time and place, and that the groups struggling against each other are also fictional, has advantages if the goal is prejudice reduction.

Furthermore, not only has *Battlestar Galactica* been a story world since the 1970s, it has been the subject of multiple television shows. After the popularity of the 2004 series, the prequel *Caprica* was launched. What we want to highlight is that fans have had time to live with these characters and story worlds. A fan may have grown up with a *Battlestar Galactica* lunchbox and a desire to be Starbuck. Then she might have watched the 2004 series and *Caprica* in adulthood. This series, like many other long-time fan favorites, lends itself to the deeper questions in life. As described, it's a great vehicle for considering prejudice. It also touches upon the meaning of religions and gods, what the most important things in life are when you are pushed to your limits, how different groups of people have different values and perspectives, and what the ethical implications of technological advancements are, to name a few. Its complex, meaningful storytelling is one of the reasons the show is beloved. So, while it may seem like *Battlestar Galactica* fans like us are just amusing nerds, we are also amusing nerds who love a story that poses the big questions. For us, this show can be used to ponder our own questions. We'll think of it when we think about things that matter in real life, such as the injustice of the quest to exterminate a race of people.

This is a big deal: We look to important stories to uncover nontrivial issues, from the *Grapes of Wrath* to *Battlestar Galactica*. And these are stories that are revisited and revisited and revisited. For example, *The Grapes of Wrath* is not only a classic work of literary fiction, but also one of the great films in American cinema and a play that is staged year after year. A great story is important to retell. If one story, like *The Grapes of Wrath* or *Our Town* or *The Glass Menagerie* is retold because many people get something out of it, then imagine what fans can get out of a continuing story that is played out over many years. Our connections with serialized story worlds that continue to add chapters and installments to them give us opportunities that a one-time story does not. To be clear, we aren't weighing in on whether *The Grapes of Wrath* or *Battlestar Galactica* is more important. It's not a contest. You don't have to give up one or the other. The pivotal question is how the psychology differs when you have an ongoing, changing, multipart story world versus a "one-off."

Obviously, people are attracted to franchises with multiple ongoing stories, just as producers of media are attracted to selling ongoing stories. Go to the mystery section of your local bookstore and you won't so much see one-off novels, but series. We all know that the same is true for movies. We tend to favor franchises, especially these days. And, like we say, part of that is because they are good business for those who sell them. But as they also offer opportunities for fans of these series to further take in and hone their understanding of the values they espouse. The longer a franchise has been around, the more situations you've seen the characters navigate, the more potential for growth and variability in the main characters. These richly developed experiences and settings become part of a reader's or viewer's network of thoughts, feelings, beliefs, and behaviors.

For example, one of the recent Marvel Cinematic Universe movies, *Captain America: Civil War* explored the timely issue of whether superheroes require oversight to minimize issues or whether superheroes should operate independently and as they see fit. (This is not the first time we've heard this story, nor will it be the last. The same description could apply to the X-men series, among others.) Characters fans have come to know and love end up on opposite sides of the argument and (because this is a superhero movie) must fight it out in fantastic, special effects–laden fashion. But ultimately, the story provides a platform for a bigger discussion that is relevant to our current world where police body cameras, privacy, and justice are important topics. For long-time fans, this clash between superheroes enables them to see the issue from multiple perspectives. Something that may not have been possible without fans' multifilm history with these characters. In the process, fans are given an opportunity to consider how they feel about these issues and whether the values of order and law are more important than the ability to fight for the little guy by whatever means necessary.

ON PREJUDICES AND VALUES ON AND OFF THE SCREEN

We live in turbulent political times where race, gender, and sexual orientation are still hotly debated issues. Lately, sexual harassment in Hollywood has risen to the forefront of American consciousness. On one level, these are cases of powerful people taking advantage of their positions, something that (sadly) happens in every industry. On another, it highlights an issue we discussed at length in Chapter 3 of this chapter: the relationship between Hollywood personalities and the roles they play.

In Chapter 3 of this volume, we talked about how the psychology of social perception applies to actors, in other words, how we understand who a person is when they "act" as more than one person. These ideas also apply to how we make sense of beloved stars who have sexually harassed or abused others.

One of the biggest cases in this category is that of actor and comedian Bill Cosby, who has been accused by roughly 50 women of drugging and sexually assaulting them. According to Cosby's accusers, these attacks happened over a period of decades (Esteban & Roi-Franzia, 2016). At the time of this writing, Cosby has been convicted of multiple counts of aggravated, indecent assault. In the summer of 2018, he was ruled by a Pennsylvania state board to be "a sexually violent predator" (Hurdle, 2018).

How have fans coped with these accusations about Bill Cosby? Well, this is a situation that really highlights how we decide what type of person someone is. Most of us know something about Bill Cosby's public persona. He's been part of the pop culture landscape for decades, first starring in *I Spy* with Robert Culp in the 1960s and then creating the animated *Fat Albert and the Cosby Kids* in the 1970s. Cosby's stand-up routine often centered on his family life, his wife Camille, and his kids. Fans will remember his well-known routine where Cosby stays home with the kids while Camille goes out, which features the kids singing, "Dad is great. He gives us the chocolate cake."

Then, in the 1980s, there was *The Cosby Show*. On the sitcom, Cosby played Heathcliff "Cliff" Huxtable, a successful doctor married to an attorney played by Felicia Rashad. *The Cosby Show* represented a watershed moment in American culture because it centered on the stable family life of a well-off Black family and was highly popular with audiences across racial boundaries.

Cosby himself, in addition to his appearances in TV and film roles, was outspoken about race relations. In the 1990s, he wrote a number of nonfiction bestsellers with titles like "Fatherhood" and "Love and Marriage." His persona, which he maintained for decades, was that of the wise father and family man—a reputation he nurtured and maintained based on the way he came across in his acting roles and public appearances.

In this context, how do fans separate out Bill Cosby, the man, from Bill Cosby, the actor, comedian, and public persona? Think about the ways Cosby and his roles intermingled. For example, one of Cosby's most famous stand-up routines is called *Bill Cosby: Himself*. In addition, the first sitcom he created and starred in during the late 1960s and early1970s was called *The Bill Cosby Show*. And, although he played Cliff Huxtable, a fictional character, on *The Cosby Show*, by titling the cultural phenomenon with his real name, not the character's name, Cliff Huxtable and Bill Cosby became even harder to separate.

If we confuse the actor and the role, in this case it seems we have every reason to do so. Bill Cosby chose to use his name to brand his work. And his stand-up comedy—where he played some version of himself—made its way seamlessly into his acting—where he theoretically played fictional characters. Given all this, it's no wonder we often believed Cosby was Cliff Huxtable, and vice versa.

So, what do we do when the persona of the wise, funny, family man is called into question when that man is accused of serious sexual violations. Again, our job is not to pick a side or assign guilt but to talk about the psychology of how fans are likely to respond to this evolving story.

What happens to you psychologically as you attempt to decide how to feel about Cosby in the wake of the accusations? Odds are that prior to these revelations of sexual misconduct you had a very positive view of Bill Cosby. This is based on a number of things: Cosby is a "funny man"; his shows featured heart-warming, relatable stories; he has traditionally been seen as a force for good; and he earned respect for being a trailblazer in American culture.

Assuming this positive perspective as your starting point, what happens when you hear allegations against Cosby in the news? The things he is accused of doing, some of which he was convicted for, are considered wrong, even repulsive. And they are highly illegal, even if you don't find them unsavory.

Now you have two thoughts in your mind to contend with, which are probably something like these:

1. I like Bill Cosby.
2. There are many accusations that Bill Cosby did terrible things over a period of decades, some of which he was judged guilty of in a court of law.

These two thoughts create cognitive dissonance, which happens when two ideas clash because they are in direct conflict with each other. When we feel cognitive dissonance, we are motivated to get rid of our discomfort by changing one of the conflicting thoughts or using strategies to minimize the situation. Here is how these dissonance reduction strategies (ways to alleviate our suffering) might look like in this case.

1. Change the first thought: "I don't like Bill Cosby anymore."
2, Change the second thought: "Bill Cosby did not do what he's accused of."
3, Minimize the severity of the problem: "It's not as bad as it sounds."
4, Add soothing thoughts: "Oh, all great men do bad things once in a while. Overall, the world is still better with them than without them."

Here is one perspective on Cosby that we find particularly pertinent, given that it comes from a prominent African American comedian, Dave Chappelle. In his stand-up routine *The Age of Spin*, Chappelle (2017) reviews the ups and downs in Bill Cosby's public life. Chappelle talks about several of Cosby's accomplishments, calling them, "No small thing." According to Chappelle, "Bill Cosby has a valuable legacy that I can't just throw away." For example, he notes that Cosby "is directly responsible for thousands of Black kids going to college." His conclusion about Cosby is as follows: "He rapes, but he saves. He saves more than he rapes, but he probably does rape."

Although stand-up comedians are known for being raw, some may find the rawness of those statements offensive. For our purposes, Chappelle's blunt words are useful because they sidestep the dissonance problem. During the period of his accusation, multiple polls reported that more Americans believed that Cosby was guilty than either not guilty or innocent until proven guilty. According to a Rasmussen poll, since the scandal became public, two thirds of Americans had an unfavorable view of Cosby (Coren, 2015). In this context, Chappelle's observations are simply matter-of-fact statements designed to boil down the situation to the basics with minimal distractions from psychological coping mechanisms—namely, that Cosby is likely guilty but that he's also done a lot of good throughout his life. As Chappelle shows, both of these statements can be true, although for most of us, it's hard to feel comfortable giving both statements equal weight.

Getting Comfortable With Contradiction

There are a number of other psychological reasons for the confusion we feel when a public person we love is accused of doing something we hate. As a rule, people have a hard time with contradictions. We prefer to make categorical judgments: right or wrong, good or bad. This too goes back to our survival mechanisms. Remember how we are wired to make assessments at an alarmingly quick speed? When we meet someone for the first time, we make several automatic judgments about the kind of person they are. One of those judgments is simply if they're good or bad. That's because, in uncontrolled circumstances, social interactions can mean life or death, leaving no time for philosophical debate or careful consideration. We need to know if we can trust someone, and we need to know *now*! The speed of these judgments makes them largely unconscious.

For example, give us your immediate gut reaction to this situation: You need a babysitter for your 11-year-old daughter. You hire one online. But when the bell rings, you open the door and see that the sitter they sent is none other than Bill Cosby. Do you let him in?

There are undoubtedly some who would say "Yes," but we're betting that for most people the answer would be a big, fat "No." Even though Cosby has never been accused of hurting a child, when you think of Bill Cosby now, your first reaction is likely to be that he is not to be trusted, period. Do you really want to risk it with someone as valuable and vulnerable as your child?

Another relevant factor is that we prefer simplicity if we can get it. We want to categorize people in an absolute way. To use some jargon, we're often low on an attribute called "tolerance for ambiguity." Many of us hate the answer, "it depends" or "sort of." We want to know who's bad, who's guilty, who's responsible. It alleviates some of our discomfort. It's reassuring to know there is a simple explanation for things.

At this point, we think we can find some truth in fiction to apply to our desire to categorize people as simply bad or good. Let's turn for answers to that venerable sleuth, one of the most beloved detectives in American TV history, Lieutenant Columbo. In "Try and Catch Me," a Season 7 episode of his namesake show, Columbo (Peter Falk) is on the trail of a famous mystery-writer-turned-murderess, Abigail Mitchell (Ruth Gordon). The detective has occasion to make a speech about his work, and he takes the time to explain how he makes sense of the murderers he's known over the years:

> Even with some of the murderers that I meet, I even like them, too. Sometimes. Like them and even respect them. Not for what they did, certainly not for that. But for that part of them which is intelligent or funny or just nice. Because there's niceness in everyone, a little bit, anyhow. You can take a cop's word for it.
>
> *Columbo*, "Try and Catch Me," Season 7, Episode 1

This sentiment rings true for many of us. Although we may not have any experience being a detective or dealing with murderers, we all have experience trying to understand how good people do bad things, ourselves likely included. This is a good example of a situation in which the fiction we watch or read contains a thread of truth. As we've discussed, the character's words did not come from nowhere; they came from real people. The writers infuse their work with their own experiences and beliefs, as well as their creativity and research. And perhaps the director and actors add their own spin on what appears in the script as well. For instance, sometimes actors contribute lines that make their way into shows. And everyone else involved from previsualization artists to fans have a role in the way a fictional idea can be integrated into a viewer's real life. That's precisely what we mean by our title, *Finding Truth in Fiction*. Fiction is created and interpreted by real people. Fiction is not a synonym for untruth; in fact, it can be a powerful vehicle for shining a light on ideas we wouldn't otherwise consider or understand.

Let's move to a different case where a public figure was accused of sexual misconduct with women—that of comedian Louis C.K. Fans have come to known Louis C.K. for his stand-up and for his roles in television and movies. He often comes off as a sad-sack middle-aged male in both his comedy routines and many of his acting roles. For instance, in the sitcom *Parks and Recreation* Louis played a cop with a crush on the main character, lovable public servant Leslie Knope, played by actress and comedian Amy Poehler (Dipold & Waliner, 2009 as shown in Figure 8.3).

On the show, Louis C.K. comes off as lovable, sweet, and kind to women. When we encounter him in his various roles, we go through that important human process of sizing up another person and deciding who they are based on the information we see. His performance as a harmless, approachable guy in *Parks and Rec* may lead us to believe, as viewers, that that's who he really is. If we watch one of his stand-up routines, which features a lot of self-deprecating humor and musings about the absurdity of life, we might get a slightly different picture of who he is. In his act, he often admits to insecurities, double-standards, and dark desires. While he comes off as someone trying to be better, his routine also makes it clear he

Figure 8.3 Comedians Louis C.K. and Amy Pohehler in *Parks and Recreation*. Sexual harassment scandals involving comedians and actors have fans asking themselves who the person is and how we should feel about them in light of their misconduct.

may not always be successful. He comes across as nice and approachable but also as someone who has demons and a dark side. Again, and especially because he writes his stand-up routine and he talks about what we believe is his real life during it, we are likely to believe that because this is the person he appears to be, this is who he is.

Now, in this instance. once a number of sexual harassment accusations by female comedians came to light, Louis C.K. publicly confirmed they were true. So, we don't have to wonder whether he did what he was accused of. Knowing these accusations are true makes his appearance on *Parks and Rec* take on a different air, making him seem less sweet and more sinister as Leslie Knope's suitor. At the same time, it confirms the darkness that seemed to be lurking in his stand-up, showing that perhaps his demons were more malignant than fans, who previously enjoyed laughing at his comedic admissions, had believed. This is hard. But one positive aspect of this case is that when a perpetrator admits he is wrong, it can ease some of the burden on the victims. Unfortunately, for the fans it can still be difficult to grapple with how to reframe their understanding of someone they previously loved.

In a monologue on her Hulu talk show, *I Love You, America*, Sarah Silverman, a friend of Louis C.K.'s, summed up the conflicting feelings we may have in this situation. She says,

> I love Louis. But Louis did these things. Both of those statements are true. So I just keep asking myself: can you still love someone who did bad things? . . . So I hope it's okay if I am at once very angry for the women he wronged and the culture that enabled it, and also sad, because he's my friend.

While Silverman acknowledges that it is the victims who matter and that anyone who acts as Louis C.K. did should be held accountable. Too often, when a perpetrator is beloved, we want to exonerate him. Because of this, we throw the victims under the bus. We don't know them, so it hurts us less to believe that if something did happen, it was their fault. We may even get some satisfaction out of the victim blaming. We get to maintain our belief that the world is a fair place—known as "belief in a just world"—and we get to feel comforted that any sexism in the system is kind of a good thing, or at least not so bad—known as "system justification." This is another way for us to ease our mental stress. We psychologically pass on the pain, deflecting what we feel and forcing it onto the victims. Of course, in these circumstances, our motives are selfish, but we may not allow ourselves to see that, at least not until the costs to us are too great—for instance, if we find out that someone we love is the victim of this perpetrator or someone like him.

All of this is a lot to deal with. Some of you may find this information exceedingly frustrating, which makes you feel bad. Others may appreciate knowing that all people have difficulty dealing with contradictions and uncertainty—it's not just you. The allegations of sexual misconduct in Hollywood and beyond have garnered passionate public attention. These stories have incited arguments and negative feelings in people around the world. Why you feel what you feel is one thing. But our main point here is that you feel something—and that something is important to you. If, for example, while thinking of Bill Cosby or Louis C.K. (or Kevin Spacey or Harvey Weinstein or Matt Lauer or—[sigh]) you feel genuine pangs of suffering, regret, or even anger, these are legitimate feelings. It hurts to see these men fall from grace and to believe that our belief in them may have been betrayed.

This is what happens when life throws a big, stinking contradiction in our faces, and the contradiction is about a person we love. Life says, "You know that person you love? He is very good. And he is very bad." We hate this. It throws us into a tizzy of cognitive dissonance. We feel motivated to do something, to change something. Our equation is out of balance, and we want to put it right.

The way we feel about an actor, a character, or another public figure in this scenario is exactly the same as we feel about a person we know. Seeing them through a screen doesn't change anything. Not really. One way we can make sense of these troubling situations is to accept the blunt reality and use it to grow. If we take this tactic, one thing we might conclude from these public conversations about these figures who disappoint us is this: Good and bad exist in the same space. They're not mutually exclusive. Maybe that's one of life's truths.

And that brings us right back around to the place where we started—the idea that fiction is valuable because it helps us discover truths. While our truth and your truth aren't always the same, what we have in common is that when we find truth in fiction, we know it. We know that the story helped us understand something important. From there, it's up to each of us to decide what to do with that knowledge. We wish you many moments of insight and delight. And, please remember, the story may not be real, but you are.

REFERENCES

10 great films about aliens visiting Earth. (2016, November 4). *BFI*. Retrieved from http://www.bfi.org.uk/news-opinion/news-bfi/lists/10-great-films-about-aliens-visiting-earth

2018 domestic grosses. (2018). *Box Office Mojo*. Retrieved from https://www.boxofficemojo.com/yearly/chart/?yr=2018&p=.htm

Barnes, B. (2017, December 31). "Last Jedi" is 2017's box office winner in a female led year. *The New York Times*. Retrieved from https://www.nytimes.com/2017/12/31/movies/last-jedi-2017-box-office-winner.html

Black, J., & Barnes, J. L. (2015). Fiction and social cognition: The effect of viewing award-winning television dramas on theory of mind. *Psychology of Aesthetics, Creativity, and the Arts, 9*(4), 423–429. https://doi.org/10.1037/aca0000031

Brewer, M. B. (1979). In-group bias in the minimal intergroup situation: A cognitive-motivational analysis. *Psychological Bulletin, 86*, 307–324.

Cameron, L., Rutland, A., Brown, R., & Douch, R. (2006). Changing children's intergroup attitudes toward refugees: Testing different models of extended contact. *Child Development, 77*(5), 1208–1219. https://doi.org/10.1111/j.1467-8624.2006.00929.x

Coren, C. (2015, July 22). Poll: 66 percent of American have unfavorable view of Cosby. *NewsMax*. Retrieved from https://www.newsmax.com/US/Bill-Cosby-poll-americans-unfavorable/2015/07/22/id/658429/

Dill-Shackleford, K. E., Drake, L. M., Gonzalez-Velazquez, C., Vinney, C., & Keller, L. (2018, October). *Evidence from a sample of youth of color that the film BLACK PANTHER can effect youth well-being and empowerment via increased ethnic identity*. Paper presented at the 2nd Digital Media and Developing Minds National Congress, Cold Spring Harbor Laboratory, Long Island, NY.

Dipold, K. (Writer), & Woliner, J. (Director). (October 1, 2009). Beauty Pageant. [Television series episode] In P. P. Daniels, G. & Schur, M. (Producers), *Parks and Recreation*. New York: NBC.

Dovidio, J. F., Gaertner, S. L., Validzic, A., Matoka, K., Johnson, B., & Frazier, S. (1997). Extending the benefits of recategorization: evaluations, self-disclosure, and helping. *Journal of Experimental Social Psychology, 33*(4), 401–420. https://doi.org/10.1006/jesp.1997.1327

Esteban, C., & Roig-Franzia, M. (2016, May 23). Bill Cosby's accusers now number 58. Here's who they are. *The Washington Post*. Retrieved from https://www.washingtonpost.com/graphics/lifestyle/bill-cosby-women-accusers/

Gerbner, G. (1999). The stories we tell. *Peace Review, 11*(1), 9–17.

Green, M. C., & Brock, T. C. (2000). The role of transportation in the persuasiveness of public narratives. *Journal of Personality and Social Psychology, 79*(5), 701–721. https://doi.org/10.1037/0022-3514.79.5.701

González-Velázquez, C. A., Dill-Shackleford, K. E., Keller, L. N., Vinney, C., & Drake, L. M. (2020). *Watching Black Panther with racially-diverse youth: Relationships between film viewing, ethnicity, ethnic identity, empowerment and wellbeing*. Manuscript submitted for publication.

Hurdle, J. (2018, July 25). State board labels Cosby sexually violent predator. *New York Times*, p. 4

Khal. (2018, March). Every record *Black Panther* has broken (so far). *Complex: Pop Culture*. Retrieved from https://www.complex.com/pop-culture/2018/03/every-record-black-panther-has-broken/

Mendelson, S. (2018, March 26). "Black Panther" broke more box office records as it topped "Avengers." *Forbes*. Retrieved from https://www.forbes.com/sites/

scottmendelson/2018/03/26/black-panther-more-box-office-milestones-as-soars-past-the-avengers/#3b699e1d61d3

Most now think Cosby likely to be guilty. (2016, May 26). *Ramussen' Reports.* http://www.rasmussenreports.com/public_content/lifestyle/people/may_2016/most_now_think_cosby_likely_to_be_guilty

Smith, S. L., Choueiti, M., & Pieper, K. (2017). Comprehensive Annenberg report on diversity in entertainment. *USC Annenberg.* Retrieved from http://annenberg.usc.edu/sites/default/files/Dr_Stacy_L_Smith-Inequality_in_900_Popular_Films.pdf

Stack, L. (2017, August 28). Ed Skrein, facing criticism, backs out of playing Asian character in "Hellboy." *The New York Times.* Retrieved from https://www.nytimes.com/2017/08/28/arts/ed-skrein-hellboy-whitewashing.html?_r=0

Tajfel, H., & Turner, J. C. (1979). An integrative theory of intergroup conflict. In W. G. Austin & S. Worchel (Eds.), *The social psychology of intergroup relations* (pp. 33–48). Monterey, CA: Brooks/Cole.

Vezzali, L., Stathi, S., Giovannini, D., Capozza, D., & Trifiletti, E. (2014). The greatest magic of Harry Potter: Reducing prejudice. *Journal of Applied Social Psychology, 45*(2), 105–121. https://doi.org/10.1111/jasp.12279

What do you think? (n.d.) *MSNBC.* Retrieved from http://www.msnbc.com/msnbc/poll-where-do-you-stand-bill-cosby#55409

Epilogue

Coping, Well-Being, and the Future of Fiction

> Stories are important, the monster said. They can be more important than anything. If they carry the truth.
> —Patrick Ness (2011) *A Monster Calls*

At this moment in history, we humans spend an immense amount of our time gazing into screens. As we watch stories on screens, our faces aglow in their light, our attention is often rapt, and our minds active, as the stories spark emotions and ideas in us. What happens in those stories can mean a great deal to us, and to those around us.

What every person on this planet has in common is the human experience: We're born, we learn, we grow, we age, we pass away. We share the same basic motives: We want to survive, to be healthy, to thrive. Our connections with others matter deeply to us. Most of us want to find a productive way to spend our days; to figure out how to lead happy, meaningful lives; and to understand something about what it all adds up to in the end. Through it all is stories.

From the holy texts of the world's religions to mythology and fairy tales to our modern novels, films, and television shows, all of these stories provide ways for us to consider our shared lives and how each of us as individuals can make the best life possible. Fans of popular media love their favorite books, movies, and shows because they are another incarnation of the timeless tales that are integral to our human understanding and survival.

Stories inspire us and even help us. The heroes of our favorite stories may be the figures of the great religious texts like Moses, Jesus, or Mohammed; they may be historical individuals like Mother Theresa, Aristotle, Cleopatra, or Gandhi; they may be the gods of mythology like Odin, Osiris, Apollo, or Diana; they may be the characters that currently ignite our cultural imagination like Luke Skywalker, Daenerys Targaryen, Gandalf, or Wonder Woman. As we discussed earlier, these are the heroes with a thousand faces, each making the hero's journey. And as we've noted, introducing young children to stories by reading to them is one of the most valuable things a parent or caregiver can do. We believe stories are an irreplaceable part of our existence. We would never mock a child for reading *Aesop's Fables* or *A Wrinkle in Time*. Given all the benefits we've discussed, we hope it's clear adults can get great value out of engaging with *This Is Us* or *The Godfather* as well.

The research we've covered throughout this book has shown how important stories can be to the human experience. When we take in a movie, television show, or book, it sparks our own memories, beliefs, perspectives, and feelings, causing some stories to resonate in a highly personal way. Our thoughts and emotions are what make stories come alive, and stories help us make sense of our lives, grapple with our struggles and, ultimately, figure out who we are.

STORIES THAT HELP US COPE, LIVE WELL, AND GROW

We've considered the many ways stories can enhance and improve our lives, but the research on this topic is still in the early stages. More and more, however, media researchers are starting to study the many positive ways stories can impact us, and they're uncovering some exciting results.

For example, recent research has started to examine how stories help us cope with our difficulties. In one study, by Elise Stevens and Francesca Dillman Carpentier (2017), participants were asked to choose a category of movie trailers to watch from four possible options: a happy category including films like *Toy Story 3*, *Superbad*, and *The Avengers*; a tender category with films like *The Vow*, *The Odd Life of Timothy Green*, and *P.S. I Love You*; an intense category including films like *The Departed*, *The Hurt Locker*, and *Black Swan*; and a serious category including films like *Seven Pounds*, *Rendition*, and *Blue Valentine*. The participants then viewed trailers from the category they chose for as long as they wanted. The study results indicated that participants chose the category that best worked with their mood and their particular style of coping. So, people who had an avoidant style of coping—meaning they tried to avoid and repress their problems—and were feeling negatively were most likely to choose the happy category. This allowed them to distract themselves from their negative mood, forget their troubles, and perhaps even improve their mood by watching happy, positive stories. On the other hand, people with an avoidant coping style who were in a positive mood were more likely to choose movies from the other three categories. In this case, people didn't need to protect themselves from their troubles because they were already feeling good, so they could handle engaging with more negative or challenging content.

In contrast, participants with an active style of coping—meaning they proactively tackle their problems to deal with and solve them—and who were in a positive mood, were a bit more likely to choose trailers from the happy category. Meanwhile, active copers who were feeling negatively were more likely to choose trailers from the other categories. These people didn't want to distract from their problems, so instead of choosing movies that would help them forget or change their mood, they chose trailers that matched their moods.

We each have different ways of dealing with our challenges. The stories that can help us deal with our issues the best vary based on our particular style of coping. So, the next time you hear someone in a miserable mood watched a comedy and wonder why they would ever bother, or that someone in a great mood watched a depressing, challenging, movie and wonder why they'd want to ruin their mood like that, you'll know it's because they're finding stories that will help them cope in the way that best fits with their personal coping style.

While we've talked a lot about the various ways fiction can improve our lives, we've focused on the emotional, cognitive, social, and behavioral effects of our consumption of stories. That's because for the most part, media psychology research focuses on these areas and doesn't pay as much attention to the physiological effects of engaging with fiction. But some research is beginning to look at this. In one study, media scholar Robin Nabi and her colleagues (Nabi, Prestin, & So, 2016) explored whether media consumption had any relationship to the hormone cortisol. Cortisol is produced when people experience stress. When stress continues over a long period of time, people's cortisol levels get higher, which can contribute to all sorts of health issues including cancer, heart disease, and poorer functioning of the immune system.

Study participants completed a survey about their media diets including how frequently they used different kinds of media and what genres they liked to watch. They also gave their perceptions of their stress levels. A couple days later, samples of their saliva were collected so the researchers could evaluate it for cortisol levels. The results of the study showed that women, but not men, who viewed more TV had lower cortisol levels and that playing more video games was associated with higher cortisol levels for both genders. Interestingly, while most of the genres the researchers asked about, including comedy, drama, and sports, didn't seem to have a relationship to cortisol levels, women who consumed more romantic stories had higher cortisol levels, while men had lower cortisol levels if they consumed more romantic stories.

These findings suggest that it may not be the content but the simple act of consuming content that impacts our stress levels. In fact, if you're a woman, watching television, although perhaps not romantic stories, might actually be good for your health, decreasing your stress and consequently decreasing your odds of some of the negative health consequences associated with increased levels of cortisol. The results also show that playing video games in general might not be good for anyone's stress level, although guys who want to reduce their physiological markers of stress might want to watch more romantic stories. Of course, the researchers also found that cortisol levels were not related to participants' perceptions of their stress levels, meaning people are not aware of their physiological stress on a conscious level. But this study may provide some good rules of thumb for the best media to relax with to decrease your cortisol levels.

In another study, Robin Dunbar and colleagues (Dunbar et al., 2016) explored whether consuming an emotionally intense TV movie, in comparison to two television documentaries, increased people's pain thresholds and their feelings of bonding with the group with whom they'd watched the film. Participants completed a survey about how much they felt they belonged in a group with the other film viewers and also were timed in how long they could hold a wall-sit pose where they held an unsupported seated position with their back against a wall.

The wall-sit test sounds pretty strange, of course. What could holding a painful position have to do with watching a TV movie? Well, this is one of the weird things researchers will do to measure things that are otherwise difficult to assess. The researchers in this study were interested in whether one of the reasons we enjoy sad or intense stories is because they activate our endorphin system, a part of our brain's system for pain management that is responsible for increasing the pleasure we feel. The thing is, the same part of the brain that manages psychological pain, like responding emotionally to sad movies, is also responsible for physical pain, like that created by a wall-sit. If the emotional arousal of a sad movie activates our endorphin system, it should also increase our ability to withstand physical pain. In addition, endorphins are important to social bonding, and when they're activated, our feelings of bonding with those around us are also enhanced. While it may seem strange, the researchers had a good reason for asking participants to do what they did.

The findings of the study showed that the people who watched the emotional movie were able to hold the wall-sit pose for longer and felt more bonded with their fellow movie-watchers after the movie ended than they had before it started. The documentary watchers, in contrast, did not increase their threshold for pain during the wall-sit and did not feel more bonded with the other documentary-watchers. Since people's personal preferences play a role in their emotional responses to stories, there were some people who watched the emotionally arousing movie that weren't moved by it. Like the people who watched the documentaries, these individuals didn't hold the wall-sit longer or feel more bonded with their fellow movie-watchers. Based on this study, it would seem that if an emotional film resonates with people, it may activate their endorphin system, increasing their pleasure, decreasing their pain, and, ultimately, heightening their feelings of belonging and bonding with the people around them, even if they don't know them. These findings indicate that one of the best ways to bond and feel like you belong with others is to experience emotionally meaningful stories together.

As we've mentioned, we've also conducted research about how stories help us cope and improve our well-being. Through our research we've found that being a fan of a popular culture story is associated with greater well-being (Vinney, Dill-Shackleford, Plante, & Bartsch, 2019) and that personally resonant stories help people cope with their personal struggles (Vinney & Hopper-Losenicky, 2017). While more research needs to happen about the numerous ways meaningful experiences with stories can enhance our health and well-being, given the numerous lists and stories online about what fans have learned and how their favorite stories have positively impacted them, it seems that, anecdotally at least, many of us have experienced the benefits of immersing ourselves in the stories we love.

For example, during a panel for the TV show *Orphan Black* at San Diego Comic-Con a few years ago, a fan got up and thanked the cast for how watching the show with her mother not only helped the fan come out of the closet and accept her sexual identity, but also helped her mother accept her daughter for who she was as well (Bianco, 2014). Similarly, in an essay, a fan of *Star Trek: Voyager* wrote about how seeing a female captain who was also a scientist was revolutionary for her as a young girl. Captain Janeway was a successful TV character she could relate to, and seeing Captain Janeway be successful made her believe she could be, too (Trendacosta, 2015). Further, the character Drax (shown in Figure E.1)

Epilogue

Figure E.1 The character Drax in *Guardian of the Galaxy, Volume 2* has inspired people on the autism spectrum by showing someone like them can be an accepted member of a group of heroes.

from the *Guardians of the Galaxy* films has inspired the autistic community since the series first premiered, because Drax's lack of ability to edit the thoughts that come out of his mouth and inability to grasp metaphors is very relatable to those on the autism spectrum. It is never explicitly stated that Drax is autistic, but for those on the spectrum, these movies give them a chance to see themselves on screen as an accepted member of a group of ragtag heroes where his differences aren't as important as who he is and what he can contribute (Rothman, 2017). Something similar can be said about Sheldon Cooper from the *Big Bang Theory*.

Stories like these abound online on websites, blogs, and social media, so clearly many people believe and acknowledge that stories can help them in important and meaningful ways. Although many people have their own stories about how a favorite film, TV show, or book impacted their lives, media research is still catching up. This is an exciting subject that we plan to continue to pursue. And we're happy that other media researchers are starting to look at the positive and inspiring sides of our association with stories, too.

STORIES THAT HELP US HEAL

In Chapter 1 of this volume we discussed how stories give us an opportunity to make sense of our emotions and experiences because we can confront them through a story without the anxiety that might accompany such challenges in real life. Some therapists have been using the power of stories to help people in a clinical setting. Bibliotherapy and cinema therapy offer methods to incorporate stories into therapy. They involve assigning either a book, poem, film, or other written or audio/visual material to a client to read or watch. Then, during therapy sessions, the therapist and client can use the story as a means for discussing the client's mental health issues. Whether the story is about superheroes, vampires, or hobbits, these techniques help people explore their issues indirectly, enabling them to displace their issues onto the story and use it as a means for addressing things that might be too threatening to confront directly (Sharp, Smith, & Cole, 2002). Bibliotherapy and cinema therapy have been found to be fairly effective forms of therapeutic treatment (Marrs, 1995).

For some people, reading a book or watching a movie can lead to self-improvement and healing even without the assistance of a therapist. People who are fans of specific popular media and become emotionally and cognitively involved with their favorite stories may be especially likely to have these experiences. If fans decide to engage in fan activities and interact with other fans, they may improve their ability to overcome challenges and obstacles in their lives even more. For example, popular culture fan researchers Lynn Zubernis and Katherine Larsen (2012) provide a provocative perspective on the power of fanfiction and fan communities to help people grow and heal. As many readers will know, fanfiction are stories fans write that use the characters, settings, relationships, and other aspects of one or more pieces of fiction, such as popular TV shows and movies, to tell new stories. These stories are often shared with other fans through online archives dedicated to fanfiction and other fan-created works. Other fans can read, comment on, and like fanfiction stories. In the process, they create a supportive and accepting fan community.

Zubernis and Larsen (2012) propose that fanfiction writers "are using the familiar characters with whom they identify to play out whatever the writers (and readers) want and need to express" (p. 100) and that this process can be therapeutic. Their assertion is based on research by psychologist James Pennebaker and his colleagues that shows that writing about emotional, stressful, or traumatic experiences improves physical and mental health (e.g., Pennebaker, 1997; Pennebaker & Graybeal, 2001). Zubernis and Larsen propose that similar benefits can come from writing fanfiction because it offers an outlet for fans to displace their emotional or traumatic experiences onto the fictional characters and scenarios about which they choose to write. Through this kind of creative expression, fanfiction writers can move from trauma participants to observers, and can redefine and reinterpret their pain from the outside in. Like people who use bibliotherapy and cinema therapy to indirectly tackle difficult topics, writing fanfiction enables fans to deal with past trauma in a way that likely feels safer and more controlled than it would if they confronted their trauma directly.

A study we conducted on *Mad Men* fanfiction provides evidence for this idea (Vinney & Dill-Shackleford, 2018). Our analysis of a corpus of fan-written stories indicated that fan writers used *Mad Men* fanfiction to reflect on difficult topics and to consider what makes life meaningful. While fanfiction most often garners attention because some of the stories include explicit depictions of sex, we found that even when stories had spicy content, writers were still wrestling with deeper issues and attempting to find meaning and purpose through their fanfic. These findings imply that fan writers use their stories to work through the various personal issues and challenges that are brought up by the fiction that inspire them to write.

Fan testimonials on the way fanfiction has impacted fans' lives offers additional support for the therapeutic benefits of this form of writing. In comments submitted to the U.S. National Telecommunications and Information Administration and U.S. Patent Office, the Organization for Transformative Works, a nonprofit that protects and advocates for fan works and also hosts a large fanfiction archive called Archive of Our Own, defended the rights of fans to create fan works from copyrighted material

(Tushnet, 2013). The comments included powerful statements from fan writers. For example, a fan named Adria wrote:

> For a few years in high school I was hovering on the edge of suicide. Fanfiction literally saved my life. Not only could I read and watch the stories I loved, but I could write them, get that pain and hopelessness out in characters and worlds that I knew as well as my own. (p. 20)

And another fan, Lauren B., said:

> Fanfiction has given me innumerable gifts, but the most important one is that it's helped me navigate my own struggles with mental illness.... [W]riting fanfiction about Buffy [from *Buffy the Vampire Slayer*]... I was able to work through some of my own pain, exploring it in the context of a character whose worth was unquestionable. (pp. 25–26)

Zubernis and Larsen (2012) also tie the potential therapeutic effects of writing and reading fanfiction to narrative therapy. You'll remember in Chapter 6 of this volume we discussed how people create a life story to give their identities continuity and coherence. In narrative therapy, therapists work with people to adjust and change the way they tell parts of their life stories to arrive at a healthier story that improves self-perceptions and eliminates negative assumptions about one's identity. Zubernis and Larsen propose that fanfiction empowers fan writers to reauthor their personal narratives by creating and controlling characters that can serve as stand-ins for them. Furthermore, when writers share and get feedback about their stories in the safe space of online fanfiction archives or other fan websites, their readers' acceptance and empathy may help fanfiction writers and other community members feel understood and less alone. As a result, fan communities may serve as a kind of support group. This is again attested to in the fan testimonials submitted in the comments by the Organization of Transformative Works to the U.S. National

Telecommunications and Information Administrations (Tushnet, 2013). A fan named Balun S. explained:

> I was an engineer, or at least I had been, I had lost my job and was dealing with the hopelessness and depression that are part and parcel of long term unemployment and dwindling savings. . . . I posted to FanFiction.net and people liked what I wrote. For the first time in years I received validation that I was a worthwhile human being! Something a job had never given me. Life was worth living again! Through my fanfiction, I worked through my emotional pain. Then I found that others shared that pain. People would read and re-read my stories to help them out of depression and suicidal thoughts. We would communicate and I helped lead them through their own dark places. I have had several people tell me that they are alive now and wanting to stay alive because of my stories and our interactions, all because we are able to connect through the shared love of a movie. (p. 25)

And another, Medillia, stated:

> My participation in *X-Men: First Class* fandom helped me deal with my disability in ways that just watching the movie would not have been able to. . . . I identified with the movie's version of Charles Xavier, a famous wheelchair user who doesn't become paraplegic until the end of the movie. . . . There are relatively few stories in pop culture about people with disabilities, fewer where they're main characters, even fewer in genre fiction. . . . [I]n [fan fiction], I found more depictions of a wheelchair user having power, respect, love and adventures than I've ever seen in "real" entertainment. . . . I have friends and allies who share my interests, and we can tell the stories and make the art we want to see, for each other. It wouldn't have worked the same for us to individually make up stories for original characters; that's lonely work and we never would have come together if not for our interest in characters we knew and loved. (pp. 37–38)

These fan accounts are inspiring and exciting. However, Zubernis and Larsen's observations about the therapeutic benefits of fanfiction and fan communities haven't been validated by formal research yet. If studies do bear out their proposals, it could open up powerful possibilities for fans who want to use their favorite stories to help them heal.

FICTION IN THE DIGITAL AGE

We've covered a lot of ground in this book and discussed the many things we get out of our interactions with fiction. How we consume stories today, however, continues to evolve as new technologies offer different ways to view, share, and produce fiction. The TV shows we can watch are no longer controlled by just three television networks, or even a plethora of cable stations—we can queue up a show or movie of our choosing in the blink of an eye through streaming services like Netflix, Hulu, or Amazon Prime. We don't have to remember to program the VCR and hope we have enough video tape to catch the latest episode of our favorite show—we can record content on DVRs or find it online or on video on demand. If we want, we can even watch or read our favorite stories whenever we want on the phones we carry in our pockets or the tablets or laptops we carry in our bags. And, in many cases, we don't have to wait a week until the network broadcasts a show's next episode—Netflix and other platforms release a show all at once, so we can binge the whole series in a matter of days. We don't have to hope our bookstore has the latest book we want to read—we can download it instantly to an e-reader. Furthermore, if we have a story we want to tell, we don't have to hope to catch the eye of someone powerful and well-placed in the entertainment industry to get it made—we can upload our videos to YouTube, share our thoughts and opinions on blogs, or self-publish our latest book, bypassing the gatekeepers and taking our stories directly to an audience through the power of the Internet.

When new technologies become popular, there's always some wariness and hand-wringing. The unfamiliar makes us nervous and when it comes to new communication technologies, we've tended to focus on the negative. As Frank Rose (2012) notes, "every new medium that has been invented, from print to film to television, has increased the transporting power of narrative. And every new medium has aroused fear and hostility as a result" (p. 36). At the same time, these new mediums were eventually integrated into our lives, and now we couldn't envision being without them. Today everything from social media to cord-cutting to streaming services to e-readers to podcasts is changing how we consume stories more rapidly than ever. Fiction remains a huge part of our lives, but it's not always clear what the changes in how we consume stories add up to, especially since we barely have a chance to catch our breath before a new technological innovation changes how we find and engage with fiction yet again.

Today there are so many choices of entertainment, we could never get through it all. Between the broadcast networks, cable, and streaming services alone, there were 487 original scripted TV shows available in America in 2017! That's a 168% increase over the number of shows available 15 years earlier (Otterson, 2018)! That's an unbelievable number of shows. And if you add in movies, novels, YouTube videos, comic books, video games, blogs, fanfiction, fan discussions, and more, we are more awash in stories and ways to consume them than ever before. A consequence of all this content is that the choice of what to watch and read (and play and listen to) is becoming increasingly personal as we look to find the stories that resonate with us the most among the almost endless options available.

Further, we have more different ways to immerse ourselves in stories and learn about story worlds than ever before. Earlier, we mentioned transmedia stories—single stories or story worlds explored across multiple media. This form of storytelling is now accepted and often expected. Over a decade ago, preeminent fan scholar Henry Jenkins (2006) observed, "More and more, storytelling has become the art of world building, as artists create compelling environments that cannot be fully explored or exhausted within a single work or even a single medium" (p. 116).

Now world building has become an established part of blockbuster entertainment, with story worlds like the Marvel Cinematic Universe, the galaxy of *Star Wars*, the *Harry Potter* series, and the CW network's ever-growing suite of DC superhero shows constantly building and expanding on their characters, worlds, and stories. While these books, movies, and television shows can be read or watched by themselves without any further information, there's a plethora of additional content available for those that seek it. From the online video that explained what Thor was doing and why he didn't appear in the otherwise superhero-heavy *Captain America: Civil War* to Universal Studios' Wizarding World of Harry Potter attractions in Orlando and Los Angeles, these additions enhance the depth and breadth of the story world, something the main story couldn't provide on its own. These things increase the complexity and expand the amount of information available about a story world. By picking and choosing which parts of a story to consume, audiences are able to explore story worlds in whatever way they choose (Jenkins, 2006). Factor in the fan art, fanfiction, discussions of fan theories, and fan interpretations of story events that are now widely available through online fan communities to those who have an interest, and the story world expands even more. Taken together, all these fragments of story help us to immerse and involve ourselves even further in our favorite fiction. This wouldn't be possible without the power of the Internet and other technologies.

For those of us who grew up before broadband, social networks, and streaming services, these developments can seem overwhelming. But they also offer unique new benefits. For example, it's now the norm for serialized television shows to contain multiple plot threads as well as dense networks of relationships between characters that viewers are challenged to keep up with from episode to episode. Instead of treating these stories as easy and disposable, people must now pay attention, keep track of a great deal of information, and remember what was happening in the story—often over a period of years (Johnson, 2005). These things challenge us cognitively and emotionally because we have to fully engage with a show to know what's happening and derive the most enjoyment from it. With additional content available across other media channels, we can also make our own decisions about the information and knowledge we want to acquire about a story. This enables us to make choices about how and to what degree to engage with any given story.

With things like live-tweeting, Facebook posts, and fan communities dedicated to our favorite shows, the experience deepens further, allowing us to share our thoughts, feelings, and perspectives on plot points, characters, and what stories mean to us in real time, or close to it. These things also enhance our engagement with the story, while at the same time creating a common ground for social connections with other fans. As we saw earlier, the accessibility of fan communities and the outlet they provide for sharing fanfiction and other story-related observations may even serve a therapeutic function.

Of course, we also must be discerning and mindful about the stories with which we engage. The new technologies, media, and new ways of telling stories now available to us make it necessary to be media literate and deliberate about how and why we use media in all its forms. We believe society would greatly benefit from teaching media literacy in grade school so children can learn the best ways to interact with and evaluate the vast swath of content that comes at them every day through different devices. All in all, however, the increased sophistication offered by transmedia stories represents a number of positives. Now it's on all of us to learn the best ways to increase the positives of transmedia while minimizing the negatives.

THE FUTURE OF FICTION

> Life's like a movie, write your own ending
> Keep believing, keep pretending
> —"The Magic Store" from *The Muppet Movie*

We are already seeing technologies develop that will lead to stories being told across even more mediums. Augmented reality enables us to catch Pokémon or run from zombies through apps like Pokémon GO or Zombies, Run! Whether we are familiar with the story of Pokémon or a fan of zombie stories prior to using them, these apps not only use a popular fictional narrative as their basis, but they also build on those narratives to explain why we would need to catch Pokémon or run from zombies. Moreover, they make us part of the story—and get us exercising at the same time.

One of the newest frontiers in fiction is likely to be virtual reality (VR). Already in New York, Los Angeles, and other locations, VR centers are offering experiences in which people can step into the shoes of characters from their favorite stories, including superheroes, government agents, and rebel spies (Shown in Figure E.2) in a galaxy far, far away (IMAX VR, n.d.; Los Virtuality, 2017; The VOID, 2016). These experiences offer an exciting new possibility in the way storytelling could evolve. And there is some evidence that storytelling with VR could lead to positive outcomes. Through VR, researchers Robin Rosenberg, Shawnee Baghman, and Jeremy Bailenson (2013) gave study participants either the power to fly or had them ride in a helicopter. During their flights, participants were assigned one of two tasks: Either find a lost diabetic child in need of insulin or tour a city. After the VR experience, all participants that "flew" were quicker to help a researcher who "accidentally" knocked over a cup of pens than those who rode in the helicopter. In fact, several of the helicopter-riding participants chose not to help the researcher at all.

Figure E.2 A scene from *Star Wars: Secrets of the Empire*, an immersive virtual reality experience where teams of four play rebel spies who infiltrate the Empire disguised as Stormtroopers.

While the word "superhero" was never mentioned during the study, the researchers took these findings to mean that the ability to fly in VR resembled the powers of a superhero like Superman, and consequently primed participants' ideas about how superheroes help people. Embodying a superhero in VR, then, helped people see themselves as someone who helps, an identity they transferred, at least for a short while, to their behavior in the real world. It's understandably hard to develop and execute studies on VR, so there aren't additional studies that we're aware of that replicate these findings in other VR contexts or explore how long these effects might last. However, the possibilities represented by these results are exciting and encouraging. In the future, VR experiences in which one embodies superheroes or other characters who help others could, at least temporarily, increase audiences' helping behaviors in the real world as well. It will be exciting to see how we adapt to, engage with, and use stories told through this new medium.

No matter what the future of fiction holds, one thing is clear: stories make us human. From our earliest days we communicated through stories. Today stories continue to make our lives richer in so many ways. They help us learn about the world, determine who we are, understand others, and connect with our fellow human beings. Fiction helps us do everything from relax and unwind to discover new things about ourselves to vicariously experience things and meet people we never would otherwise. Stories are something we all have in common, and while there are always negatives, we believe that on balance, stories play an immensely positive role in our lives. A world without stories would be a darker and less rich place.

As the world becomes more decentralized and information continues to proliferate, fiction may become even more important to us as we search for ways to bring coherence to our lives, common ground on which to bond, and perspectives that help us make sense of the world. Clearly, the way we tell and take in stories is still in flux. The story of fiction is still unfolding.

We can't wait to see what happens next.

REFERENCES

Bianco, M. (2014, July 28). One fan's powerful question brought "Orphan Black" star Tatiana Maslany to tears at Comic Con. *Mic*. Retrieved from https://mic.com/articles/95084/one-fan-s-powerful-question-brought-orphan-black-star-tatiana-maslany-to-tears-at-comic-con?utm_campaign=social&utm_medium=main&utm_source=policymicFB#.SYLtBuLIR

Dunbar, R. I. M., Teasdale, B., Thompson, J., Budelmann, F., Duncan, S., van Emde Boas, E., & Maguire, L. (2016). Emotional arousal when watching drama increases pain threshold and social bonding. *Royal Society Open Science, 3*, 1–11. https://doi.org/10.1098/rsos.160288

IMAX VR. (n.d.) [Home Page]. Retrieved from https://imaxvr.imax.com/

Jenkins, H. (2006). *Convergence culture: Where old and new media collide*. New York, NY: New York University Press.

Johnson, S. (2006). *Everything bad is good for you: How today's popular culture is actually making us smarter*. New York, NY: Riverhead Books.

Los Virtuality. (2017). [Home Page]. Retrieved from http://www.losvirtuality.com/index.html

Marrs, R. (1995). A meta-analysis of bibliotherapy studies. *American Journal of Community Psychology, 23*(6), 843–870. https://doi.org/10.1007/BF02507018

Nabi, R. L., Prestin, A. & So, J. (2016). Could watching TV be good for you? Examining how media consumption patterns relate to salivary cortisol. *Health Communication, 31*(11), 1345–1355. https://doi.org/10.1080/10410236.2015.1061309

Ness, P. (2011). *A monster calls*. Somerville, MA: Candelewick Press.

Otterson, J. (2018, January 5). 487 scripted series aired in 2017, FX chief John Landgraf says. *Variety*. Retrieved from http://variety.com/2018/tv/news/2017-scripted-tv-series-fx-john-landgraf-1202653856/

Pennebaker, J. W. (1997). Writing about emotional experiences as a therapeutic process. *Psychological Science, 8*(3), 162–166.

Pennebaker, J. W., & Graybeal. A. (2001). Patterns of natural language use: Disclosure, personality, and social integration. *Current Directions in Psychological Science, 10*(3), 90–93.

Rose, F. (2012). *The art of immersion: How the digital generation is remaking Hollywood, Madison Avenue, and the way we tell stories*. New York, NY: W. W. Norton.

Rosenberg, R. S., Baughman, S. L., & Bailenson, J. N. (2013). Virtual superheroes: Using superpowers in virtual reality to encourage prosocial behavior. *PLoS One, 8*(1), 1–9. https://doi.org/10.1371/journal.pone.0055003

Rothman, M. (2017, May 9). Why "Guardians of the Galaxy Vol. 2" hero Drax resonates with the autism community. *ABC News*. Retrieved from http://abcnews.go.com/Entertainment/guardians-hero-drax-resonates-autism-community/story?id=47283318

Sharp, C., Smith, J. V., & Cole, A. (2002). Cinematherapy: Metaphorically promoting therapeutic change. *Counselling Psychology Quarterly, 15*(3), 269–276. https://doi.org/10.1080/09515070210140221

Stevens, E. M., & Dillman Carpentier, F. R. (2017). Facing our feelings: How natural coping tendencies explain when hedonic motivation predicts media use. *Communication Research, 44*(1), 3–28. https://doi.org/10.1177/0093650215587358

Trendacosta, K. (2015, January 16). Why *Star Trek: Voyager* meant the world to me. *io9*. Retrieved from https://io9.gizmodo.com/why-star-trek-voyager-meant-the-world-to-me-1679736359\

Tushnet, R. (2013, November 13). Comments for the Organization for Transformative Works (OTW). Retrieved from http://www.transformativeworks.org/wp-content/uploads/old/Comments%20of%20OTW%20to%20PTO-NTIA.pdf

Vinney, C., & Dill-Shackleford, K. E. (2018). Fan fiction as a vehicle for meaning making: Eudaimonic appreciation, hedonic enjoyment, and other perspectives on fan engagement with television. *Psychology of Popular Media Culture, 7*(1), 18–32. https://doi.org/10.1037/ppm0000106

Vinney, C., Dill-Shackleford, K. E., Plante, C. N., & Bartsch, A. (2019). Development and validation of a measure of popular media fan identity and its relationship to well-being. *Psychology of Popular Media Culture, 8*(3), 296–307. https://doi.org/10.1037/ppm0000188

Vinney, C., & Hopper-Losenicky, K. (2017, April). *More than escapism: How popular media helps fans learn, cope, and live*. Popular Culture Association/American Culture Association Annual Conference, San Diego, CA.

The VOID. (2016). Star Wars™: Secrets of the Empire. Retrieved from https://www.thevoid.com/dimensions/starwars/secretsoftheempire/

Zubernis, L., & Larsen, K. (Eds.). (2012). *Fandom at the crossroads: Celebration, shame and fan/producer relationships*. Newcastle upon Tyne, England: Cambridge Scholars.

NAME INDEX

Tables, figures and Boxes are indicated by *t*, *f* and *b* following the page number
For the benefit of digital users, indexed terms that span two pages (e.g., 52–53) may, on occasion, appear on only one of those pages.

Abigail Mitchell (*Try and Catch Me*), 236
Abrahams, D., 69
Abrams, A., 130–31
Ackles, Jensen, 14
Adams, Ellery, 2–3
The Adventures of Mary-Kate and Ashley (television show), 75
Aesop's Fables, 244
The Age of Spin (television show), 234–35
Albus Dumbledore (*Harry Potter*), 4, 91
Alderson, B., 49
Alison (*Orphan Black*), 67
Allan, David, 40
Allemand, A., 208–9
Almost Famous (movie), 160
The Amazing Race (television show), 28
Amy (*Doctor Who*), 138–39
Anderson, D. R., 195–97
Andress, Ursula, 69
Anne of Green Gables, 148
Annie (movie), 183
Apollo (Greek god), 244
Appel, Markus, 42
Archie (*Riverdale*), 201

Aristotle, 128, 140–41, 142, 143, 144, 145, 148, 149, 244
Arnett, Jeffrey Jenson, 158, 159, 160, 162, 164, 165, 199
Aronson, Elliot, 128
Aronson, V., 69
Arquette, Patricia, 206
Arrested Development (television show), 53–55, 62
Arthur Fonzarelli (*Happy Days*), 62
Ashe, D., 5
Atomic Blonde (movie), 69
Atran, S., 133
Austen, Jane, 8–9, 18
Avalon, Frankie, 129
Avatar (movie), 12, 148–49
The Avengers (movie), 117–18, 244–45

Baby Einstein (television show), 194
Back to the Future (movie), 31
Baghman, Shawnee, 258
Bailenson, Jeremy, 258
Baker, Becky Ann, 206–7
Bandura, Albert, 201–2, 223–24
Bardo, A. R., 209–10

NAME INDEX

Barnes, B., 218
Barnes, Jennifer, 30–31, 221
Barriga, C. A., 111–12
Barry, Gene, 228–29
Barry Zuckerkorn (*Arrested Development*), 62
Bartsch, Anne, 18, 43–44, 153–54, 208
Batman, 25, 110
Batman Forever (movie), 203
Battlestar Galactica (television show), 25, 229–31
Baumeister, Roy, 157, 159
Beach, Lee Roy, 121, 123, 124
Beach Blanket Bingo (movie), 129
Beauty and the Beast (movie), 31, 218
Belk, Richard, 167, 170
Bella Swan (*Twilight*), 169
Belle (*Beauty and the Beast*), 31
Bem, Daryl, 85
Beowulf, 146
Beren, J., 111–12
Bernini, M., 49
Bernsen, Corbin, 52–53
Bettencourt, B. Ann, 97
Bianco, M., 248–49
Bielby, Denise, 7, 176, 209–10
Big (movie), 133–34
The Big Bang Theory (television show), 43–44, 248–49
The Big Lebowski (movie), 3
The Big Sick (movie), 217
Bilandzic, Helena, 92, 96–97, 99–100, 104, 105, 108–9, 110–12, 114–15
Bill Cosby: Himself (television show), 233
Bissell, Byron, 121, 123, 124
Black, Jessica, 30–31, 221
Black Panther (movie), 12, 217, 218
Black Swan (movie), 244–45
Black Widow (*The Avengers*), 25
Black-ish (television show), 217
Blade (movie), 105–6
Blade Runner (movie), 43–44, 129
Blascovich, Jim, 136
Blue Is the Warmest Color (movie), 160
Blue Valentine (movie), 244–45

Blue's Clues (television show), 185, 196–97
Bonatsos, A., 68–69
Bonnie and Clyde (movie), 65
Bonus, J. A., 208
Bort, R., 63–64
Boston Legal (television show), 80
Boyhood (movie), 161, 206, 207
The Brady Bunch (television show), 98
Branaugh, Kenneth, 85–86
Brand, R. J., 68–69
Branscombe, Nila, 168–69
Breakfast at Tiffany (movie), 69
The Breakfast Club (movie), 160
Breaking Bad (television show), 8–9, 97
Bree (*Desperate Housewives*), 94–96
Breen, A. V., 176–77
Brehm, Jack, 126–27
Brett, Jeremy, 134
Brewer, Marilyn, 227–28
Bring It On (movie), 160
Broadchurch (television show), 71
Brock, Timothy, 10, 113–14, 221
Brockmeier, Jeanne, 152
Bronfenbrenner, U., 195
Brooks, J. A., 64–65
Brown, Jane, 160, 162, 163–64, 170
Brown, R., 226–27
Brown, Steven, 87–88
Browning, Logan, 216
Bruce, Nigel, 134
Bruce Banner (*The Avengers*), 187, 188
Bruner, Jerome, 171–72, 184–85
Buffy (*Buffy the Vampire*), 210–11
Buffy the Vampire Slayer (television show), 8, 22–23, 45, 135, 154–55, 172–73, 200, 210–11, 252
Burton "Gus" Guster (*Psych*), 52–53
Busselle, Rick, 92, 96–97, 99–100, 104, 105, 108–9, 110–12, 114–15

C. K., Louis, 237–40
Cairney, K., 176–77
Call Me by Your Name (movie), 160, 217
Calvert, S. L., 195–97, 202–3

NAME INDEX

Camello, M. L. G., 25
Cameron, James, 12, 142, 148
Cameron, L., 226–27
Campbell, Joseph, 140, 146, 147, 148, 149
Cantor, Joanne, 185–86, 187–88, 192, 207–8
Capozza, D., 50, 221
Capra, Frank, 39, 41–42, 58–59
Caprica (television show), 230
Captain America: Civil War (movie), 117–18, 231, 255–56
Captain America (*The Avengers*), 117–18
Captain Benjamin Sisko (*Star Trek*), 12
Captain Janeway (*Star Trek*), 248–49
Captain Jean-Luc Picard (*Star Trek*), 55
Captain Kirk (*Star Trek*), 7, 14–15, 35, 76–79, 80
Carell, Steve, 13
Carpentier, Francesca Dillman, 244–45
Carstensen, L. L., 207–8
Casablanca (movie), 2, 129
Castiel (*Supernatural*), 205–6
Castro, Fidel, 82
Cayer, Deborah, 47
Chandler (*Friends*), 13
Chaplin, Charlie, 8–9
Chappelle, Dave, 234–35
Charles Xavier (*X-Men*), 253
Charlie (*West Wing*), 52–53
Charlie and the Chocolate Factory (movie), 183
Charlton, Kelly, 97
Chekhov, Anton, 30, 154–55
Choueiti, M., 217
Christakis, Dimitri, 194–95
Christie, Agatha, 85–86
Chuck Lumley (*Night Shift*), 62
Clarence (*It's a Wonderful Life*), 39
Clayton Forrester (*War of the Worlds*), 228–29
Cleopatra, Queen of Egypt, 244
Clipmaster, P., 237
Clueless (movie), 124–25
Coco (movie), 217
Cohen, Jonathan, 11, 13–14, 25

Colbert Report (television show), 79
Cole, A., 250
Cole, K., 172–73
Coleridge, Samuel Taylor, 112–13
Collier, J. G., 10–11
Collins, Misha, 205–6
Colman, Olivia, 71–72
Coltrane, Ellar, 161
Conger, E. E., 195–96
Coogler, Ryan, 217
Coren, C., 235
Cosby, Bill, 232–35, 236, 239–40
The Cosby Show (television show), 232–33
Cosette (*Les Misérables*), 148
Cosima (*Orphan Black*), 67
Côté, J. E., 158
Crain, W., 188
Cramer, P., 159
Crazy Ex-Girlfriend (television show), 171
Crazy Rich Asians (movie), 217
Crockett, Peter, 87–88
The Crown (television show), 156
Cruise, Tom, 228–29
Csikszentmihalyi, Mihalyi, 51
Culp, Robert, 232
Cumberbatch, Benedict, 64, 134
Cylons (*Battlestar Galactica*), 229

Daenerys Targaryen (*Game of Thrones*), 244
Damon Salvatore (*The Vampire Diaries*), 174–75
Daniels, Jeff, 37–38
Danny Latimer (*Broadchurch*), 71
Darth Vader (*Star Wars*), 2, 53, 223
Das, Ranjana, 115
The DaVinci Code (movie), 53
Day, L., 5
Days of Our Lives (television show), 63, 84–85
Dead Poet's Society (movie), 97
Dean Winchester (*Supernatural*), 14
Dear White People (television show), 216, 217
dela Paz, J., 130

Denny Crane (*Boston Legal*), 80
The Departed (movie), 244–45
Deshong, H., 68–69
Desperate Housewives (television show), 94
Dexter (television show), 65
Diana (Greek goddess), 244
Diana (*Wonder Woman*), 2
DiCaprio, Leonardo, 36–37
Die Hard (movie), 37–38, 105
A Different World (television show), 21
Dill, Karen, 97
Dillane, Stephen, 156
Dill-Shackleford, Karen, 12, 14–15, 23, 24, 26–27, 31, 44, 49, 55, 56–57, 125–27, 130, 131–32, 134, 138, 139, 153–54, 200–1, 218, 221b, 222b, 248, 251
Djikic, Maja, 23–24, 29–30, 36–37, 48, 154–55
Doc Brown (*Back to the Future*), 31
Doctor Who (television show), 9–10, 23, 35, 36, 138–39, 209–10
Don Draper (*Mad Men*), 9, 68–69, 110–11, 125–26
Donna Noble (*Doctor Who*), 138–39
Donna Reed (*It's a Wonderful Life*), 97
Dora the Explorer (television show), 195–96
D'Orazio, R., 68–69
Dorothy (*Wizard of Oz*), 53
Douch, R., 226–27
Doug Stamper (*House of Cards*), 63–64
Douglas, Michael, 87
Dovidio, John, 227–28
Downey, Robert, Jr., 64, 134
Downton Abbey (television show), 8, 126
Dr. Abe Saperstein (*Parks and Recreation*), 62
Draco Malfoy (*Harry Potter*), 50, 222b, 223–51
Dracula (movie), 133–34
Drake, Lawrence, 218
Drax (*Guardians of the Galaxy*), 248–49
Drew Baird (*30 Rock*), 68–69
Duffett, Mark, 176
Dunbar, Robin, 247
Dykers, C. R., 160

Eat Pray Love (movie), 151
Edidin, R., 54
Edward (*Twilight*), 169
Elena (*The Vampire Diaries*), 201–2
Elizabeth Bennet (*Pride and Prejudice*), 18–19
Ellen Ripley (*Alien*), 37
Elliot (*Mr. Hacker*), 107
Elliott (*E.T.*), 37
Elliott, G. R., 158
Empire (television show), 65, 217
Ensign Chekov (*Star Trek*), 79–80
Erikson, Erik, 156, 158, 204–5, 209–10
Esteban, C., 232
E.T. (*E.T.*), 37
Everwood (television show), 201
Ewoldsen, David, 14, 15, 25, 72
Eyal, Keren, 13–14

The Facts of Life (television show), 21
Falk, Peter, 236
Family Matters (television show), 83
Farley, Chris, 37–38
Farrell, Will, 91–92
Fat Albert and the Cosby Kids (television show), 232
Faulkner, J., 133
Feldman, S. S., 158
Fender, J. G., 194–95
Fernyhough, Charles, 49
Ferris Bueller's Day Off (movie), 160
Feshbach, S., 128
Fey, Tina, 68–69
Fiennes, Ralph, 80–81
Finnegan's Wake (Joyce), 146
Firefly (television show), 45
Firth, Colin, 18–19
Fisher, D., 79–80
Fisherkeller, JoEllen, 160–61
Fitzgerald, Kaitlin, 28–29
Flanagan, M., 29
Flores, Jason, 22
Fonda, Jane, 219
Fong, K., 162
Ford, Harrison, 69

NAME INDEX

Foster, Jodie, 5
Frank, Anne, 177
Frank Underwood (*House of Cards*), 63–64
Frankenstein (movie), 133–34
Frasier (television show), 98
Frasier Crane (*Frasier*), 98
Freeman, G., 29
Freeman, J. B., 64–65
Freeman, Martin, 134
Freeman, Morgan, 4
Fresh Off the Boat (television show), 217
Freud, Sigmund, 128
Friday Night Lights (movie), 97
Friends (television show), 13–14
Frodo (*Lord of the Rings*), 48
From Russia with Love (movie), 69
Frozen (movie), 151
Full House (television show), 74–75
Funicello, Annette, 129

Gabriel, Shira, 154–55
Gabrielle (*Desperate Housewives*), 94–96
Gaiman, Neil, 1
Game of Thrones (television show), 8–9
Gandalf (*Lord of the Rings*), 244
Gandhi, Mahatma, 244
Gardner, Wendi, 168
Garmon, L. C., 164–65, 199–200
Geen, Russell, 128
General Hospital (television show), 210
George Bailey (*It's a Wonderful Life*), 39–41
George Bluth Sr. (*Arrested Development*), 54–55
Gerbner, George, 216
Gerrig, Richard, 102, 104, 113
Get Out (movie), 217
Ghost in the Shell (movie), 218
Gilbert, Daniel, 113
Gilbert, Sophie, 22
Giles, David, 5, 13, 128, 159–60, 189, 198–99
The Gilmore Girls (television show), 36, 97
Gilovich, Chad, 52–53

Giovannini, D., 50, 221
The Glass Menagerie (Williams), 230–31
Glee (television show), 13
Glenn (*Superstore*), 197–98
Glover, R. J., 164–65, 199
The Godfather (movie), 244
Goldstein, Thalia, 27
Gonzalez-Velazquez, Carlos, 218
The Good Wife (television show), 30–31
Goodwin, Ginnifer, 120
Gordon, Ruth, 236
Grace and Frankie (television show), 217, 219
The Graduate (movie), 36
Graesser, Arthur, 96–97, 99, 104–5
Graham Sutherland (*The Crown*), 156
Grandmother Willow (*Pocahontas*), 149
Grapes of Wrath (Steinbeck), 230–31
Graybeal, A., 251
Greathouse, Scott, 97
Green, Melanie, 10, 28–29, 113–14, 154–55, 221
Grey's Anatomy (television show), 111–12
Griffith, Melanie, 37–38
Groene, Samantha, 7–8, 168–69
Groot (*Guardians of the Galaxy*), 53
Grossberg, Lawrence, 169–70
Guardians of the Galaxy (movie), 53, 248–49
Guster, Burton, 52–53

Hagrid (*Harry Potter*), 147, 223
Hall, Alice, 109–10
Hall, Deirdra, 63
Hamilton (play), 110
Hamm, Jon, 68–69
Hammack, P. L., 174
Han Solo (*Star Wars*), 129
Handscombe, Claire, 6
Hanks, Tom, 59, 80–81, 133–34
Hannah (*Girls*), 206–7
Happy Days (television show), 62, 97
Hardwicke, Edward, 134
Harrington, C. Lee, 7, 176, 209–10
Harris, Ed, 106–7

NAME INDEX

Harris, V. A., 82
Harry Potter and the Chamber of Secrets (movie), 223
Harry Potter and the Deathly Hallows (movie), 91
Harry Potter and the Sorcerer's Stone (movie), 2, 4, 154–55, 221*b*
Harry Potter (*Harry Potter*), 2, 46, 47, 50, 111–12, 115, 147–79, 221*b*, 222*b*, 222, 223–25
Harry Potter (movie), 224–26, 227–28
Hartmann, Tilo, 29, 43–44
Hawkes, R., 66
Hawkins, J., 93
Heathcliff Huxtable (*The Cosby Show*), 232–33
Heintz, K. E., 193, 194–95
Hemsworth, Chris, 69
Henry Spencer (*Psych*), 52–53
Hepburn, Audrey, 69
Hercule Poirot, 85–86
Hermione Granger (*Harry Potter*), 50, 223–51
Hettinger, Vanessa, 7–8, 168–69
Hill, Dulé, 52–53
Hills, Matt, 154
The Hills Have Eyes (movie), 208
Hirsh, J., 130
Hitchcock, Alfred, 8–9, 11, 91–92
The Hobbit (movie), 146
Hofer, M., 208–9
Hoffner, Cynthia, 186, 202–3
Hogg, Jerri Lynn, 23, 26–27, 125–26
Holland, Norman, 51
Hopper-Losenicky, Kristin, 12, 23, 26–27, 115, 125–26, 154, 172, 248
Horton, D., 13
Hotel Rwanda (movie), 208
Houran, J., 5
House of Cards (television show), 63–64
How to Get Away With Murder (television show), 217
Huang, S., 47
Huckleberry Finn, 148
Hulk (*The Avengers*), 187, 188

The Hunger Games (movie), 3, 17–18
Hurdle, J., 232
The Hurt Locker (movie), 244–45

I Love You, America (television show), 239
I Spy (television show), 232
Ilsa (*Casablanca*), 2
The Incredible Hulk (movie), 187, 192
Independence Day (movie), 129–30, 228–29
Indiana Jones (*Indiana Jones*), 12, 37
Indiana Jones (movie), 69
Interview with the Vampire (movie), 135
iRobot (movie), 69
Iron Man (*The Avengers*), 117–18
Isbouts, Jean-Pierre, 23–24
IT (movie), 189–90, 191–92
It Happened One Night (movie), 41–42
It's a Wonderful Life (movie), 39–41, 42, 58, 97, 174–75

Jack (*Nursery Rhyme*), 121
Jack (*Three's Company*), 56–57
Jack (*Titanic*), 142, 143
Jacob (*Twilight*), 169
Jacobs, E. L., 195–96
Jake Sully (*Avatar*), 12, 148, 149
James, Jesse, 52
James, William, 122–23, 166–67, 228
James Bond, 12
Jane Eyre (Brontë), 146, 148
Janet (*Three's Company*), 56–57
Jaws (movie), 192
Jeff (*Superstore*), 197–98
Jeff Jeffries (*Rear Window*), 11
Jenkins, Henry, 255–56
Jenson, J., 7
Jesus Christ, 244
Jill (*Nursery Rhyme*), 121
Joan of Arc, 17–18
Joey (*Friends*), 13
Johansson, Scarlett, 218
John Smith (*Pocahontas*), 149
John Wick (movie), 105

NAME INDEX

Johnson, S., 256
Johnson B. K., 25
Jonathan Byers (*Stranger Things*), 131
Jones, E. E., 82
Jones, R. A., 162
Jonny Appleseed, 53
Josselson, Ruthellen, 171
Joyce Byers (*Stranger Things*), 131, 132
Jung, Carl, 147
Jurassic Park (movie), 129–30

Katniss Everdeen (*The Hunger Games*), 17–18, 91–92
Kaufman, Geoff, 10, 12, 22, 29
Keeping Up With the Kardashians (television show), 8–9
Keller, Helen, 177
Keller, L., 218
Kelly, Michael, 63–64
Kermit the Frog (*Sesame Street*), 51
Kim, Hyekyung, 112–13
King, Martin Luther, Jr., 227
King, Stephen, 189–90
Klettke, B., 96–97
Kobayashi, Tsukasa, 135
Koenig, Walter, 79–80
Kominsky Method (television show), 87
Krakowiak, K. Maja, 28
Krcmar, Marina, 194
Krull, Douglas, 113
Kukkonen, Karin, 108
Kung Fu Panda (movie), 151

LaBeouf, Shia, 66
Lady Bird (movie), 160
Lady Edith (*Downton Abbey*), 126
Lady Mary (*Downton Abbey*), 126
The Lady With the Toy Dog (Chekhov), 30
Lane Kim (*Gilmore Girls*), 36
Lange, R., 5
Larsen, Katherine, 7, 10–11, 26, 154, 250–51, 252–53, 254
Larsen, Steen, 26
Larson, R., 159, 162, 199–200
Lauer, Matt, 239–40

Laura Winslow (*Family Matters*), 83
Lautner, Taylor, 169
Law, Jude, 134
Lee, Angela, 168
The LEGO Batman Movie (movie), 53
Lennon, John, 5
Leslie Knope (*Parks and Recreation*), 237, 238–39
Lewis, C. S., 182
Libby, Lisa, 12, 22
Lieberman, Matthew, 136
Lieutenant Columbo (*Try and Catch Me*), 236
Life, Animated (movie), 6
Life of Pi (movie), 129–30, 151
Lin, S.-F., 10–11
The Lion King (movie), 36, 151
Lisjak, Monika, 168
Lithgow, John, 156
Liu, Lucy, 134
Liz Lemon (*30 Rock*), 68–69
Lloyd, B. T., 160
Lord of the Rings (movie), 48
Loreen (*Girls*), 206–7
Lorelai Gilmore (*Gilmore Girls*), 97
Lorre, Chuck, 87
Lost (television show), 30–31, 103, 104
Luckie, Mark, 21
Luke Cage (*Luke Cage*), 174–75
Luke Skywalker (*Star Wars*), 11, 144, 147–79, 223, 244
Lynette (*Desperate Housewives*), 94–96

Mad Men (television show), 9, 23, 24, 26–27, 68–69, 110–11, 125–26, 251
Magliano, J. P., 99
Malone, P. S., 113
Maltby, John, 5, 159–60, 198–99
Man in Black (*Westworld*), 106–7
Mar, Raymond, 17, 23–24, 27, 30–31, 130, 162
Mares, M.-L., 207–8
Marge Simpson (*The Simpsons*), 97
Marion Cunningham (*Happy Days*), 97
Markus, Hazel, 159–60

Married with Children (television show), 97
Marrs, R., 250
Mars Attacks! (movie), 228–29
Martin, George R. R., 3
Martin, M., 208–9
Martin Crane (*Frasier*), 98
Marty (*Back to the Future*), 31
Mary Margaret (*Once Upon a Time*), 120
The Mary Tyler Moore Show (television show), 177
Maslany, Tatiana, 66–68
Massie, A., 52
The Matrix (movie), 36
Max (*Where the Wild Things*), 20
Mayer, John, 9
McAdams, Dan, 40–41, 157, 158, 171, 174–75, 176–77
McCall, Cade, 136
McCutcheon, L. E., 5
McDonald, Daniel, 10–11, 26
McLean, Kate, 171, 174, 175, 176–77
McLernon, Dennis, 84, 85–86
Mellmann, K., 13, 26, 30
Meltzoff, A. N., 194
Memento (movie), 101–2
Mendelson, S., 217
Menninghaus, W., 27–28
Meredith Grey (*Grey's Anatomy*), 111–12
Meyer, S., 154–55
Michael (*Arrested Development*), 54–55
Michael Scott (*The Office*), 13
Michelle Tanner (*Full House*), 74–75
Miller, Jonny Lee, 134
Mister Rogers' Neighborhood (television show), 185
Moby-Dick (movie), 146
Mohammed, Prophet, 244
Monica (*Friends*), 13
A Monster Calls (book), 243
Monteith, Cory, 13
Moonlight (movie), 217
Moore, Alan, 151
Moses (Biblical leader), 133, 244
Mowgli (*Jungle Book*), 148

Mr. Darcy (*Pride and Prejudice*), 18–19
Mr. Robot (*Mr. Robot*), 107
Mr. Robot (television show), 107
Mr. Smith Goes to Washington (movie), 41–42
Mrs. Robinson (*The Graduate*), 36
Mulholland, A., 97
The Muppet Movie (movie), 257
Murder on the Orient Express (movie), 85–86
Murray, K. J., 202–3
Mylod, M., 120

Nabi, Robin, 246
Near Dark (movie), 135
Nededog, J., 36–37
Ness, Patrick, 243
Neville Longbottom (*Harry Potter*), 4
Neytiri (*Avatar*), 149
Night of the Living Dead (movie), 133–34
Night Shift (television show), 62
Niles Crane (*Frasier*), 98
Nimoy, Leonard, 14–15, 77–78, 79–80, 152–53
Ninio, A., 184–85
No Country for Old Men (movie), 145
Nolan, Christopher, 102
Norenzayan, A., 133
Nurius, P., 159–60
Nymphomaniac (movie), 66

Oatley, Keith, 17, 23–24, 26, 27, 29–31, 36–37, 116–18, 130, 154–55
Obi-Wan Kenobi (*Star Wars*), 147
The Odd Life of Timothy Green (movie), 244–45
Odin (Norse god), 244
Oedipus Rex (Aristotle), 141–42, 144
Offer, D., 162
The Office (television show), 13
Office Space (movie), 36
Ohler, Jason, 23–24
Olde, B., 96–97
Oliver, Mary Beth, 18, 29, 42, 43–44, 207–8

NAME INDEX

Oliver Twist, 148
Olsen, Ashley, 74–75
Olsen, Mary-Kate, 74–75
Once Upon a Time (television show), 120, 174–75
Orange is the New Black (television show), 217
The Originals (television show), 182–83
Orphan Black (television show), 66–68, 248–49
Osiris (Egyptian god), 244
Otterson, J., 255
Our Town (movie), 230–31

Parks and Recreation (television show), 49, 62, 237–39
Paul Bunyan (*American Folklore*), 53
Peg Bundy (*Married with Children*), 97
Pennebaker, James, 251
The Perks of Being a Wallflower (movie), 124–25
Peskin, J., 162
Peterson, Jordan, 23–24, 30–31, 36–37, 130, 154–55
Phoebe (*Friends*), 13
Piaget, Jean, 158, 188
Pieper, K., 217
Pierroutsakos, Sophia, 193–94
Pillow, B. H., 113
Plante, Courtney, 44, 153–54, 248
Pocahontas (movie), 77–78, 149
Poe, Edgar Allan, 100–1
Poehler, Amy, 237
Pose (television show), 217
The Poseidon Adventure (movie), 129–30
Potocki, B., 10–11
Potter, W. James, 109
The Practice (television show), 80
Prestin, Abby, 246
Pretty Woman (movie), 105
Pride and Prejudice (Austen), 18, 129
Princess Leia (*Star Wars*), 129
The Property Brothers (television show), 73
P.S. I Love You (movie), 244–45

Psych (television show), 52–53
Puckrik, K., 62
Pulp Fiction (movie), 101–2
Punky Brewster (television show), 8–9

Queen Elizabeth II (*The Crown*), 156
Queer Eye (television show), 28
Quinto, Zachary, 77–78

Rachel (*Friends*), 13, 14
Raney, Arthur, 43–44
Rapp, D. N., 113
Rashad, Felicia, 232–33
Rathbone, Basil, 134
Reagan, Ronald, 5
Rear Window (movie), 11
Rebel Without a Cause (movie), 8–9
Reed, Donna, 39
Regina, Evil Queen (*Once Upon a Time*), 174–75
Rendition (movie), 244–45
Rey (*Star Wars*), 12
Reysen, Stephen, 168–69
Rhoda (television show), 177
Richard Parker (*Life of Pi*), 130
Richert, Rebekah, 193, 194–97
Rick (*Casablanca*), 2
Rick Deckard (*Blade Runner*), 129
Rideout, Vicky, 184, 193
Riverdale (television show), 182–83, 201
Robb, M. B., 193, 194–95
Robbins, Tim, 4
Rocky (movie), 48
The Rocky Horror Picture Show (television show), 3
Roday, James, 52–53
Roi-Franzia, M., 232
Romeo & Juliet (movie), 129, 142
Romero, George, 133–34
Ron Weasley (*Harry Potter*), 223–51
Roots (television show), 25
Rory (*Doctor Who*), 138–39
Rory Gilmore (*Gilmore Girls*), 36
Rose (*Titanic*), 142, 143
Rose, Frank, 254–55

Rosenberg, Robin, 258
Ross (*Friends*), 13
Rothman, M., 248–49
Rowling, J. K., 154–55, 221*b*
Roz Doyle (*Frasier*), 98
Rubin, A. M., 43–44, 161–62
Rutland, A., 226–27
Ryder, Winona, 131

Sally Draper (*Mad Men*), 125–26
Sam (*Lord of the Rings*), 48
Samantha White (*Dear White People*), 216
Sanders, Meghan, 7–8, 46, 168–69
Sandvoss, Cornel, 7
Sandy Kominsky (*Kominsky Method*), 87–88
Santa Claus, 189
Sarah (*Orphan Black*), 67
Sarge, M. A., 10–11
Saturday Night Live (television show), 7, 37–38, 81–82, 169
Saving Private Ryan (movie), 208
Say Anything (movie), 160
Schaller, M., 133
Schimmel, K. S., 7
Schindler's List (movie), 110
Scooby Doo (television show), 23
Scott, Drew, 73–74, 75–76
Scott, Jonathan, 73–74, 75–76
Seilman, Uffe, 10–11, 26
Sendak, Maurice, 20
Sesame Street (television show), 51, 124, 185
Sestir, Marc, 154–55
Seven Pounds (movie), 244–45
Shackleford, Lee, 139–49
Shakespeare, William, 8–9
Shapiro, Michael, 111–13
Sharp, C., 250
Shatner, William, 7, 14–15, 35, 76–77, 78–80, 81–82
Shatner's Raw Nerve (television show), 14–15, 79–80

Shatner's World (television show), 79
Shawn Spencer (*Psych*), 52–53
The Shawshank Redemption (movie), 4, 127, 174–75
Sheahen, L., 47
Sheldon, K. M., 69–70
Sheldon Cooper (*Big Bang Theory*), 248–49
Sherlock (television show), 134
Sherlock Holmes, 17–18, 51–52, 134–35
Shuri (*Black Panther*), 12
Shuster, Joe, 147–48
Siegel, Jerry, 147–48
Silver, N., 10
Silverman, Sarah, 239
Simba (*The Lion King*), 36
The Simpsons (television show), 97
Singer, Jerome, 136, 137, 138
Singer, R. D., 128
Sixteen Candles (movie), 124–25, 160
Skrein, Ed, 218
Slater, Michael, 10, 14, 15, 24–25, 42, 72
Sleeping Beauty (movie), 133
Smith, Daniel, 57–58
Smith, E. I., 193
Smith, J. V., 250
Smith, S. L., 217
Smith, Will, 69
Snowden, Monique, 21–22
So, J., 246
Something Wild (movie), 37–38
Song, L., 184–85
Spacey, Kevin, 239–40
Sparks, Glenn, 185–86, 187, 188, 192
Speechless (movie), 217
Spencer, Shawn, 52–53
Spider-Man, 25, 86–87, 110, 174–75
Spielberg, Steven, 228–29
Spock (*Star Trek*), 77–78, 152–53
Square Pegs (television show), 8–9
Stack, L., 218
Stand by Me (movie), 129–30
Star Trek: Deep Space Nine (television show), 12

NAME INDEX

Star Trek (franchise), 3, 8, 14–15, 76–77, 78–80
Star Trek: The Next Generation (television show), 55
Star Trek: The Original Series (television show), 7, 35, 78–79
Star Trek: The Wrath of Kahn (movie), 14–15
Star Trek: Voyager (television show), 248–49
Star Wars Episode IV: A New Hope (movie), 144
Star Wars (franchise), 8–9, 11–12, 53, 146, 209–10
Star Wars: The Last Jedi (movie), 218
Starbuck (*Battlestar Galactica*), 230
Stathi, S., 50, 221
Steele, Jeanne, 160, 162, 163–64, 170
Stefan (*Family Matters*), 83
Steve Urkel (*Family Matters*), 83–84
Stevens, Elise, 244–45
Stever, Gayle, 204–5
Steward, James, 39
Stewart, Jimmy, 58–59
Stewart, Patrick, 55
Stranger Things (television show), 91, 129–33, 146
Streep, Meryl, 59
Strong, B. L., 195–96
Strouse, G. A., 202–3
Suchet, David, 85–87
Suicide Squad (movie), 65
Sun, Y., 208
Superbad (movie), 244–45
Supergirl (television show), 115–16, 160
Superman, 25, 110, 115–16, 147–48, 259
Supernanny (television show), 28
Supernatural (television show), 8, 14, 182–83, 205–6
Superstore (television show), 197–98
Survivor (television show), 28
Susan (*Desperate Housewives*), 94–96
Suskind, Owen, 6
Suskind, Ron, 6

Swain, Lisa, 26–27
Swinton, Tilda, 218

Tajfel, H., 168, 227–28
Tami Taylor (*Friday Night Lights*), 97
Tamis-LeMonda, C. S., 184–85
Tarantino, Quentin, 101–2
Tate, Catherine, 138–39
T'Challa (*Black Panther*), 218
Tennant, David, 71–72, 138–39
10th Doctor (*Doctor Who*), 138–39
Terminator (movie), 105
The Texas Chainsaw Massacre (movie), 208
Thelma and Louise (movie), 36
Theresa, Mother, Saint, 244
Theron, Charlize, 69
13 Reasons Why (television show), 160
30 Rock (television show), 68–69
This Is Us (television show), 244
Thor (movie), 69
Thor (*The Avengers*), 117–18
Thorne, Avril, 174, 175
Three's Company (television show), 56–57
Titanic (movie), 36–37, 142, 143
TJ Hooker (television show), 80
Tomlin, Lily, 219
Tony Stark (*The Avengers*), 64
Toy Story 3 (movie), 244–45
Transformers (movie), 66
Tree of Souls (*Avatar*), 149
Trendacosta, K., 248–49
Trifiletti, E., 50, 221
Tronick, E. Z., 195
Troseth, Georgene, 193–94
Try and Catch Me (television show), 236
Tsay-Vogel, Mina, 7–8, 28, 46, 168–69
Turner, J. C., 227–28
Tushnet, R., 251–53
12 Years a Slave (movie), 174–75
Twilight (franchise), 154–55, 163, 169, 182–83, 211
Two Face (*Batman*), 203

Unbreakable Kimmy Schmidt (television show), 65
Undercover Boss (television show), 28

Valkenburg, Patty, 137–38, 185–86, 187–88
The Vampire Diaries (television show), 174–75, 201–2
Veronica Mars (television show), 48
Vertigo (movie), 91–92
Vezzali, L., 50, 221, 223
Vinney, Cynthia, 8, 9, 12, 14, 23, 26–27, 36, 44, 45, 105–6, 115, 125–26, 131, 135, 153–54, 166, 172, 182–83, 189–92, 200, 210–11, 218, 221b, 248, 251
Voldemort (*Harry Potter*), 47, 111–12, 223, 224–25
Voort, Tom van der, 137–38
The Vow (movie), 244–45
Vozzola, E. C., 164–65, 199

The Walking Dead (television show), 11, 163
Walster, E., 69
Walter White (*Breaking Bad*), 97
Wang, Qi, 152, 173–74
War of the Worlds (movie), 105, 228–29
Wartella, E. A., 193, 194–95
Watson, 52–53, 134
Weinstein, Harvey, 239–40
Welles, Orson, 228
Wells, H. G., 228
Wenzel, William, 102, 104
West Side Story (movie), 129
The West Wing (television show), 6, 30–31, 52–53
Westworld (television show), 106–7
Whedon, Joss, 172–73
When Harry Met Sally (movie), 105, 129
Where the Wild Things Are (movie), 20

White, A. B., 160
White, Jaleel, 83–84
Will and Grace (television show), 43–44
Will Byers (*Stranger Things*), 131, 132
Williams, Robin, 97
Willis, Bruce, 37–38
Willow (*Buffy the Vampire Slayer*), 210–11
Willy Wonka & the Chocolate Factory (movie), 99, 109
Wilson, B. J., 128
Winkler, Henry, 62
Winslet, Kate, 36–37
Winston Churchill (*The Crown*), 156, 157
The Wizard of Oz (movie), 53
Wohl, R. R., 13
Wolverine (movie), 65
Wonder Woman (movie), 2, 110, 218, 244
The Wonder Years (television show), 124–25
Woods, Kelsey, 14, 15, 72
Wooley, J. K., 29
Woolley, J. D., 189, 190–92
A Wrinkle in Time (movie), 244

X-Men: First Class (movie), 253

You Can't Take It with You (movie), 41–42
Young, A. F., 154–55
The Young and the Restless (movie), 210
Yuan, Ye, 87–88

Zehnder, S. M., 202–3
Zeigarnik, Bluma, 126
Zeitchik, S., 161
Zimmerman, F. J., 194–95
Zoeterman, S., 23–24, 36–37, 154–55
Zubernis, Lynn, 7, 154, 250–51, 252–53, 254
Zunshine, L., 30
Zwaan, Rolf, 99, 100–1

SUBJECT INDEX

Tables, figures and boxes are indicated by t, f and b following the page number

For the benefit of digital users, indexed terms that span two pages (e.g., 52–53) may, on occasion, appear on only one of those pages.

active style of coping, 245
actors
   actor/role perceptual problem, 62–64, 73
   adolescent identity development in, 161
   attraction to, 68–72
   confusing roles with, 75–82
   contradictions between roles and behavior of, 235–40
   creation of characters, 84–88
   effect of role on, 83–88
   fundamental attribution error, 81–82
   message in media and, 58–59
   multiple roles played by, 66–68
   person perception, 64–66
   PSR-personae, 14–15
   regeneration of characters, 23
   sexual misconduct by, reactions to, 232–35, 237–40
   twins, 73–75
adolescents
   characters as role models for, 201–3
   connecting to peers through media, 200
   coping strategy, media as, 199–200
   identity development in, 158–59
   media practice model, 162–64
   parent communication with, basing on stories, 200–1
   relationships with stories, 198–203
   repeated exposure to stories, effect on identity, 164–65
   role of fiction in identity development, 159–62
   sensation seeking among, 199
ads, realism of, 112
adulthood
   changes in media preferences during, 207–9
   generativity in, 204, 205–6
   life stories, 171–77
   media in navigation of, 204–7
   relationships with stories, 203–7
   stories as anchors throughout, 209–12
affiliation, symbols of, 169–70
African Americans
   life-changing stories for, 21–22
   portrayal in stories, 217–18
age stereotypes, 219
Agta stories, 57–58
alien stories, 55, 105, 115–16, 228–30

allegories, 115–18
anchors, stories as, 209–12
appreciation, 43–46
appropriation, 163–64
attractiveness of actors, 68–72
attributions, 81
augmented reality, 257–58
authentic emotions triggered by stories, 126–27
autism, using stories to overcome, 6, 248–49
autobiographical memories, triggered by fiction, 26–27
avoidant style of coping, 244–45

beauty of actors, attraction to, 68–72
becoming-a-fan narratives, 176
behavior
    daydreaming, 136–39
    effect of virtual reality on, 257–58
    imitating characters, 4–6
    impact of story on personal lives, 29
bibliotherapy, 250
bonding
    effect of media on, 247–48
    over shared experiences, 35–38
books
    experiential crossing while reading, 49–50
    healing through, 250–54
    personality shifts after reading, 29–30, 154–55
    reading to children, 184–85
    reducing prejudice through, 221–26
    repeated exposure to, effect on identity, 164–65
    theory of mind, developing, 30–31
bottom–up analysis, 64–65
brands, identity and, 168
breaking the fourth wall, 49–50

Castro speech study, 82
catchphrases, sharing, 53–55
catharsis hypothesis, 128
catharsis through stories, 128, 142–43, 144

causal continuity, 100–4
celebrities. *See also* actors
    charity work inspired by, 205–6
    development of attachments to, 198–99
    worship of, 5
centration, 185–86
changes in the self, 154–55
character identification. *See* identification
character models, 105–9, 117–18
characters. *See also* identification
    adolescent identity development in actors, 161
    attraction to, 68–72
    daydreaming about, 138–39
    dual empathy, 10–11
    effective creation of, 141–42
    experience-taking, 12
    experiential crossing, 49–50
    fear of, 187–88, 189–92
    imitating in personal lives, 4–6
    intimacy with, 17–18
    parasocial breakup, 13–14, 16*t*
    parasocial interactions with, 13, 16*t*
    parasocial relationships with, 13–15, 16*t*
    person perception, 64–66
    regeneration of, 23
    relationships between, revisiting, 134–35
    retrospective imaginative involvement, 15, 16*t*
    as role models, 201–3
    transformations in, effect on young children, 187–88
charity work, 205–6
children
    autism, using movies to overcome, 6
    distinguishing fantasy from reality, 189–92
    identity development in, 158
    incidental learning by, 197–98
    learning from screen stories, 192–98
    perceptual boundedness, 185–86
    reading to, 184–85
    relationships with stories during development, 183–88

screen time recommendations, 184, 185
symbolic communication in screen
   media, understanding of, 193–94
time spent on media, 184
visual cues, reliance on, 186–88
watching media with, 185, 194–95
Chinese culture, identity in, 173–74
choice of stories
   during adolescence, 161–62
   media practice model, 163
   by older adults, 207–9
   repeated exposure, 164–65
cinema therapy, 250
cliffhangers, 126
climax of story, 142, 144
clowns, fear of, 189–91
cognitive development in children
   general discussion, 183–88
   learning from screen stories, 192–98
cognitive dissonance, 233–35
coming of age stories, 160
communication
   among fans, 44–46
   bonding over shared experiences, 35–38
   catchphrases, sharing, 53–55
   healing through stories, 250–54
   parent-adolescent, basing on
      stories, 200–1
completion of story, need for, 126
complication phase, 143–45
concrete operations stage of cognitive
   development, 188
continuity, dimensions of, 100–4
continuity, law of, 123
contradictions between behavior of actors
   and roles, 235–40
coping strategy, stories as,
   199–200, 244–46
correspondence bias, 82
cortisol levels, effect of media on, 246–47
counterintuitive narratives, 132–34
creative speculation, story discontinuity
   and, 103–4
cultivation theory, 216
cultural touchstones, meaning in, 39–41

culture
   effect on identity, 151–53
   master narratives, 174–76
   role in construction of life
      stories, 173–75

Dark Triad personality type, 41–42
daydreaming, 136–39
departure phase, 148
depression
   fanfiction, therapeutic benefits
      of, 250–54
   life-changing stories for, 22–23
digital age, fiction in, 254–57
disbelief, suspension of, 112–14
dissonance, cognitive, 233–35
distancing-embracing model, 27–29
diversity in media, 217–19
dreams, stories fulfilling, 135–36
dual empathy, 10–11

educational benefits of media
   after age 2, 195–98
   before age 2, 192–95
emerging adulthood, identity development
   during, 158–59
emotions
   authentic, triggered by stories, 126–27
   catharsis through stories, 128,
      142–43, 144
   caused by sexual misconduct of actors,
      232–35, 237–40
   distancing-embracing model, 27–29
   gratifications from engagement with
      stories, 43
   imitating characters in personal
      lives, 4–6
   lessons from stories, 47, 47t
   reactions to stories, 26–29
   well-being among fans, 43–46
empathy, 30–31
endorphin system, effect of media
   on, 247–48
eudaimonic motivation, 43–44, 54–55
expectancy violation theory, 97

experience-taking, 12
experiential crossing, 49–50
extensions of identity, 165–70
external realism, 110

fairy tales, 133–34
fandom, 3–4
   adolescent friendships based on, 200
   becoming-a-fan narratives, 176
   bonding between, 35–38
   celebrity worship, 5
   changes over time, 210–11
   changing view of, 8
   charity work inspired by
      celebrities, 205–6
   confusion between actors and
      roles, 62–64
   daydreaming about characters, 138–39
   derogatory view of fans, 7
   fanfiction, therapeutic benefits
      of, 250–54
   focus on real-life elements of
      stories, 115
   identity and, 153–54
   impact of story on personal lives, 4–6
   social identity theory, 168–70
   stories as anchors throughout
      adulthood, 209–12
   symbols of affiliation, 169–70
   technological advancements
      and, 255–57
   well-being linked to, 44–46, 248–49
fanfiction, therapeutic benefits of, 250–54
fantasy stories
   ability of children to distinguish reality
      from, 189–92
   focus on real-life elements of, 115
   metaphors and allegory in, 115–18
   realism of, 110
fear of characters, 187–88, 189–92
fiction. *See also* stories
   autobiographical memories triggered
      by, 26–27
   in digital age, 254–57
   emotional reactions to, 26–29
   exploring other worlds and people
      through, 10–20
   future of, 257–59
   history, distinguishing from, 51–53
   identity and, 159–62
   life-changing stories, 21–23
   personal nature of, 26–31
   personality shifts due to, 29–30
   physiological effects of, 246–48
   ubiquitousness of popular
      culture, 6–10
fictionality, 114–15
Florence Nightingale position, 175
flow state, 51
fourth wall, breaking, 49–50
franchises, 230–31
friendships. *See also* parasocial
      relationships
   during adolescence, 198–99, 200
   among fans, 44–46
   learning about in stories, 40, 47*t*, 48*t*,
      50, 56–57
functionalism, 122–23
fundamental attribution error, 81–82
future of fiction, 257–59

gender
   cortisol levels, effect of media
      on, 246–47
   diversity in media, 217–18
   wishful identification and, 202–3
generativity, goal of, 204, 205–6
genres. *See also specific genres*
   realism in, 109–12
   schemas for, 105
Gestalt psychology, 122–23
gratifications, fulfilled with
      entertainment, 43

healing through stories, 250–54
hedonic motivation, 43–44, 54–55
hero's journey, 146–49, 244
history, distinguishing from
      fiction, 51–53
honeymoon script, 98

SUBJECT INDEX

identification
  changes over time, 210-11
  defining, 11, 16t
  dual empathy, 10-11
  experience-taking, 12
  normality of, 19-20
  self-concept and, 12
  wishful, 201-3
identity
  changes in, 154-55
  defining, 154-57
  development of, 158-59
  effect of culture on, 151-53
  extending through stories, 165-70
  fan identities, 153-54
  fiction and, 159-62
  media practice model, 162-64
  narrative identity, 171-77
  self-socialization and repeated exposure to stories, 164-65
  social identity theory, 168-70
imagination
  daydreaming, 136-39
  identification and, 12
  predicting outcomes with, 124-25
  relationships, understanding through, 125-26
  simulation and, 23-25
imitating characters in personal lives, 4-6, 12
immigrants, overcoming prejudice towards, 50-51, 223-24, 225-26
incidental learning, 197-98
inclusion of self in others, 226-30
incorporation, 163-64
insight, gaining from fiction, 46-51
integrity, goal of, 204
interaction with media, 163, 195-96
interpretation of meaning, 41-46, 162
intimacy
  with characters, 17-18
  during young adulthood, 204-5
involvement, role in realism, 110

journeys of self-discovery, 151

learning from screen stories
  before age 2, 192-95
  after age 2, 195-98
LGBTQ persons, overcoming prejudice towards, 224-26
life lessons, learning from fiction, 46-51, 47t, 48t
life stages, importance of stories during, 182-83. *See also* adolescents; adulthood; children
life stories, 171-77
life-changing stories, 21-23, 48
love of stories, 120-22
love stories, 9, 105, 126, 129, 246-47

make-believe play of children, 116-17, 189
making meaning from fiction
  adult media preferences, 207-9
  appreciation, 43-46
  bonding over shared experiences, 35-38
  gaining insight, 46-51
  getting the message, 56-59
  history, distinguishing from fiction, 51-53
  learning lessons, 46-51
  personal interpretations of, 41-46
  sharing stories, 53-55
  themes, connecting to, 39-41
master narratives, 174-76
mate value, attractiveness in, 69-70
meaning. *See* making meaning from fiction
media. *See* stories
media literacy, 56-59, 257
media practice model, 162-64
media realism, 109-12
media selection
  during adolescence, 161-62
  media practice model, 163
  by older adults, 207-9
  repeated exposure, 164-65
media types, impact on mental models, 108
memories, triggered by fiction, 26-27

mental models of fiction
  building blocks of, 96–99
  character model, 105–9
  dimensions of continuity, 100–4
  fictionality, 114–15
  mental models, discussion of, 91–96
  mental models quiz, 92–93, 95t
  metaphor and allegory, 115–18
  problems created by, 98–99
  realism in stories, 109–12
  schemas in, 96–97, 104–5
  scripts in, 96–97, 98–99
  story world model, 105–9
  suspension of disbelief, 112–14
message in media, understanding, 56–59
metaphors, 115–18
method acting perspective, 87–88
minimally counterintuitive
  narratives, 132–34
monomyth, 146–49
mothers, person schema of, 97
movies
  autobiographical memories triggered
    by, 26–27
  distancing-embracing model, 27–29
  diversity in, 217–19
  fan identities constructed
    around, 153–54
  gratifications from engagement with, 43
  healing through, 250–54
  impact of story on personal lives, 6, 29
  older adult's preference for meaning
    in, 207–9
  repeated exposure to, effect on
    identity, 164–65
  well-being among fans of, 44–46

narrative consistency, role in realism, 110
narrative genres. See also specific genres
  realism in, 109–12
  schemas for, 105
narrative identity, 171–77
narrative realism, 110–11
narrative therapy, 252–53
narrative thought, theory of, 121, 123

narratives. See also stories
  becoming-a-fan, 176
  master, 174–76
  minimally counterintuitive, 132–34
  versus story, 121
news versus fiction, emotional reactions
  to, 27–28

observational learning, 201–3
older adults, media preferences of,
  204, 207–9
ongoing stories, 230–31, 256
orphan alone in the world story, 147–48
out-groups, overcoming prejudice
  towards, 50–51, 227–30

pain thresholds, effect of media on, 247–48
parasocial breakup, 13–14, 16t
parasocial interactions (PSIs), 13, 16t, 196
parasocial relationship–character (PSR-C),
  16t, 72
parasocial relationship–personae (PSR-P),
  16t, 72
parasocial relationships (PSRs)
  in children, 196–97
  defined, 16t
  general discussion, 13–15
  intimacy through, 204–5
  parasocial breakup, 16t
parents
  autism, using movies to overcome, 6
  basing communication with adolescents
    on stories, 200–1
  reading to children, 184–85
  screen time recommendations for
    children, 184, 185, 198
  watching media with children,
    185, 194–95
perceptual boundedness, 185–86
perceptual organization, Gestalt principles
  of, 123
perceptual persuasiveness, role in
  realism, 110
perceptual problems with actors and
  roles, 73

SUBJECT INDEX 281

confusing roles with actors, 75–82
effect of roles on actors, 83–88
twins, 73–75
performed narratives, 140
person perception
confusing actors and roles, 75–82
general discussion, 64–66
multiple roles of actors, 66–68
twin actors, 73–75
personal lives
anchors, stories as, 209–12
healing through stories, 250–54
impact of stories on, 4–6, 29, 48
life stories, 171–77
role of fiction in adolescent identity development, 159–62
personal nature of fiction, 26–31
personality
effect of roles on actors, 85–88
imitating characters in personal lives, 4–6, 12
interpretation of meaning based on, 41–42
shifts in, 29–30, 154–55
wishful identification and, 203
personality attributions, 81
physical attractiveness stereotype, 68–72
physiological effects of fiction, 246–48
popular culture. *See also* fandom
extending identity through stories, 167
fanfiction, therapeutic benefits of, 250–54
gaining insight from, 46–51
mental health and identification with characters, 19–20
metaphors and allegory in, 115–18
narrative identity, effect on, 176–77
social messages, understanding, 56–59
ubiquitousness of, 6–10
well-being among fans of, 44–46, 248–49
prejudice
behavior of actors, 232–35
contradictions between behavior and roles of actors, 235–40

cultivation theory, 216
diversity in media, 217–19
recategorization theory, 227–30
reducing through stories, 50–51, 221–26
self-in-other framework, reducing with, 226–30
serialized story worlds, reducing through, 230–31
preoperational stage of cognitive development, 188
pretend play of children, 116–17, 189
proximity, law of, 123
PSIs (parasocial interactions), 13, 16t, 196
PSR-C (parasocial relationship–character), 16t, 72
PSR-P (parasocial relationship–personae), 16t, 72
PSRs. *See* parasocial relationships
psychological realism, 127
psychosocial needs, fulfilling with entertainment, 43–44

racial prejudice
diversity in media, 217–18
reducing through stories, 221–26
realism in stories, 109–12
reality, distinguishing fantasy from, 189–92
recategorization theory, 227–30
redemption stories, 40–41, 127, 174–75
refugees, overcoming prejudice towards, 225–27
regeneration of characters, 23
relationships, understanding through stories, 125–26
repetitive viewing
by children, 196–97
identity development and, 164–65
resolution phase, 143–45
retelling of stories, 146–49
retrospective imaginative involvement (RII), 15, 16t
role models, characters as, 201–3
role schemas, 96–97

roles
    actors playing multiple, 66–68
    attraction to, 68–72
    behavior of actors off-screen, 232–35
    confusing actors with, 75–82
    contradictions between behavior of actors and, 235–40
    effect on actors, 83–88
    effect on adolescent identity development, 161
    twin actors, 73–75
romantic stories, 9, 105, 126, 129, 246–47

schemas
    filling in story gaps with, 104–5
    general discussion, 96–97
science fiction
    focus on real-life elements of stories, 115
    metaphors and allegory in, 115–18
    prejudice, reducing through, 228–30
    realism of, 110
screen time recommendations
    for children, 184, 185
    for tweens, 198
script writing, 139–45
scripts, 96–97, 98–99, 104–5
selection of stories
    during adolescence, 161–62
    media practice model, 163
    by older adults, 207–9
    repeated exposure, 164–65
self-change, 48
self-concept. See also identity
    fan identities, 153–54
    identification and, 12
self-discovery, journeys of, 151
self-in-other framework, 226–30
self-perception theory, 85
self-schemas, 96–97
self-socialization, 164–65
sensation seeking, 199
sense of self. See identity
serialized story worlds, 230–31, 256
sexual misconduct of actors
    dealing with contradictions between roles and, 237–40
    fan reactions to, 232–35
sexual orientation, overcoming prejudice towards, 224–26
shared story experiences, bonding over, 35–38
sharing stories, 53–55
similarity, law of, 123
simulation, 23–25
situation model, 99–100
    dimensions of continuity, 100–4
    schemas, filling in gaps with, 104–5
soap operas, 63, 210
social cognitive theory, 223–24
social identity theory, 168–70
social messages, understanding, 56–59
social perception, 64–66, 232
    confusing actors and roles, 75–82
    twin actors, 73–75
social relationships, learning through stories, 196–97. See also friendships
social schemas, 96–97
social skills, development of, 30–31
social-emotional selectivity theory, 207–8
societal norms and values, understanding through story, 57–59
spatial continuity, 100–4
spiritual lessons, learning from stories, 47, 47t
Stanislavski method, 87–88
stereotypes. See also prejudice
    cultivation theory, 216
    of fans, 7, 153–54
    filling in story gaps with, 104–5
    mental models and, 98–99
storied relationships, 134–35
stories
    adolescent relationships with, 198–203
    adult relationships with, 203–7
    child relationships with, 183–88
    continuity, dimensions of, 100–4
    as coping strategy, 244–46
    distancing-embracing model, 27–29
    emotional reactions to, 26–29

exploring other worlds and people through, 10–20
extending identity through, 165–70
gaining insight from, 46–51
healing through, 250–54
impact on personal lives, 29, 48
importance of, 122–23
learning lessons from, 46–51
life-changing, 21–23
love of, 120–22
mental health and involvement in, 19–20
versus narrative, 121
personality shifts due to, 29–30
physiological effects of, 246–48
psychosocial needs fulfilled with, 43–44
role in identity development, 159–62
self-socialization and repeated exposure to, 164–65
shared experiences, 35–38
sharing, 53–55
simulation and imagination, 23–25
structure of, 143–45
"their story is our story" motto, 2–6
transmedia, 255–57
well-being and, 248–49
story arcs, 40–41, 174–75
story world model, 105–9
story worlds
 fictionality and, 114–15
 imagination and, 2
 mental models of, 94–96, 95t, 108–9
 retrospective imaginative involvement, 15
 serialized, 230–31, 256
 transmedia stories, 255–56
 transportation, 10–11
stress, effect of media on, 246–47
structure of story, 143–45
suffering, emotional reactions to, 27–29
superheroes, 25
 hero's journey, 146–49, 244
 metaphors and allegory in stories about, 115–18
 serialized story worlds, 230–31, 256

virtual reality, effect on behavior, 257–59
supernatural stories, 130–34
survival stories, 129–32
suspension of disbelief, 112–14
symbolic communication, screen media as, 193–94
symbols of affiliation, 169–70

technology, evolution of, 254–57
television, effect on imagination, 137–38
television shows
 autobiographical memories triggered by, 26–27
 distancing-embracing model, 27–29
 diversity in, 217–19
 educational benefits in children, 192–98
 fan identities constructed around, 153–54
 gratifications from engagement with, 43
 impact on personal lives, 6
 increase in number of, 255
 mental models quiz, 94, 95t
 older adult's preferences in, 208
 theory of mind, developing, 30–31
 time spent watching, 6, 7–8
 well-being among fans of, 44–46
temporal continuity, 100–4
"their story is our story" motto, 2–6
theory of mind, 30–31, 67–68, 221
theory of motivation, 126–27
theory of narrative thought, 121, 123
therapeutic use of fiction, 250–54
time spent watching television, 6, 7–8
timelessness of stories, 120–22
 authentic emotions triggered by, 126–27
 catharsis through stories, 128
 completion of story, need for, 126
 daydreaming, 136–39
 dreams, stories fulfilling, 135–36
 hero's journey, 146–49
 imagination, 124–25
 love stories, 129
 minimally counterintuitive narratives, 132–34

timelessness of stories (*cont.*)
  retelling of stories, 146–49
  storied relationships, 134–35
  survival stories, 129–32
  understanding relationships through stories, 125–26
  writer perspective on, 139–45
top-down analysis, 64–65
transformations in characters, effect on young children, 187–88
transmedia stories, 9–10, 255–57
transportation, 10–11, 113–14
trauma
  emotional reactions to, 28–29
  fanfiction, therapeutic benefits of, 251
true stories, realism of, 110
TV commercials, realism of, 112
tweens, relationships with stories, 198–203
twin actors, 73–75

uses and gratifications approach to media, 43–44

values, 216–19
  behavior of actors, 232–35
  contradictions between actors and roles, 235–40
  cultivation theory, 216
  diversity in media, 217–19
  understanding through story, 57–59
  using story to reduce prejudice, 219–31
violence in media
  adult media preferences, 207–9
  catharsis hypothesis, 128
  daydreaming and, 137–38
virtual reality (VR), 257–58

wall-sit test, 247–48
websites, mental models of, 92–93
well-being
  effect of stories on, 248–49
  fan experiences linked to, 44–46
  in older adults, 207–8
Western culture, identity in, 152, 157, 173–75
"what if" scenarios, 124
willing construction of disbelief, 113
wisdom, gaining from fiction, 46–51
wishful identification, 201–3
world building, 255–56
writer perspective, 139–45
writing fanfiction, therapeutic benefits of, 250–54

young adulthood
  media in navigation of, 204–5
  media preferences in, 207–8

Zeigarnik effect, 126